A Century of Design

Florian Hufnagl (Ed.)

A Century of Design

Insights Outlook
on a Museum of Tomorrow

DIE NEUE SAMMLUNG State Museum of Applied Arts, Munich

ARNOLDSCHE

Copyright 1996 © ARNOLDSCHE and
Die Neue Sammlung, Staatliches Museum
für angewandte Kunst, Munich

ARNOLDSCHE Verlagsanstalt GmbH,
Senefelderstraße 8,
D-70178 Stuttgart/New York

Published by
Dr. Florian Hufnagl

Texts by
Stephan Braunfels
Detlev von der Burg
Dr. Florian Hufnagl (FH)
Dr. Ellen Maurer (EM)
Dr. Corinna Rösner (CR)
Prof. Dr. Willibald Sauerländer
Volker Staab
Dr. Joseph Strasser (JS)

With the assistance of
Cornelia von Buol M.A.,
Michaela Kreuter M.A.,
Dagmar Rinker M.A.,
Andrea Saul M.A.

Edited by
Dr. Corinna Rösner, Die Neue Sammlung

Copyedited by
Dirk Allgaier

Translated from German by
Claudia Lupri, Cologne

Graphic design by
Silke Nalbach, Stuttgart

Offset reproductions by
Die Repro, Tamm

Printed by
EBS, Verona

This book was printed on 100 % chlorine-
free bleached paper and thus meets the
TCF standards.

Die Deutsche Bibliothek
CIP-Einheitsaufnahme

Insights: outlook on a museum of
tomorrow / Die Neue Sammlung,
State Museum of Applied Arts. Publ. by
Florian Hufnagl. [Texts by Stephan
Braunfels ... Transl. from German by
Claudia Lupri]. – Stuttgart: Arnoldsche,
1996
Dt. Ausg. u.d.T.: Einblicke – Ausblicke

ISBN 3-925369-59-7

NE: Hufnagl, Florian [Hrsg.]; Neue
Sammlung <München>

Made in Europe, 1996

Table of Contents

Exhibition poster designed by
Mendell & Oberer, Munich, on
the occasion of the presentation
of the competition results for
the planned new museum
building on the site of the
former Türkenkaserne in
Munich, 1992

For a Museum of Tomorrow

Florian Hufnagl

"Für ein Museum von morgen" was the name of an exhibition we presented in the fall of 1974, in which new acquisitions from the years 1964 to 1974 were shown. Behind the hopeful, programmatic title stood the intention to illustrate to a broad public for the first time that the museum had been promised its own new building since the late twenties with almost constant regularity – but that its realization was just as consequently postponed into a distant future with changing arguments.[1] Now that the construction of the planned museums in Munich and Nürnberg is apparently about to finally begin, it seems meaningful to not only indicate with this historically significant exhibition title[2] the difficult path, characterized by many set-backs, the museum has had to take in the past, but above all to point out the opportunity rendered by the Free State of Bavaria having two newly erected museums of modernism in Munich and Nürnberg in a few years. Here unique collections will be housed and fine art, architecture, and design shown under a single roof for the first time. Thus a dream that was already alive at the beginning of the 20th century and the idea that has been a leitmotif in intellectual history – the idea of the "unity of the arts" – could become reality shortly before the end of the century.

In Munich the Staatsgalerie moderner Kunst, the Staatliche Graphische Sammlung, the Architekturmuseum of the Technische Universität, and our institution will then – without giving up the identity of the individual institutions – be able to show the art of our century in an interplay of all its facets. Joint temporary installations on the various exhibition levels of the central domed room, which cuts through the whole building like a screw, as well as in the ground floor rooms for special exhibitions, will be framed by the individual collections of the various institutions.

In Nürnberg an independent state museum of a new type will be built at the same time. It will not be an art museum after traditional pattern, in which the so-called fine arts stand alone, instead fine and applied art, visual art and design as of 1945, will be combined in its rooms. With the inclusion of the Designforum Nürnberg and the Institut für moderne Kunst it will be considered a center for the reflection of artistic culture. Contributions from various sides are necessary in order to achieve a new whole. Thus this new museum in Nürnberg will receive the city's "Sammlung internationaler zeitgenössischer Kunst" (Collection of International Contemporary Art), which has been built up since 1967, as a loan. In addition to that a Nürnberg entrepreneur, art dealer, and

Planned extension of Die Neue Sammlung in the courtyard of the Bayerisches Nationalmuseum based on the design by Prof. Paolo Nestler, 1965/67 Model

Author: P. Kreuzeder

Author: G. Green

Designs for a gallery of the
21st century on the site of the
former Türkenkaserne
Work submitted for a diploma
under the chair of Prof. Friedrich
Kurrent
Technische Universität
München, 1981/82

collector intends to give the museum a collection. The Bayerische Staatsgemäldesammlungen will be lending the new museum in Nürnberg
exhibitions for a limited period of time or groups of works from its holdings and be jointly planning temporary exhibitions. It will be the
contribution of our house to install a permanent design exhibition that
will refer to the collection of fine art since c. 1945 with emphasis on
the most recent trends. In consideration of the broadened concept of
design since 1945, we will be showing a selection of design objects from
the fifties to the nineties. Temporary exhibitions, which can also extend
chronologically beyond the narrower framework of the permanent
installation, will offer additional accents and incentives.

Three months after the Bavarian council of ministers had decided that
both new museum buildings would be erected within the framework
of competitions for realization, open nationwide with invitations to
internationally renowned architects abroad, I was appointed director of
Die Neue Sammlung. I had been working at the museum for a decade
already and had been responsible for its re-organisation together with
and under the former director Dr. Hans Wichmann. The professional
pre-requisites were thus favorable, since I like no other knew the
strengths, but also the weak points. Although neither the personnel and
spatial nor the financial limitations have essentially changed, and due to
the intimate knowledge of the collection holdings gained during the
previous ground-laying work, it was possible to set decisive accents. These
will be indispensable when the hidden treasures from this internationally
renowned institution will be presented to a broad public for the first
time after 70 years of collection history.

It sounds absurd, but almost each of my predecessors had to, for instance,
do without voluminous and space consuming corpus furniture! To the
present day our collection is stored, from the perspective of conservation
adequately, but so compactly and distributed over such a number of
external storage sites, that it is impossible to lay it out and prepare the
presentation for the planned new buildings. To resolve that is one of
the most urgent tasks before the opening of the two museums.

It was and is my interest to bring about the art historical establishment
of design – unfortunately a somewhat overloaded word today – within
the history of forms and styles of the 19th and 20th centuries, but above
all to also show the inspiration coming from China and Japan, which
influenced the applied arts through the world exhibitions. The sensational acquisition of a piece of furniture by E.W. Godwin from the year
1867 is paradigmatic for this. Hermann Muthesius had already recognized
its significance around 1900 and it can be considered the earliest known
precursor of modern furniture design. Its purchase was made possible
with the support of the committee of directors from special funds
and with the generous assistance of the Ernst von Siemens Foundation.
Of similar decisive importance was the acquisition of a "bibliothèque" from 1928 by Jacques-Emile Ruhlmann, a designer standing in
the classical tradition of the French ebonists. With this bookcase he
created unit furniture that could be combined as desired – precursor of
all that furniture that was to characterize our living and working
world after 1945.

Two new acquisitions point to the area of industrial design. The radial
engine of the American company Pratt & Whitney, to be dated to 1928
and lovingly restored in the MTU apprentice workshop over the years,

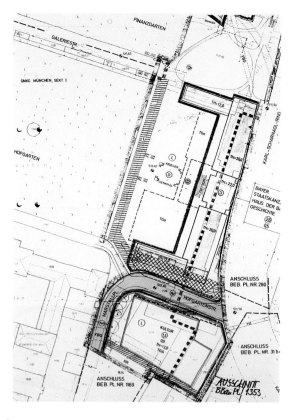

Ground plan of the building project for Die Neue Sammlung and the Staatsgalerie moderner Kunst on the northern Marstall-gelände (site of the former royal stables) of the Hofgarten (royal gardens) decided on by the Bavarian council of ministers on 19 November 1985

Author: Markus Allmann

Author: Anne Hugues

Designs for a new building for Die Neue Sammlung and the Staatsgalerie moderner Kunst on the northern Marstallgelände of the Hofgarten
Work submitted for a diploma under the chair of Prof. Friedrich Kurrent
Technische Universität München, 1985/86

has since the thirties repeatedly been considered a sensational example of the "classical" unpretentious design of an industrial product that does not have to slavishly follow fashionable tastes with cheap showmanship. The streamlined forms of the Tatra 87 of 1934/38 anticipated developments that have only taken hold in products in the last years of our century. The desk design by the French sculptor Maurice Calka from the late 1960's, the lamp developments by Yonel Lébovici or the sofa by the Italian Nani Prina, may indicate the direction with which we want to make our contribution to the Nürnberg museum.

In the years 1991 to 1995 we were able to permanently supplement the 23 departments of our extensive collection holdings with about 4,200 objects and groups of objects. About two-thirds of these objects were gifted to our institution! Here I would like to thank all those numerous donors from around the world, who responded to my often not very modest requests with great consideration and understanding. Examples which might be held up are the donation of the Munich entrepreneur Alexander Tutsek, who gave us a valuable collection of furniture from the Glasgow School of Art, or the MBB company, which donated a 24 m long rotor blade of a wind energy plant – objects that represent six or seven digit sums. The donors have rendered an outstanding service of lasting value to the museum and the projects we have taken up. Their names appear in a roll of honor after the catalog of selected new acquisitions.

I thankfully acknowledge the assistance of my colleagues representative for all Dr. Corinna Rösner and Dr. Josef Strasser – who actively and with great commitment supported me during my impatient efforts for acquisitions, exhibitions, and publications. I extend my gratitude to Pierre Mendell and Klaus Oberer, who with great success have left their mark on the graphic presentation of our house since 16 years now, and I am indebted to Angela Bröhan for the numerous photographs of the objects in our collection, which are not easy to place in the right light.

It may not surprise that my final acknowledgements are extended to the Stiftung Pinakothek der Moderne, State Minister Hans Zehetmair, the moving spirit behind the project, and the Bavarian government. Without their committed efforts, without the support from the side of the state and from private hands the fulfillment of the dream, "Museum of Tomorrow", whose construction is about to begin, would have continued to remain a dream.

1 Cf. Pinakothek der Moderne: eine Vision des Museums für Kunst, Architektur und Design des 20. Jahrhunderts in München.
Publ. by Stiftung Pinakothek der Moderne. Munich/New York, 1995, p. 24f.

2 Cf. the german exhibition titles: Für ein Museum von morgen (1974) and Einblicke Ausblicke. Für ein Museum von morgen (1996). Transl.

Pinakothek der Moderne
Just Catching Up or a Chance for the Future?

Willibald Sauerländer

This article is based on the text of a lecture that was held at the Kunst- und Antiquitätenmesse (Art and Antiques Exhibition) in Munich in November 1995. The text has not been altered for the printed version, although developments in the last few months have changed the date for the corner-stone ceremony and the name of the museum project. The ceremonial laying of the corner stone is now being planned for the fall, not the spring of 1996. The name "Pinakothek der Moderne" has been given up and replaced with "Museum der Moderne." Nevertheless it seems useful even now to remind of the promising alternatives: a gallery for paintings or an integrated presentation of modernism from architecture and design to paintings and sculpture. This contribution can be seen as a decisive plea for the second integrated solution. The nature of the problem, which continuous to exist, was most easily explained on the basis of the name that has in the meantime been given up: Pinakothek der Moderne. The respective passages were thus not re-written. From the integrated museum concept the idea almost inevitably arises that the house, in which several collections have grown together into one entity, could become an independent museum of modernism.
It is the wish-thinking of an art historical outsider who can pursue his thoughts without having to consider administrative or technical constraints. I immediately accepted Dr. Hufnagl's offer to include this essay in a publication of Die Neue Sammlung, because it seemed to make sense. The impression should not arise, however, that this independent contribution is a targeted vote for the interests and desires of a single collection participating in the museum project. My text was written "procul negotiis", and in this spirit it should be read.   March 1996 W.S.

When in the early summer of 1993 the new building project for the third pinacotheca – the Pinakothek der Moderne, as it is officially called – was being threatened with being postponed due to the ever decreasing government budgets, when the highest authorities were saying "desirable, but not urgent," something amazing happened. People got together, took the initiative, collected millions, and could finally convince the hesitant government that the desirable is also urgent. In this spring of 1996[1] the construction of the third pinacotheca will begin, so it was promised – and we have no cause to doubt this. Thus it was a citizens' initiative that confirmed and strengthened Munich's reputation as a city of the arts. It wanted to make visible that even the "Athens" on the river Isar no longer wants modernism, the 20th century, excluded from the spectrum of its large and magnificent museums. And these initiatives developed along, as it seems to me, typical Munich lines: not as protest and demonstration, but rather as a friendly and clever attempt to entice the penny-pinching government to expand its official sponsorship to the exotic and terrifying territory of modern art. Thus one was successful – not least of all thanks to an active minister of culture – but only relatively successful, as we should not forget, inspite of the construction soon beginning.

In view of the coming project there is thus some cause to be pleased and hopeful, and as an indication of this we may certainly also value the fact that the organizers of the Kunst- und Antiquitätenmesse München have decided to turn over their 1995 profit to the Pinakothek der Moderne and to thus join the above mentioned project in an exemplary manner. Old and new, which we were long accustomed to seeing as opposites, seem to be reconciled, and the antiques see fit to help the moderns on their way, more precisely: to help them to a museum! Thus it is a happy occasion that has led to this contribution, and words of encouragement and assurance will, rightly so, be expected from the author. It seems to me that I can best fulfil these expectations in attempting to speak of the venture, the chance, but also of the risks that are hidden in this belated Munich project for a Pinakothek der Moderne at the end of the century, but also of the dangers and the half-heartedness that still threaten to overshadow this project. I can do so with the audacious uninhibitedness of an outsider who has no practical experience in museum work, who is in the enviable position of being retired, and thus no longer holds any active public responsibility and cannot become anything anymore – indeed, even in the outsider role of an art history professor who through his own work is more closely acquainted with older art history than with modernism. But perhaps exactly for the above mentioned reasons I can speak with a frankness that is denied others – insiders, those more knowledgable – for a variety of reasons.

Let us continue our considerations first of all with the name with which one has baptized the future museum: the "Dritte Pinakothek" or the "Pinakothek der Moderne."[2] This designation links up with a noble local tradition and is in keeping with an impressive topographical constellation. To the side of the Alte Pinakothek by Leo von Klenze, of the Neue Pinakothek by Alexander von Branca opposite – which, with its multiple arcades, hugs and subordinates itself to Klenze's majestic building – a third pinacotheca, precisely that of modernism, is to find its place on the adjoining land of the former Türkenkaserne (barracks) to the East. In more ways than one, this name can be considered a happy and promising choice. It points to a continuity of patronage and collecting that reaches back in Munich to the time of the Wittelsbach dynasty and far beyond the 19th century. Three art museums next to one another – one old, one new, and now one modern – that cannot, after all, be found in any other place in Germany, indeed in the whole world, as one may determine with some satisfaction. Something of the pride of the old Isar Athens resounds in the baptism of the new museum. Modernism is to be wedded and reconciled with the old. Not a break, but a careful forward-pressing continuity is desired. That makes local sense, has its specific Munich stamp. But as with any claim to tradition, with the renaissance of the honorary title Pinakothek one also takes a historical burden upon oneself. To become modern and yet remain with the old, that is an understandable familiar desire, but one will have to keep an eye on the price that the realization of the outer shell as well as the contents of the new museum threatens to demand.

But there is another aspect to the name Pinakothek der Moderne. The term Pinakothek, which has been taken from the Greek, means – as one knows – a collection of pictures, i.e. a gallery of paintings. It was used in the same way already by the ancients, as one can read in the treatise of the Roman theoretician of architecture Vitruvius: "the pinacothecas are to be layed out like exedras," or also "the pinacothecas, which require an even light, should be oriented towards the North" – a requirement that, by the way, continues to exist in the building of museums in the 19th and 20th century. Following Italian examples, King Ludwig I then chose this term for the royal picture gallery in Munich, in order to differentiate it from the somewhat older Glyptothek, for which the collection of Greek and Roman sculpture was designated. Thus the coining of these names corresponds to the genre of the respective art museums in the Isar Athens dreamed up and created by the king. If one takes this historical etymological genesis as starting point, then the Pinakothek der Moderne may be seen as the gallery of modern paintings, wholly in keeping with the Alte Pinakothek and Neue Pinakothek, which do indeed both shelter large collections of paintings. Purposely or not, this term makes clear where the emphasis – the magnetism – of the new institution will lie: on a collection of paintings of the 20th century, on the painting of classical modernism. That is certainly understandable, it is in keeping with the prolonged genesis of the new project and is also justified by the impressive holdings of modernist works that the

Bayerische Staatsgemäldesammlungen (Bavarian State Collections of Paintings) presides over. Let us remember the genesis once more:
The desire for a new building came from the Staatsgemäldesammlungen, which recognized early on that the newly erected Neue Pinakothek would be much too small to hold the art of the 19th as well as the 20th century. In addition, one wanted to put an end to the grotesque and shameful situation that exactly in Munich the works of the German expressionists, the Beckmanns, and Klees should be exhibited in Hitler's art temple, which had once been erected against classical modernism. It was the adminstration of the Staatsgemäldesammlungen who, already at a time when one could still hope for a construction site in the Hofgarten, demanded a new building. Let us come to the holdings: One likes to speak of the failings that are supposed to have and have occurred during the building up of the Staatsgalerie moderner Kunst after 1945 and especially after 1970. Indeed, missing out on the opportunity to attract the Ströher collection to Munich betrays a regrettable lack of courage to let oneself in for something new, something not of long-standing. Here the burden of tradition became noticeable in a manner not altogether uncharacteristic for Munich. One was victim of the, apparently never ending, impact of classicism in the city of Klenze and Hildebrandt. In view of this new museum project, one should, even today, keep this failing as a portent in mind. But having said that, it must now be emphasized that the holdings of the Staatsgalerie moderner Kunst are astoundingly rich in the area of 20th century German painting, for one, and that the activities of the patrons associated with the Galerie-verein (Gallery Association) have also ascertained that there is a link to the present, for the other – at least up to a certain degree and with an emphasis on German works, which seems meaningful. Thus it is understandable, indeed, it suggests itself that the upcoming museum be called Pinakothek der Moderne and that in that context one thinks first of all of a gallery of classical modern painting, which towards the year 2000 will open its portals, and which will expand the collections of the Alte Pinakothek and Neue Pinakothek into the 20th century. In good old Munich tradition the new would link up with the old.
But it is exactly at this point that the danger becomes clear: one might be sacrificing the unique opportunity to create a museum of the 21st century to the presentation of a modernism that has become historical. Let me attempt to expand on that from two different angles.
As everyone knows there are in connection with the projected building logistical problems as well. At more than one place in our Munich the collections have grown faster than the spaces which are available to hold them, thanks to enthusiastic patronage and active curators. The Graphische Sammlung is still housed in an emergency shelter of the post-war period, in the former administration building of the NSDAP (National Socialist German Workers' Party) in the Meiserstraße. There its holdings – valuable holdings – are insufficiently protected against the dust of the nearby street, and there are at the moment almost no exhibition areas at all. For representative expositions, the graphics curators have to find space elsewhere: as for the Dutch drawings from Cambridge at the Städtische Galerie in the Lenbachhaus in 1995. This is a shameful situation that is not acceptable in the long run and that does not give the state representatives, who are responsible for the care of the collections, a good testimonial. One may not be able to make a grand display with

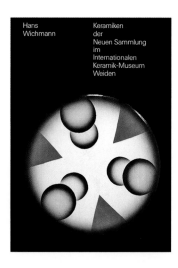

Catalog of the contribution of Die Neue Sammlung to the exhibition at the Internationales Keramik-Museum Weiden, 1990 Branch museum of Die Neue Sammlung

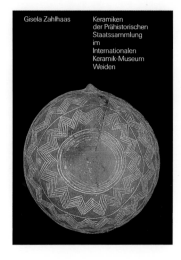

Catalog of the contribution of the Prähistorische Staats-sammlung to the exhibition at the Internationales Keramik-Museum Weiden, 1990 Branch museum of Die Neue Sammlung

Since some time Die Neue Sammlung has carried out a series of exhibitions and projects together with other museums and institutions, in order to present exhibition themes in as integral a manner as possible. Striking examples were the following exhibitions:

Pilot project with objects from Die Neue Sammlung and the Staatsgalerie moderner Kunst exhibited within the rooms of the permanent collection of 20th century holdings in the Haus der Kunst, Munich 1984.

Exhibition on the architect and designer Arne Jacobsen in cooperation with the Danish museum of architecture and the Dansk Design Center, Copenhagen, 1994

precious drawings, but they often say more than some outsized daub that fills a whole wall. But the Graphische Sammlung remains a special case.

The growth problems of which I have spoken can, however, be shown in an exemplary manner with two large, very original, collections of which Munich can be proud. There is for one the Architekturmuseum of the Technische Universität, which has grown out of a study collection for architects, but is today, with 300,000 drawings and 100,000 photographs, the largest specialized collection of its type in Germany. It ekes out a rather cinderella-like existence in the buildings of the Technische Universität and must seek its exhibition spaces outside of the institution, in the Stadtmuseum.

But above all, there is Die Neue Sammlung, the only really modern museum in Munich, founded in 1925. It had its origins in the early Werkbund movement; its oldest works stem from the former collection "Moderne Vorbilder" of the Munich Werkbund. Perhaps it is charac-teristic that the classical Munich opened itself very early and most freely to the area of applied art – not painting or sculpture. Today Die Neue Sammlung is with its approximately 40,000 objects one of the largest collections of modern applied art. Indeed, it claims to be the most significant collection for industrial design in the world. Thus there is here an amazing potential for the modernization of the Munich museum landscape. As you all know, these treasures are currently hidden away in storage, and for exhibitions Die Neue Sammlung has at its disposal only a historical annex of the Bayrisches Nationalmuseum, a certainly pretty, but not exactly modern building.

At the time that the decision for the new building was made, all these logistical museum problems had to be solved by the administration for state culture. It was a practical and thoroughly sensible decision of the administration to accomodate all these homeless collections on the property of the former Türkenkaserne. After the completion of Stephan Braunfels' planned building the Staatsgalerie moderner Kunst, the Graphische Sammlung, the Architekturmuseum, and Die Neue Sammlung are one day to be housed next to one another.

But what the space problems of the various collections, what the logistical constraints over the detour of the administration have be-stowed upon us here – a co-habitation of museums – that holds in it the unique opportunity to break away from the concept loaded with tradition, to transform being next to one another into being together and thus to create in Munich something that does not exist anywhere else: a museum of the 20th century on the threshhold to the 21st century that brings together architecture and design, sculpture and painting in a conceptually orchestrated presentation.

Let me attempt to expand on that historically. The history of European and American museums reflects specializations of various types: speciali-zation based on the so-called art genres – namely, sculpture, painting, arts and crafts, graphics – or specialization based on epochs and cultural groups – namely, antiquity and middle ages, Africa and East Asia. These specializations make sense within the context of the respective collections, are sometimes even desirable for reasons of conservation, and yet they too often tear apart the historically as well as aesthetically useful and meaningful relationships. Most of the museums specialized in the 20th century are collections of painting and sculpture. Even when

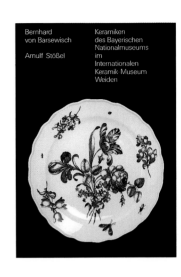

Catalog of the contribution of the Bayerisches Nationalmu-seum to the exhibition at the Internationales Keramik-Museum Weiden, 1990 Branch museum of Die Neue Sammlung, Munich

they – like the Museum of Modern Art in New York – have large departments of architectural drawings, photography, or film, the presentation always follows the ideal of a classical art collection: it shows only paintings and sculpture. Objects of design, which have been of pathbreaking significance for art of the 20th century, one has to look for in arts and crafts museums or even in technical collections. One only needs to think of such phenomena in 20th century art history as Jugendstil, Bauhaus, de Stijl, of Léger or op art in order to recognize that in the period of classical modern design, sculpture, painting, and architecture were together part of the "modern movement." As far as I can tell, the museums of modern art – at least those that I think to know – hardly ever deal with these relationships between design and fine art, which are so enlightening for the art history of the 20th century. From Basel to Düsseldorf, from the Tate Gallery in London to the Musée d'Art Moderne de la Ville de Paris, one always enters treasure houses of painting and sculpture – admittedly with much enjoyment and being offered a many-sided program appealing to the sensitive fantasy of the visitor. But now it is the happy coincidence, banal logistical requirements have wanted it so, that here in Munich painting, sculpture, and design will be housed under one roof. I ask myself, is it only the amateurish wish of an outsider far removed from practical museum work when he imagines to himself: it should not just be cleanly divided departments adjacent to one another within one building, but Staatsgalerie and Die Neue Sammlung should develop a concept for a joint-presentation of their collections? Munich, of all cities the classicistic Munich, would then have the perhaps only museum in the world that would lay down the barriers between applied and fine art. It would be able to prove to its visitors that 20th century images and design products formed, over large areas, a structured whole. In fact the museum could well continue to be called Pinakothek der Moderne. Why should we have this lovely name, which has become established in Munich, taken away from us? But it would not be a pinacotheca in the traditional sense any more, instead it would demonstrate what has been true for large areas of the art of the 20th century: Factory and academy are in the world of modernism no longer opposites. Indeed, in this context the audacious outsider even dares to abandon himself to impudent administrative dreams. Could one not imagine that such a house would free itself from the association with other long-established collections and would come to be, in cooperation with architecture, design, and fine art, a museum of modernism on its own, even run independently, indeed, to also be a museum of the present

open to perspectives of the future? Dreams? Perhaps. But when the coming Pinakothek der Moderne is already being called a vision, then one should spur on the vision to translate this chance for a "musée total" of modernism into fact, a chance that has been played into our hands here in Munich by a logistical coincidence – or should I say: fortuna? But let me now attempt to describe the second angle mentioned above, the opportunities and dangers of a Pinakothek der Moderne on the threshhold to the 21st century. I do so carefully and step-by-step since we are dealing here with a problem that is for the moment still very unclear and fluctuating. Munich is on the point of catching up with its museum of modernism at that moment in which one is speaking of the end of modernism with helpless emphasis and gossipy eagerness in many European and American discussions. Is Munich then, in that it opens up to modernism with a museum, once again too late? In answer to this question, let me once again begin etymologically! At the time that the term *modernus, modern* with the meaning *new*, was coined in late antiquity – at first of course only in Latin – it referred from the very beginning, either in succession or in polemic, to *antiquus*, to the old, which was supposed to be superseded or overcome by the new, the modern. One celebrated the age of Charlemagne, in differentiation to the preceding Merovingians, as the "saeculum modernum". At the time that in France at the end of the 17th century the "Querelle des Anciens et Modernes" broke out, literature and art were concerned with the rebellion of the moderns against the ancients, in this case against the overwhelming canonical validity of the models from classical antiquity. In Swift's well-known satire "The Battle of the Books", the tomes and works of ancient and modern authors battle one another on the shelves of an imaginary library like soldiers in a war. Thus modern is a term of progress, which is against the old – and tradition – and wants to do away with it and displace it. The closer we come to the newer time, the epoch of the revolutions beginning in 1789, the more dynamic, radical, impatient the use of the term of modernism becomes; the deeper are also the fears of the reactionaries of the manifestoes and concepts of the moderns. But never before has the demand for modernism, which leaves behind the old and burns its ships, unfolded such furious creative potency as in architecture, design, painting, and sculpture since the beginning of the 20th century. Whether with the Blue Rider or the futurists, with Le Corbusier or El Lissitzky, it always had to do with storming beyond tradition and replacing it with modernism, the new per se, the spiritual, the suprematistic, the futuristic. Only, at some point after the mid-

First joint exhibition with the Architekturmuseum of the Technische Universität München on the architectural photographs by Klaus Kinold, 1995

century the ancients were no longer there, modernism had been robbed
of its counter player in tradition, and the renewals began to run dry
and to become independent. Once the avant-garde, modernism now
became history, was put in museums and in a paradoxical twist was even
canonized by the epithet classical. This modernism, that began as the
avant-garde at the beginning of our century, has at its end, since there is
nothing left of the old that has to be overcome, become the old itself.
If one now applies this fact to the Pinakothek der Moderne, then one will
have to ask the question: Will it not, after its completion on the threshhold of the new millenium, be a historical museum, so to speak, a second
Neue Pinakothek? Can the art mecca Munich never escape the fate of
being the Isar Athens of those museums that guard the art of the past?
In order to find an uncertain answer to this ambivalent question, I will
return to the title that I selected for this small contribution: "Pinakothek
der Moderne – Just Catching Up or a Chance for the Future?" Yes, in
Munich there is the need for an appropriate and relevant presentation
of the works of classical modernism, and that is the primary reason that
the new building is being constructed. Said a little bit more pointedly:
what has been right for Dürer and Rubens for a long time already, is only
proper for Beckmann and Klee now. There is absolutely no reason to
be ashamed of this need to catch up, to have doubts about it, just
because the old, the classical, modernism has become historical in the
nineties of this century. On the contrary, one could argue: An art-enthu-
siastic public, large sections of the population have in the meantime
practice in dealing with the works of classical modernism and desire an
art museum for the expressionists, the new objectivity, for Picasso, and
the surrealists. Museums are there in order to, amongst other things,
sensitize their visitors and – venia sit verbo – to give enjoyment, and
there is no doubt that the pinacotheca of classical modernism, urgently
necessary and having to catch up, has an existential justification.
But that is only one side of the coin; because not only does one wish,
as described above, an imaginative concept for the Munich house of
modernism linking the presentation of fine and applied arts, painting
and design, with one another, the upcoming museum will also be
exposed to completely different odds and risks that it cannot ignore
without impunity. Every museum that has the name of modernism in its
title, is a bit of a centaur, is placed in a never-ending dilemma. Curators
guard museums and museums preserve, they are holding institutions
for that which is valuable, noteworthy – but historically finalized. With
the concept of the modern there is, however, inspite of all reservations
noted above, still the idea of a renewal, of the unexpected, of an
adventure. Modernism, or better yet the present, brings with it a
moment of unexpectedness, a disruption into the museum, certainly also
a bit of life. One could experience that impressively, for instance, at
the Museum of Modern Art in New York around 1970. In the way that
Alfred Barr had perfectly orchestrated it, the MOMA, as it is lovingly
referred to in Manhattan, was the most beautiful monument to classical
modernism in the world. But in the restless sixties the younger New
York artists began to denounce this monument as being academic and
elitist. I remember how Flavin's neon tubes were exhibited at the MOMA
in the spring of 1970 – it was on the one hand fascinating. On the other
hand, the puristic shell of Barr's museum with its selected sequences
of masterworks, its Mondrians and cubists arrayed like strings of beads,

was disrupted in an irritating manner, was exposed to new, irritating means of perception. And then there were even years in which the just founded Whitney Museum on Madison Avenue made the MOMA seem a bit like an old aunt, a bit dusty. It will be exciting to observe how the Pinakothek der Moderne will deal with this dilemma between the old and the new, between classical modernism that has become historical and contemporaneity that is shaken by radical crisis-like changes completely open to new perspectives. The concept of a pinacotheca, of a gallery of paintings, may still be able to integrate Baselitz and Lüppertz, but it will be burst open by all those experiments that deal with the interrelationship between an optical theatrical production and visitors, and that do not destroy our whole conception of art, as many augurs announce, but fundamentally change it. We are building the Pinakothek der Moderne at a moment in which the theatrical productions of art are being inspired and moved in a completely new way by the media, science, research in medicine, physiology, neurobiology, perceptual psychology. They have long time since left the idyllic territory of the traditional painting, have fled from the art museums and are exploring completely different questions, established somewhere between science and aesthetics, about the ever more complicated human being. Here it still needs to be seen whether we will create in Munich a Pinakothek for the modernism of yesterday or whether an institution will be created that is open to the new, the unexpected. Since one has to, at any rate, wish for such an institution oriented towards the future, that seems to be once again a reason to think about whether the Pinakothek der Moderne should not stand as an independent, independently controlled, institution next to the other, historically stamped, museums.
But let me return to those memories of the year 1993, with which I initiated my contribution. In the art mecca Munich, which is often vituperated against as being anti-modern, we have experienced how a citizens' initiative was formed for the Museum der Moderne. This citizens' initiative – and I stubbornly cling to this term not esteemed everywhere – has reminded the public, that art – and particularly contemporary art – is not just a desirable decoration of daily life ruled by the restrictions of economy, but an urgent need in a time in which people – and above all young people – seek an emotional orientation. This citizens' initiative has in the meanwhile settled down to effective, indeed many sigh already, all too effective, and mundane sponsoring by establishing the Stiftung Pinakothek der Moderne. Now, they who wish to succeed must do without such, not actually unpleasant per se, moral scruples. But an uncomfortable feeling of a completely different and more fundamental sort, which steals up on one in view of the financial procedures for the new building of the Pinakothek der Moderne, must here be addressed yet after all. Hereby I once again use my position as outsider in order to speak as openly as possible. The sponsoring of art through private initiative, through individual patrons, financial institutions, and firms is an enrichment, which cannot be sufficiently praised, of the artistic life in the communities and Länder, and particularly here in our home-town Munich. It takes place with a generosity, liberality, and tolerance that lets any concerned rumors of undue influence of money on culture seem philistine. But this private sponsoring is an enrichment and an additional support, it does not – and should not – take the place of the responsible bodies nor replace the basic

maintenance of our museums. On the whole it is certainly still like that. But recently we have been able to observe in some places – particulary in some neighbouring European countries as well – a developing tendency towards a desire to privatize museums, almost like Telekom![3] Immediately one points to American models without reflecting that in the United States, government and the individual have a completely different relationship to one another than in the old world, and that the social commitment of all private incomes there is a much weaker one – with consequences that can be insistently demonstrated in view of the slums, public schools, health service. The American museums could also tell a thing or two about what happens when the much acclaimed private supporting body is suddenly no longer so interested. We have in Germany a long-standing tradition of public support for our large museums. The government is not only responsible for having the garbage picked up, according to good tradition it also equips institutions of intellectual and artistic life with the essentials. Without the activities of the libraries, theaters, and museums, the life of its citizens would be emotionally stunted. The initiative to the very welcome private sponsorship, in comparison, can only be an enrichment of the publicly funded basic equipping of our museums, to which, last but not least, the buildings belong. That is how it is, and thus – one hopes – it should remain even at those times when public finances are at a low ebb.

Now let me attempt to return from these all too noble sentences to the current pragmatic problem of the project Pinakothek der Moderne.

In an exceptional situation a private initiative has supported the government – that was and is good. But not only must that remain an exception, this amazing citizens' initiative should demonstrate to everyone – including the parliament and government: Here one is dealing with a unique plan that will determine the status of Munich, a city of the arts, in the since 1989 enlarged republic: the last large museum building in the vicinity of our pinacothecas. We should not fool ourselves: At some point in time, after the turn of the millenium, that other Northern Athens on the Spree (i.e. Berlin) will have brought the imposing battery of its museums up-to-date, and then the art mecca Munich will have to be able to withstand this concentrated competition. That is why we have to say today: We hope for an integrative museum of modernism that brings painting and design together, we hope for a museum that links the presentation of classical modernism with a true openness for the future, but for that we need a generously equipped building that has not been curtailed by budget scissors! One would regret it bitterly in future, if this unique opportunity for a modern museum in Munich were to be curtailed due to saving measures, if the second phase of construction, which is indispensable for the completion of the exterior shell as well as for the contents of the upcoming institution, were to be postponed or even endangered. Let me conclude with a somewhat emotive anecdote. In the terrible time of the war a motion was introduced in the British House of Commons to curtail the expenditures for culture. Prime minister Churchill stood up and called out angrily: "Goddam what are you thinking we are fighting for!" That is how it is. That is how it is in Munich today as well. The modern Munich needs high tech, Garching,[4] BMW, but also the uncurtailed Pinakothek der Moderne, even in meagre times. The one goes with the other!

1 According to an announcement
   in the Abendzeitung (Munich) of
   27 January 1996, p. 8, the Bavarian
   minister president Dr. Edmund
   Stoiber named the fall of 1996 as
   the date for beginning the construction. The Bavarian minister of
   culture Hans Zehetmair announced
   the more precise date, according
   to the Süddeutsche Zeitung of
   2 February 1996, p. 11, as being
   September 1996.

2 According to an announcement
   in the Süddeutsche Zeitung of
   9 February 1996, p. 11, the future
   name has been determined:
   Museum der Moderne – Kunst.
   Architektur. Design (Museum of
   Modernism – Art. Architecture.
   Design).

3 Germany's telecommunication
   service, formerly under the German
   Federal Post Office, privatized since
   1 January 1995. Trans.

4 Site of a test reactor. Trans.

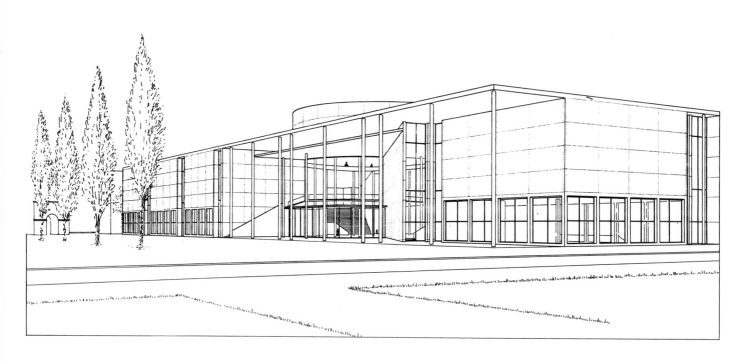

View of the planned Museum
der Moderne from the northwest.
Architect: Stephan Braunfels,
Munich

Museum der Moderne
Art. Architecture. Design.

Stephan Braunfels

In the immediate vicinity of the Alte Pinakothek and the Neue Pinako-thek is the site for the planned museum complex with over 22,000 m² on the property of the former Türkenkaserne (barracks) in Munich. It links the Maxvorstadt[1] laid out on a grid plan, with the irregularly round old city.

"Where is the entrance?" is thus the key question of the design. Should the new museums orient themselves completely toward the Alte Pinakothek and Neue Pinakothek in the northwest and have their back toward the city center, or should they face the inner city? In answer, the design allows for access to the museum complex from both sides. The one entrance is the large loggia in the northwest – facing the two other art museums. Visitors coming from the city center can, however, also approach the museum area from the southeast – through a large gate. Here they are greeted by a large winter garden, where the Café-Restaurant and evening entrance to the lecture hall can also be found. The two entrances are linked by a diagonal axis that leads visitors directly into a central hall.

Already before entering the museum inquisitive visitors can look through large high skylights on the sides, down into the reception hall of Die Neue Sammlung, which has a total exhibition area of just about 3,000 m². In this hall 400 m² large and 9 m high, are the largest objects of the collection, such as cars and aircraft components, which Die Neue Samm-lung collects on the basis of aesthetic not technical criteria.

The series of lower, artificially lit rooms is concluded with a 9 m high hall for street furniture, which leads back to the ground floor. This two-storied hall is in the immediate vicinity of the Architekturmuseum and is framed by galleries leading to that museum's temporary exhibition rooms.

Thus it is possible for the Architekturmuseum and Die Neue Sammlung to supplement one another as well as displaying joint exhibitions.

The concern to link the various museums in the building – in the basement, Die Neue Sammlung; on the ground floor, the Architektur-museum, Staatliche Graphische Sammlung, and all temporary exhibition rooms; on the second floor finally, the Staatsgalerie moderner Kunst – not just by stacking the three levels on top of one another, but to link them vertically as well, is emphasized by the staircase. Funnel-like it expands upwards and downwards, and leads visitors diagonally through the whole house from Die Neue Sammlung in the basement up to the

Access to the exhibition rooms
of Die Neue Sammlung in the
planned Museum der Moderne.
Architect: Stephan Braunfels,
Munich

Staatsgalerie moderner Kunst on the second floor. With this stairwell integrating the rotunda, an extraordinary sculpture-like interior space is created, linking all parts of the building over a length of 100 m and a difference in height of 12 m.

Above the encircling gallery connecting the first and second circuits of the collection of paintings, the rotunda receives a further exhibition space. From here one can look down into the central foyer on the ground floor from a height of about 14 m. Similar to the Guggenheim Museum in New York, this uppermost gallery level receives its light from a domed skylight, which vaults the open rotunda hall with an internal diameter of 18 m. This uppermost gallery is intended for temporary exhibitions or installations of contemporary art.

The total represented concept also attempts to respond to a question central to all modern museum structures: Should the architecture of a museum completely recede into the background, in order to just serve art, or may, indeed should, the museum building be an architectural work of art?

The size of the total complex as well as the particular urban development context, inviting the diagonal cut through the building, make it possible to create a composition of exciting room sequences for the "social" areas of the museum – such as rotunda, entrance loggia, winter garden, as well as the large staircases – and to allow diverse views. In the actual exhibition rooms the architecture should, in contrast, recede: simple clear rooms lit from above, rectangular or square in various proportions suitable to the art works, white plastered walls and a stone floor as restrained as possible, and nothing else, so that in the exhibition rooms everything is concentrated on the art, not on the building.

Like on the inside, the outer appearance of the building should be powerful and sculpture-like on the one hand, while integrating with the urban development, being experienced as part of a larger museum city, on the other. The walls encircling the museum complex will close the urban development wound of the Maxvorstadt and recreate the original street spaces.

The large entrance gate facing the city on the corner of Türkenstraße and Gabelsbergerstraße is to be understood as the entrance into the whole museum district – consisting of Alte Pinakothek, Neue Pinakothek, as well as the Museum der Moderne – not just to the new museums. By not creating a building set up like a single solitaire, which might have been twice as large as the Alte Pinakothek, and through conscious restraint in the impression of height, the Alte Pinakothek is to retain its unique placement in the center of this museum landscape.

1 A district developed as a suburb of
Munich in the early 19th century.
Trans.

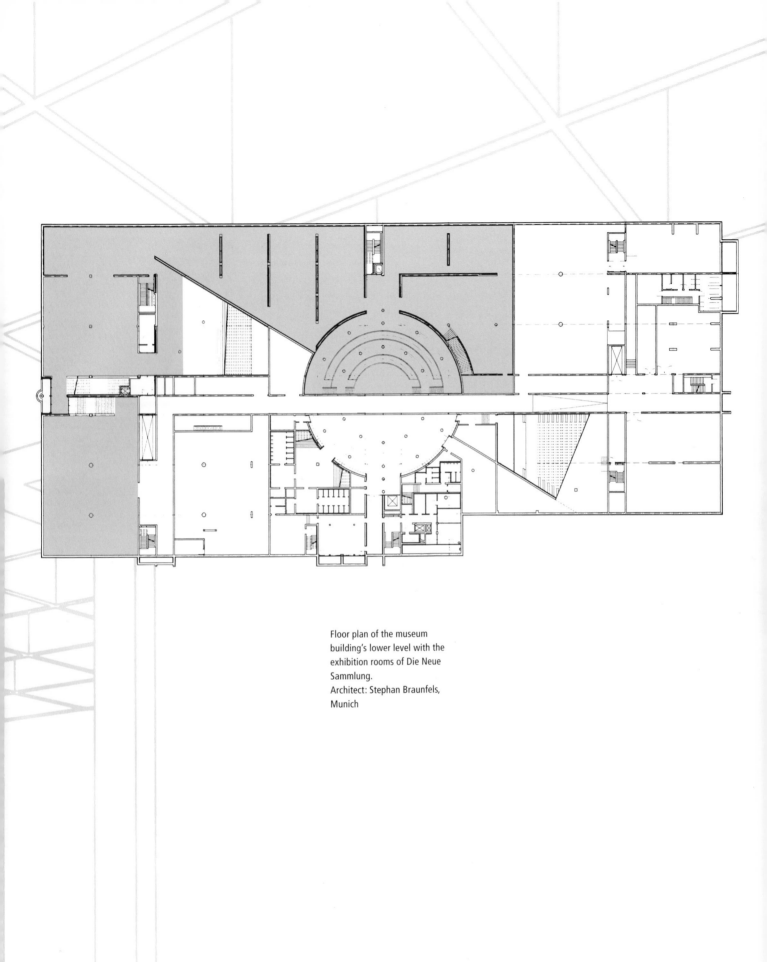

Floor plan of the museum
building's lower level with the
exhibition rooms of Die Neue
Sammlung.
Architect: Stephan Braunfels,
Munich

Neues Museum Franken.
View from the east.
Architect: Volker Staab, Berlin

Neues Museum Franken

Volker Staab

At the edge of Nuremberg's old town, within the ring of the city wall and not far from Nuremberg's central station, is the property on which the new building of the museum is to be erected. At first glance the site does not seem predestined for such a public function, most of it being in the middle of the block, disconnected from the lively streets. The object-like free-standing building volumes that the tradition of museum buildings seem to prescribe – one might think of Schinkel's Altes Museum or the Neue Nationalgalerie by Mies van der Rohe in Berlin – had no chance on the cramped Nuremberg site. But as is so often the case, it was this particularly difficult location that offered at the same time charm and inspiration for the proposed urban development and architectural concept.

Thus the volume of the buildings is seen as being part of the existing old town block, subordinated to the outer edges of the grown structure of the block. The simple, but decisive architectonic intervention is the cut through the block, which materializes in a steel and glass facade of c. 100 m, and which opens up the rooms and building volumes, bursting the scale of the locality.

Due to this cut in the block, the property is linked to the public street system, and a signet-like spatial entry into the middle of the museum property and to the square in front of the museum is created. From here the museum can be experienced in its full dimensions. To supplement the museum building, an additional angled building, which hides the fireproof walls on the Luitpoldstraße, spatially formulates the small entry street from that side and with its south front helps to essentially determine the museum square.

The urban development theme of the cut-open block is continued as architectural theme on the interior. Behind the transparent membrane of the glass facade, cut-open and intact room structures are alternated and in this way transport the contents of the museum into the public space. In the materialization as well, the cut and intact structures are shown in the alternation between exposed concrete left rough and wall surfaces plastered or covered.

Corresponding to the functions, the building is structurally divided in three different areas: in the old building with supplementary new building on the Luitpoldstraße, rooms for the administration as well as the Institut für moderne Kunst; in the self-contained cube in the center of the site, the area for temporary exhibitions, the foyer, and the

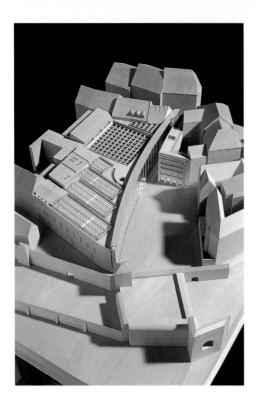

View of the planned Neues
Museum Franken in Nuremberg
from a bird's-eye view. Architect:
Volker Staab, Berlin

lecture hall; in the two-storied structure opening toward the square, the
contemporary art and design collection.
It is part of the concept of the museum complex that the two institutions
thematically related to the museum – the Institut für moderne Kunst
and the Design Forum Nürnberg – be integrated within the new buildings.
The latter is housed, separate from the museum building, in the angle-
shaped construction. On the ground floor of this building is the museum
café, which will thus also help bring the museum square to life after
opening hours.

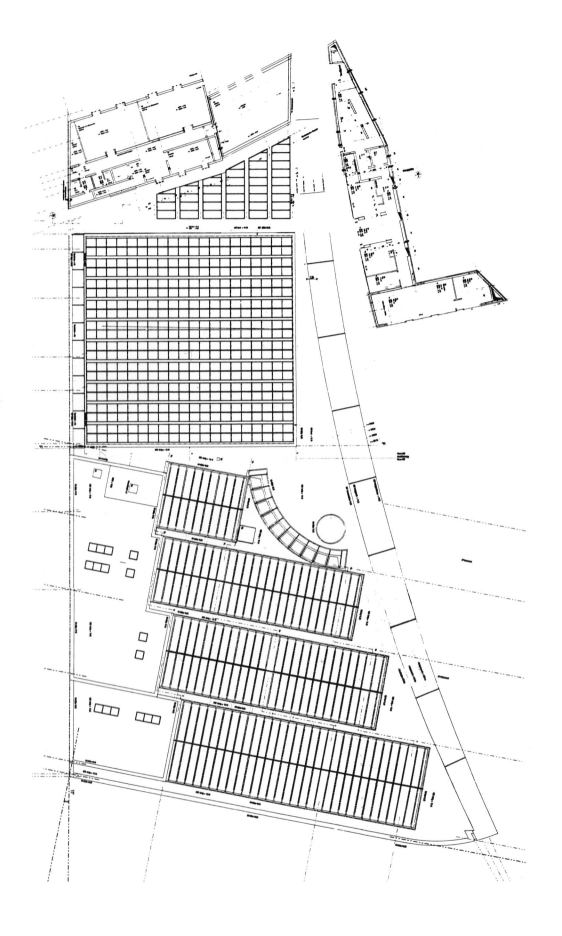

Neues Museum Franken. View of
the top. Architect: Volker Staab,
Berlin

Fund-raising poster of the
Stiftung Pinakothek der Moderne

Fund-raising poster of the
Stiftung Pinakothek der Moderne

Foundation Pinakothek der Moderne

The Bavarian government has – after some initial hesitation – decided to build the Pinakothek der Moderne. The Foundation Pinakothek der Moderne contributed to this to a great extent, as it came to be a not to be overheard voice of the residents of Munich from all walks of life. In order to begin with the construction, private initiative is required. At least DM 20 million are supposed to supplement public monies and must come from donations. The Pinakothek der Moderne will be the Museum of the 20th century for Munich. With it Munich will finally join the international art metropolises. On 22,000 m² one will be able to see:

Flyer for a concert in benefit of the Foundation Pinakothek der Moderne

1. Painting from the beginning of this century to today. Especially the first third of this century is one of the most creative phases of German painting altogether. World-famous works are lying in depots. Donations of valuable works have been made dependent on the building of an appropriate museum.
2. Die Neue Sammlung with outstanding examples of design from all periods of this century.
3. Valuable works from the Graphische Sammlung, at the moment not visible for the most part and endangered in temporary archive storage.
4. The most important exhibits of the Architekturmuseum of the Technische Universität such as drawings, etchings, models from significant architects who have left their mark on Germany and Europe.

With the new building on the property of the former Türkenkaserne (barracks) a rare and rich spatial ensemble will be created: Antikensammlung and Glyptothek, Lenbachhaus, Alte Pinakothek, and Neue Pinakothek, right down to the art of the 20th century. Thus Munich is returned to its position among the top art cities, which it had long held and deserves.
The non-profit Foundation Pinakothek der Moderne is calling for donations for the new museum building, in close cooperation with the actual initiator of the museum project, the minister of culture Hans Zehetmair. It sees itself as a citizens' initiative for Munich, the city of culture, and for the economic site Bavaria, and can, after almost two years of activities, look back on a successful balance. Up to December 1995 around DM 15 million were donated or promised. A few very large donations and hundreds of small contributions were made.

From the very beginning the "Idee π" reached the business world, the population, and the media. With events, joint advertising, and other models of cooperation, the foundation managed to be in the public eye again and again. Now the realization of the vision is coming closer. The breaking of the ground is planned for the second half of 1996. More than ever it is necessary to reach the commitment of private circles and persons, in order to achieve the goal of 20 million.
But even thereafter the financial partnership with the public will be challenged. Not only does an adequate furnishing of the museum have to be financed, the second building phase, until now not budgeted for, has to be completed.
We ask of you: please contribute as well!

Detlev von der Burg
Executive Member of the Foundation Board

Foundation Pinakothek der Moderne
Ainmillerstraße 11
80801 Munich
Telephone 49 (0) 89/33 51 50, Telefax 49 (0) 89/33 51 68

View from the planned Museum
der Moderne to the northwest
onto the Alte Pinakothek.
Architect: Stephan Braunfels

Abbreviations

ø	diameter
acc. no.	accession number
cat.	catalog
cc	cubic centimeter
cf.	compare
cm	centimeter
co. cat.	company catalog
coll. cat	collection catalog
d.	depth
et al.	et alii, and others
exh. cat.	exhibition catalog
h.	height
hp	horsepower
h.s.	height of seat
ill.	illustration, illustrated
max.	maximum
no.	number
pub.	publisher, published by
sel. lit.	selected literature
vol.	volume
w.	width, with

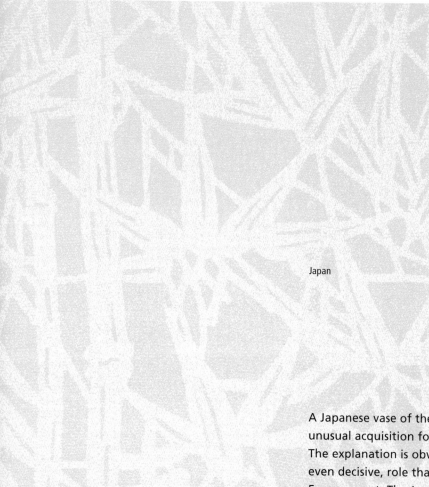

Japan

A Japanese vase of the 18th century may seem at first glance a somewhat unusual acquisition for a museum of applied arts of the 20th century. The explanation is obvious, however, if one thinks of the immense, in fact even decisive, role that the art of Japan played in the genesis of modern European art. The Japanism beginning at the end of the 19th century not only changed the fine arts – compare the paintings by van Gogh, Gauguin, etc. – but also the applied arts. Japanese works like this vase were for a number of French ceramists the decisive challenge and inspiration that, in the end, led to the genesis of modern ceramics. Juxtaposing the works of perhaps Carriès or Jeanneney illustrates this convincingly. Japanese artisanry, especially ceramics, was being collected by many artists including Carriès; Jeanneney began working in ceramics himself only through his collecting. The provenance of our vase proves it to have been part of such a collection. It comes from the collection of Louis Gonse, who as editor and publisher of the journal Gazette des Beaux Arts, as art critic and collector, was one of the most important pathbreakers for Japanism in France. Gonse not only organized several exhibitions of Japanese art, in addition he also wrote such important and influential publications as L'Art Japonais, 1883, a book which had numerous editions and came to be an early standard work on Japanese art. JS

Hanaike (Flower Vase for
Tea Ceremony)
Japan, 18th Century
(Edo Period 1615–1868)

Iga ceramics, thrown and
formed; dark brown coarse-
grained body; brown enamel
glaze, thick blue-green
treacle glaze with white
speckles
H. 21.9 cm, ø 10.7 cm
Made in the Province of Iga
(today the Mie Prefecture)
Provenance: Collection of
Louis Gonse, France
Acc. no. 463/92

India

The two ship's lamps coming from India are examples of a purely functional aesthetic, often characteristic of instruments and tools of the 18th and 19th century. In the case of the ship's lamps the principle of the Cardan joint determines the design: In a sphere consisting of round metal rods and metal bands two rings rotate inside one another, with pivot pins staggered at 90°. The inner ring holds the actual mount for the oil lamp. Geronimo Cardano (1501–1576), the Italian nature philosopher, physician and mathematician is considered the inventor of this principle, which holds the position of such objects as lamps, compasses, clocks, etc., constant in a continually swaying environment. The manual, hardly ever changing, production of such lamps over centuries was kept up longer in a less industrialized and less developed country like India than in Europe. JS

Two Ship's Lamps
India, 19th Century

Metal
ø 16.5 and 13.5 cm
Acc. no. 241/93-1,2

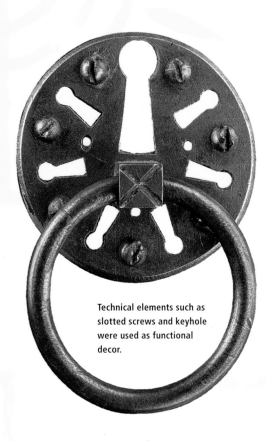

Technical elements such as slotted screws and keyhole were used as functional decor.

Edward William Godwin
Sideboard, 1867–1869

Black lacquered pine with a gold linear decor, silver-plated metal hardware
H. 171 cm, w. 153 cm, d. 48 cm
Made by William Watt, London
Acquired with the assistance of the Ernst von Siemens-Stiftung
Acc. no. 470/93

Extent and scope of the influence of Asia on European modernism in architecture, painting and the applied arts, have even at the end of the 20th century been only insufficiently researched. Characteristic for this is the furniture of the English architect Edward William Godwin, until recently totally unknown, which was designed shortly before or at least at the same time that historicism dominated Europe. Under the influence of Japanese art, furniture was created that was fundamentally different from the contemporaneous historicizing furniture in its basic severe forms, in its combination of simplicity and aesthetic refinement as well as in the renunciation of all three-dimensional ornamentation. It stands, in the mid-19th century, as the forbear of furniture art of the 20th century, as it were, and found adequate succession only decades later in the designs of Charles Rennie Mackintosh and Josef Hoffmann. FH

Sel. Lit.: Tätigkeitsbericht der Ernst von Siemens-Stiftung 1983–1993. München 1993, 88–89 ill. – Dry Graham, Ein Meisterwerk des anglo-japanischen Stils. In: Kunst & Antiquitäten 1994, no. 12, 20–22 ill. – [exh. cat.] Arts and Crafts. Von Morris bis Mackintosh – Reformbewegung zwischen Kunstgewerbe und Sozialutopie. Institut Mathildenhöhe. Darmstadt 1994, 325–326 ill. [reversed] – Pinakothek der Moderne: eine Vision des Museums für Kunst, Architektur und Design des 20. Jahrhunderts in München. Pub. Stiftung Pinakothek der Moderne. München/New York 1995, 288 ill.

Gold linear decor on the left
side of the top section.
Godwin used stepped lines
and stylized sunflowers on
later designs as well, incl. on
an organ case in a church in
Bristol (1870) and on the
curtain of a sideboard, which
is illustrated in the catalog of
the manufacturer William
Watt, published in 1877.

Edward William Godwin

1833 Bristol – 1886 London
Student of W. Armstrong. As of 1854
architect in Bristol. 1864–1871
collaboration with H. Crisp. 1865 office in
London, worked for Jeffrey & Co. and
later for the cabinet-maker Collinson &
Lock. As friend of Whistler, he organized
an exhibition for him in 1874. Aside
from architectonic concepts and stage
sets he also designed furniture, etc.

Christopher Dresser

1834 Glasgow – 1904 Mülhausen, Alsace
Studied 1847–1853 at the School of
Design at the Somerset House in London,
including botany under John Lindley.
Lectures on Botany. After his appointment
as professor to the University College in
London had fallen through, Dresser
turned to design. As of the mid-1860's
works as "industry designer." Travels to
the USA and to Japan.

Christopher Dresser, one of the most important pathbreakers for modern design in the 19th century, designed this unusual candleholder with its captivatingly bold form. A generation before Peter Behrens – at the same time as William Morris (1834–1896) and John Ruskin (1819–1900) – Dresser geared his work purposefully towards industry and thus towards the design of industrial mass production. His for the times very progressive point of view is also mirrored in his art theoretical works and is, as the following quotation shows, still valid today: "It will now be apparent that even a common object may result from such careful consideration that its form will at once suggest its use; but the object will only reveal the purpose for which it was created with definiteness of expression when it perfectly answers the end proposed by its formation. The advice which I must give to every designer is to study carefully exactly what is required, before he proceeds to form his ideas of what the object proposed to be created should be like … The designer must be a utilitarian, but he must be an artist also. We must have useful vessels, but the objects with which we are to surround ourselves must likewise be beautiful; and unless they are beautiful, our delicacy of feeling and power to appreciate Nature, which is full of beauties, will be impaired." (Dresser, Christopher, Principles of Decorative Design, London, 1873, p. 124, 128) JS

Sel. Lit.: [exh. cat.] Christopher Dresser. Kunstgewerbemuseum. Köln 1981, 59, ill. no. K 30, ill. 91 – Halén Widar, Christopher Dresser. Oxford 1990, 178 ill. – Durant Stuart, Christopher Dresser. London 1993 [cover ill.] – [exh. cat.] Arts and Crafts. Von Morris bis Mackintosh – Reformbewegung zwischen Kunstgewerbe und Sozialutopie. Institut Mathildenhöhe. Darmstadt 1994, 319 ill.

Christopher Dresser
Candleholder, 1894

Galvanically silver-plated
metal and ebony
Stamped on base: H & H,
eagle / 9656 / RD No 228142
12.7 x 14 cm, h. 11.3 cm
Made by J.W. Hukin & J.T.
Heath, Birmingham/London
Acc. no. 429/94

Ernest Chaplet

1835 Paris – 1909 Choisy-le-Roi, France
Began his ceramic training at the age
of 13, including porcelain painting,
at the Manufacture Nationale de Sèvres.
Then employed there until 1852 and as
of 1853 by Emile Lessore in Paris.
1857–1874 worked at the fayence
manufactory Laurin in Bourg-la-Reine,
where he developed the barbotine
method of painting on fayence
1871–1872. Sold this method to the
atelier of Charles Haviland in Auteuil,
where he began to work in 1875.
Took over the artistic and technical
directorship in 1881, in 1885 the
directorship of the atelier as a whole.
As of 1881 stoneware production with
colored glazes, 1885 development
of the sang-de-bœuf glaze. In 1887 sold
the atelier and stoneware production
recipes, subsequently worked only with
porcelain glazes. Participated in numerous
salons and exhibitions (e.g. Paris
world exhibitions 1889 and 1900)
receiving the highest awards. In 1905
loss of sight.

Ernest Chaplet
Bowl, c. 1890

Thrown and built stoneware,
gray, extremely coarse-
grained body; on the interior:
irregular sang-de-bœuf glaze
Blind-stamp on base
H. 6.5 cm, ø 28.2 cm
Acc. no. 455/95

Pierre Adrien Dalpayrat

1844 Limoges, France – 1910 Limoges
As of 1867 lived in Bordeaux, then in
Toulouse, Monte Carlo, and Limoges
working as porcelain painter and
ceramist; in 1889 he settled in Bourg-la-
Reine near Paris, where he dedicated
himself to the perfection of his Japanese
inspired ceramics and the development of
the famous "Dalpayrat red," which in
combination with other colors achieves a
marble-like effect and was introduced
at the Salon of 1892 with great success;
collaborated with Adèle Lesbros
and Voisin, with Maurice Dufrêne and
Constantin Meunier, et al.

Pierre Adrien Dalpayrat
Vase, c. 1890

Thrown and formed fine
stoneware, light gray body;
dark blue, violet and green
glaze
Blind-stamp on base
H. 37 cm, ø max. 21 cm
Acc. no. 219/93

French ceramics of the last decade of the 19th century mark a decisive
turning point in the history of applied arts. Under the influence of
East Asian examples one finally turned away from the historicizing
repetition of styles. The ceramics of Japan had become known in Europe
through the world exhibitions in the last decade of the 19th century.
With their unusual forms and richly nuanced irregular glazes, they represented a challenge for many French ceramists. Aside from Jean Carriès
(1855–1894) and Paul Jeanneney (1861–1920), of whose work Die
Neue Sammlung also owns some examples, it was amongst others Ernest
Chaplet who used Japanese work as a basis for his experiments, for
instance, with sang-de-bœuf glaze made on a copper oxide basis. To
research the glaze so characteristic of the art of East Asia and whose
composition was not known in Europe at that time was the goal of many
ceramists of the late 19th century. Chaplet was one of the first to achieve
convincing results and to develop his own sang-de-bœuf glaze, for
which the bowl illustrated here is a particularly charming example. Pierre
Adrien Dalpayrat – awarded the gold medal at the world exhibition in
Chicago in 1893 – also worked with the development of new glazes
in his workshop founded in Bourg-la-Reine in 1889. His so-called "Rouge
Dalpayrat," a copper oxide based stoneware glaze with flame-shaped
formations, came to be famous. JS

Koloman Moser

1868 Vienna – 1918 Vienna
1886–1892 studied at the Akademie der
Bildenden Künste in Vienna and
1892–1895 at the K.K. Kunstgewerbeschule Wien; was already at this time
illustrating for the journal "Wiener
Mode" and making ex libris for the
publisher Martin Gerlach. One of the
founders of the Vienna Secession in 1897;
planned in 1898 the stained glass
windows for the Secession building.
Numerous cover designs for the journal
"Ver Sacrum." As of 1899 teacher and
from 1900 to 1918 professor at the K.K.
Kunstgewerbeschule Wien. Founded
together with Josef Hoffmann the Wiener
Werkstätte in 1903 and was editor of
the associated journal "Hohe Warte".
Moser's work covered a broad spectrum
of furniture designs, graphics, textiles,
glass, leather, book covers, toys, metalwares, ceramics, and leatherwork.

The painter, graphic artist, and designer Koloman Moser is considered
together with Josef Hoffmann and Otto Wagner a protagonist of the
constructive Viennese Jugendstil. As a founding member of the Wiener
Secession (1897) and the Wiener Werkstätte (1903), he played a
decisive role in the breakthrough of modernism at the beginning of
the 20th century. As of 1899 Moser devoted his attention to designing
glass windows, tableware, and vases commissioned by the company
E. Bakalowits Söhne. In contrast to the at that time common glass
production of his contemporaries, usually still lavishly covered with
historicizing decoration, Moser restricted himself to a simple metal collar
and on the effect of the optical glass. The decanter was made in
conjunction with tableware no. 100 "Meteor", which is considered
together with the "Münchner Service" by Peter Behrens (1898) as one of
the first really modern sets of drinking glasses. Already in 1900 the set
"for the simple household" was awarded the 1st prize in the competition
for craft objects from the Hoftiteltaxfonde (an imperial foundation); in
1901 it was being sold at La Maison Moderne in Paris.
The glasses were made by the company Meyr's Neffe in Adolf/Winter-
berg, which delivered blanks to such Vienna companies as E. Bakalowits
Söhne or J. & L. Lobmeyr. In the Bakalowits' pattern book carafes
(i.e. without stoppers) of the same shape but without collars can be
found under the model numbers 368 and 369. According to the partic-
ulars made there, the various parts of the sets were created between
1899 and 1900 (see Neuwirth, Waltraud, Das Glas des Jugendstils:
Sammlung des Österreichischen Museums für Angewandte Kunst, Vienna
Munich, 1973, p. 414). JS

Koloman Moser
Glass Decanter, 1899/1900

Optical colorless glass with
silver-plated metal collar
H. 20.3 cm, max. ø 15 cm
Made by E. Bakalowits Söhne,
Vienna
Acc. no. 214/92

Archibald Knox

1864 Isle of Man – 1933 Isle of Man
Studied from 1878 to 1884 at the Douglas
School of Art, Isle of Man. In 1897 moved
to London, taught at the Redhill School of
Art, London, assisted by Christopher
Dresser in the metal trades. From 1898 to
just before the begin of World War I in
1914 designs for Liberty & Co., London;
sold his works there up to the thirties. As
of 1898 also textile designs, including
those for Bromley, Philadelphia, in 1912.
1911–1939 Knox Guild of Craft and
Design, founded by Knox. Returned to the
Isle of Man in 1913.

Under the name "Cymric," in other words "Welsh," Liberty & Co. in London introduced its own program of silver and jewelry for the first time. The name Cymric, which no doubt can be understood within the context of enthusiasm for Celtic "simplicity" at the time, was coined in 1898 by the Welshman John Llewellyn who was appointed to the management of Liberty and was also responsible for buying this program. A small exhibition of approximately 80 items of silver was held on the premises of this company. In the catalog one can read that these pieces give an idea about the nature of this new movement in silver articles, about the originality of this style, about its impressive fusing of decor and usefulness, that its charm is derived from its characteristic forms and from the fact that it is completely hand-made. This guarantees, one reads, the much desired individuality, which is at the same time a prerequisite for the arts and crafts. Most of the designs for these first "Cymric" pieces came from the famous Silver Studio, which at that time was being managed by Rex Silver. Some of the designs seem to stem from Archibald Knox, but it is not known whether he worked for the Silver Studio or whether he simply sold his designs to Liberty through the studio. Because of the anonymity of the products sold at Liberty, his designs can often be identified only on the basis of stylistic comparison or due to being named in contemporary journals or exhibitions. Securely documented are numerous designs from the period after 1901, including the service of Die Neue Sammlung, which undoubtedly belongs to the most outstanding objects by Knox. Simplicity, but of utmost refinement, characterizes the design of the individual pieces. Accentuated only by the inset turquoise stones, Knox's service thus stands succinctly apart from the often lavish products of the same period, overloaded with craftsmanship. The most successful designs for "Cymric" silver and "Tudric" pewter, made as of 1901, stem almost exclusively from Archibald Knox. They were decisive for the spread of the Liberty style throughout England and on the continent. CR/JS

Sel. Lit.: Tilbrook Adrian J., The Design of Archibald Knox for Liberty & Co. London 1976, no. 131, 144 ill. – Arwas Victor, Liberty Style. London 1983, 132–133, no. S 78 ill. – Morris Barbara, Liberty Design 1874–1914. Weingarten 1991, 74 ill. [comparable service] – [coll. cat.] Jugendstil. Badisches Landesmuseum. Karlsruhe 1987, 91 ill. – Martin Stephen A.(pub.), Archibald Knox. London 1995, 109 ill. [spout and handle of the pot changed; d. 1903]

Archibald Knox
Tea Service, 1902
Silver 925/1000 and turquoise

Teapot
Stamped on base: L & Co /
anchor (= Birmingham) lion /
C (= 1902) / CYMRIC; on edge
on inside of lid: lion, C
H. 21.5 cm, max. w. 12.5 cm

Sugar Bowl
Stamped on base: L & C,
anchor, lion, g (= 1906) / 5703
H. 4 cm, ø 9.5 cm

Sugar Tongs
Stamped inside: 5 103 /
CYMRIC / L & Co, anchor, lion,
d (= 1903)
L. 10.5 cm

Made by W.H. Haseler,
Birmingham
Acc. no. 497/92-1,2,3,4

Pitcher
Stamped on base: H. GREAVES
NEW ST B'H A M. / L & Co,
anchor, lion, C (= 1902) /
CYMRIC
H. 10.9 cm, max. w. 8 cm

Henry van de Velde

1863 Antwerp – 1957 Zurich
1881–1884 studied painting at the
Académie des Beaux Arts in Antwerp. In
1889 member of the artist group Les
Vingt in Brussel. In 1890 switched to arts
and crafts, and architecture. Designed
central buildings for the art nouveau
movement, such as his own house
Bloemenwerf in Uccle (1892–1895). After
the presentation of his interiors at the
Internationale Kunstausstellung Dresden
in 1897, numerous commissions in the
German language region, including the
Folkwang-Museum in Hagen (1898–
1902). In 1901 artistic advisor at the
court of Weimar and 1906–1914
directorship of the arts and crafts schools
in Weimar. In 1907 founding member of
the Deutscher Werkbund. In 1917 moved
to Switzerland; in 1925 founded the
Institut Supérieur d'Archictecture et des
Arts Décoratifs.

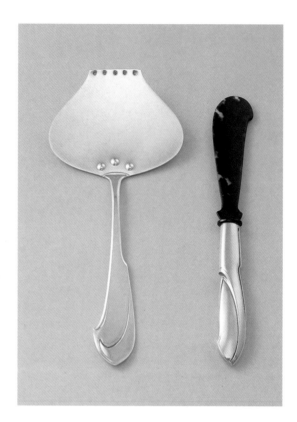

Henry van de Velde
Paté Slice and Caviar Knife of
the Cutlery Series Model I,
1902

Silver 925/1000 and tortoise-
shell
Stamped: 925, crescent moon,
crown
L. 20.5 and 19.5 cm
Made by Koch & Bergfeld,
Bremen, for Th. Müller, Weimar
(as of 1903)
Acc. no. 80/92

With the appointment of the Belgian Henry van de Velde as artistic
advisor of Grand Duke Wilhelm Ernst von Sachsen-Weimar in 1902, one of
the most outstanding artist personalities of the Jugendstil came to
Weimar. His seminars on crafts and his design activities were to further
the existing workshops and small industry and thus make Weimar to a
center of European art and culture again. Van de Velde was commissioned, by request of the grand duke, to design the silverware consisting
of 335 pieces that the grand duke was to receive from his land for his
wedding on April 30, 1903. The Weimar court jeweler Theodor Müller was
responsible for having van de Velde's design of the fall of 1902 carried
out. Because of the limited capacities of his workshop, he gave the
contract to the Bremen silverware factory Koch & Bergfeld. Since the
forms of the individual pieces of cutlery were too complicated for
machine production, they had to a large extent be made by hand in the
Bremen company's smithy for cutlery. Already in the fall of 1903
the silver could be shown to the public in the Kunstgewerbemuseum zu
Weimar. The cutlery, originally created as a single commission for the
grand duke, was made in subsequent years for other people, including
Karl Ernst Osthaus, as well. JS

Sel. Lit.: [coll. cat.] Metallkunst. Bröhan Museum. Berlin 1990, 482–483, no. 519 ill. [further
literature] – Sänger Reinhard W., Das deutsche Silberbesteck. Stuttgart 1991, 208–216 ill.
[incl. preliminary sketches and final drawings]

Pieces such as this big vase with its sensational luster glaze established the international fame of the Hungarian manufacturing plant Zsolnay and was very successful at, for instance, the world exhibition in Paris in 1900.

After Vilmos Zsolnay (1828–1900) had taken over the factory from his brother in 1865, he soon began to employ various artists and to develop numerous new glazes. In 1893 the first pieces with the iridescent eosin glaze were created in collaboration with the chemist Dr. Vince Wartha, professor at the Technical University Budapest. Aside from Sándor Apáti Abt (1870–1916) and József Rippl-Rónay (1861–1930), it was above all Lajos Makk who designed decorations and forms in the "modern style." The vase from Die Neue Sammlung, datable on the basis of its model number, also stems from Makk (cf. Makus, Horst, [Kat. Aust.] Keramik aus Historismus und Jugendstil. Staatliche Kunstsammlungen Kassel 1981, p. 209, no. 192 w. ill.). JS

Lajos Makk

1876 – 1916
Worked at the manufacturing plant
Zsolnay in Pécs around 1900.

Lajos Makk
Vase, Model No. 5916, 1900

Thrown fine stoneware, light
gray body; dark gray irides-
cent glaze with a pattern
of dots in green and red tones
Stamped on base: trademark,
5916, M, 23
H. 45.5 cm, ø 25 cm
Made by Keramische Fabriken
Vilmos Zsolnay, Pécs
(Fünfkirchen), Hungary
Acc. no. 8/93

Ernest Archibald Taylor

1874 Greenock – 1951
Attended the Glasgow School of Art and
the Glasgow and West of Scotland
Technical College, at which he taught
furniture design from 1900 to 1906. Until
1906 designs for interiors and furniture,
which were carried out by Wylie &
Lochhead in Glasgow. Then moved to
Manchester, where devoted himself
exclusively to glass painting. In 1911 he
moved to Paris, in 1916/17 returned to
Scotland.

The stringently, inspite of the floral elements, tectonic secretaire
represents an important example of the furniture designs of the Glasgow
school, which was formed in the late 1890's around a group of young
graduates from the Glasgow School of Arts. With Charles Rennic Mackintosh taking the lead, they developed their own Japanese inspired style,
which was pathbreaking for the continental European and especially for
the Viennese Jugendstil.
Ernest Archibald Taylor's most important designs were created in collaboration with Wylie & Lochhead who, as the Glasgow counterpart to
Liberty & Co. in London, had a significant part in the breakthrough of the
new art movement. The significance of Taylor was recognized early on:
Muthesius considered him already in 1904 one of the decisive representatives of the Glasgow School of Arts. Taylor himself took a vehement
stance against the separation of fine and applied arts in his many-
sided work as well as in his statements: His concern, similar to the aims
of the Arts and Crafts Movement, was that the lost unity of the arts be
restored. JS

Sel. Lit.: Pinakothek der Moderne: eine Vision des Museums für Kunst, Architektur und
Design des 20. Jahrhunderts in München. Pub. Stiftung Pinakothek der Moderne.
München/New York 1995, 47 ill.

Ernest Archibald Taylor
Secretaire, between 1901 and
1905

Mahogany, French oak,
mahogany root wood, lead
glass, and metal
H. 122 cm, w. 103.8 cm,
d. 46.5 cm
Made by Wylie & Lochhead
Ltd., Glasgow
The secretaire is part of an
extensive collection of
valuable furniture that the
Munich industrialist Alexander
Tutsek donated to Die Neue
Sammlung for the museum
building planned on the site
of the former Türkenkaserne
(barracks).
Acc. no. 22/93

Joseph Maria Olbrich

1867 Troppau – 1908 Düsseldorf
Attended the Staatsgewerbeschule in
Vienna, graduating in 1886. Architectural
studies at the Akademie der bildenden
Künste in Vienna between 1890 and 1893,
leaving with the Prix de Rome. Travels
to Italy and Tunesia. 1894–1899 employed
by Otto Wagner in Vienna. In 1897 one
of the founders of the Vienna Secession,
for which he also constructed the
exhibition building in 1898. From 1899 to
1907 planned and directed the artists'
colony Mathildenhöhe in Darmstadt. In
1903 founding member of the Bund
Deutscher Architekten, in 1907 one of
the founders of the Deutscher Werkbund.
In addition to his work as architect,
numerous designs for furniture, textiles,
glass, and ceramics.

Shortly after being appointed to the Darmstadt artists' colony,
J.M. Olbrich began to work with the Lüdenscheid metalwares factory
Eduard Hueck. Aside from Olbrich, Peter Behrens and Albin Müller also
delivered designs to this company between 1901 and 1906 and thus
established its significance at the beginning of the century. Amongst the
most popular works were undoubtedly the pewter objects designed
by Olbrich, as, for example, a plate with a rose motif. But most successful
was the two-armed candelabrum, it came to be a synonym for the
Darmstadt Jugendstil, so to speak – as Olbrich with his objects and buildings left a permanent mark on the image of the Darmstadt artists' colony
on the whole. JS

Sel. Lit.: [coll. cat.] Metallkunst. Bröhan Museum. Berlin 1990, 234, no. 237 ill. [further
literature] – Rudoe Judy, [coll. cat.] Decorative Arts 1850–1950. British Museum. London
1991, 87, no. 226, ill. 91

Joseph Maria Olbrich
Two Candelabra, c. 1901

Polished pewter
Stamped on base: EDELZINN
E: HUECK 1819 (in circle),
JO Monogram (in square)
H. 36 cm, w. 19.1 cm,
d. 11.3 cm
Made by Eduard Hueck KG,
Lüdenscheid
Acc. no. 15/96-a, b

Otto Wagner

1841 Penzing/Vienna – 1918 Vienna
Studied in 1857 at the Wiener Technische
Hochschule, in 1860 at the Berliner
Bauakademie and 1861–1863 at the
architecture school of the Akademie der
bildenden Künste in Vienna, where he
taught from 1894–1913. 1899–1905
member of the Vienna Secession.
Comprehensive architectural projects
such as in Vienna, for example the
stations of the city railroad (1894–1907),
the postal savings bank office building
(1904–1906), and the Steinhof Landes-,
Heil- und Pflegeanstalt (asylum) with
church. In addition to his buildings, he
planned as of 1890 interiors and
furniture. Wagner also designed textiles,
glass, silverware and wrought-iron work.

In 1894 Otto Wagner was named professor at the Vienna Akademie.
Under the motto "nothing that is not practical can be beautiful," he
pleaded in his inaugural lecture for a new approach to architecture
independent of the past and formed by rationalism. In the same year yet
he received the commission for one of his best known works, the
architectonic design of the Vienna Stadtbahn buildings. The contract also
covered designs for the complete installation, furnishing, lighting, and so
forth. From the former furnishing only a few examples have survived,
amongst them the bench designed in 1898. The form details on the sides,
each cast in one piece, are variations of motifs on the cast iron Stadtbahn
columns. In 1914 they could still be seen in the comprehensive catalog
of Kitschelt's Erben together with benches by Josef Hoffmann. JS

Sel. Lit.: [co. cat.] Preis-Tarif der ersten kais. kön. priviliegierten Eisenmöbelfabrik u.
Metallgießerei A. Kitschelt's Erben. R. Kitschelt. no. 16. Wien 1915, 156 ill. – Asenbaum Paul,
Haiko Peter, Lachmayer Herbert and Zettl Reiner, Otto Wagner. Möbel und Innenräume.
Salzburg/Wien 1984, 153–154, ill. 192

**Otto Wagner
Bench for the Viennese Stadtbahn (city railroad), 1898**

**Cast iron and white lacquered
oak
H. 86.5 cm, w. 156 cm,
d. 52.5 cm
Made by August Kitschelt's
Erben, Vienna
Acc. no. 466/90**

1905/1906

Josef Hoffmann's designs for garden benches, made several years after Wagner's Stadtbahn bench and also produced by the same manufacturer in several variations, are characterized by a more severe approach to form in comparison to those of Wagner. Hoffmann dispenses with reliefs and thus with decoration of the sides, which exist only in the arrangement of the vertical bars. Whether Hoffmann's designs were made on the basis of a definite commission is not known. On the still existing preliminary sketch (see cat. Zürich) is the inscription "Tegethof," which one has not been able, however, to connect with any specific project yet. JS

Sel. Lit.: [co. cat.] Preis-Tarif der ersten kais. kön. priviliegierten Eisenmöbelfabrik u. Metallgießerei A. Kitschelt's Erben. R. Kitschelt. no. 16. Wien 1915, 155, no. 563 ill. – [exh. cat.] J. Hoffmann Wien. Jugendstil und 20er Jahre. Museum Bellerive. Zürich 1983, 61, ill. 41, 114, no. 53 [preliminary sketch]

Josef Hoffmann

1870 Pirnitz/Mähren – 1956 Vienna Student of Karl von Hasenauer and Otto Wagner at the Vienna academy. In 1897 one the founders of the Vienna Secession. In 1899 professor of architecture at the Wiener Kunstgewerbeschule. Together with Koloman Moser he founded the Wiener Werkstätte in 1903, remained its artistic director up to 1931. In 1905 resigned from the Secession. In 1912 one of the founders of the Österreichischer Werkbund, which he directed until 1920.

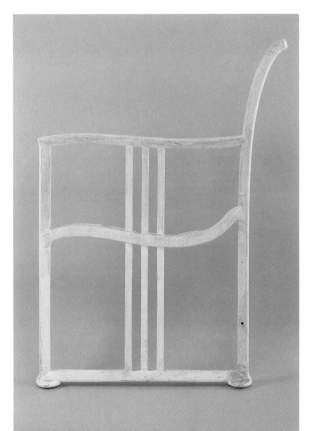

Josef Hoffmann
Garden Bench, 1905/1906

White lacquered cast iron and oak
H. 89 cm, w. 169 cm, d. 64 cm
Made by August Kitschelt's Erben, Vienna
Acc. no. 431/90

Josef Hoffmann

1870 Pirnitz/Mähren – 1956 Vienna
Student of Karl von Hasenauer and Otto
Wagner at the Vienna academy. In 1897
one the founders of the Vienna Secession.
In 1899 professor of architecture at
the Wiener Kunstgewerbeschule. Together
with Koloman Moser he founded the
Wiener Werkstätte in 1903, remained its
artistic director up to 1931. In 1905
resigned from the Secession. In 1912 one
of the founders of the Österreichischer
Werkbund, which he directed until 1920.

At the time of the transition between Jugendstil and the twenties, Josef Hoffmann reached the peak of his many-sided work. It was also at this time that his interest in glass began. In 1910 Stefan Rath, proprietor of the company Lobmeyr, was successful in gaining Hoffmann as designer for his company. After Hoffmann first occupied himself with black and white decorations (Broncit glassware), he made designs for cut glass which, as these examples show, belong to his most challenging works. In 1914 such cut glasses were shown at the Cologne Werkbund exhibition. In contrast to the tableware "The Patrician," which Hoffmann also designed for Lobmeyr and which is still being produced today, the elaborately cut glasses of this set remained commercially unsuccessful. Of the glasses produced in a very limited number of pieces, only a few examples still exist. JS

Sel. Lit.: Deutsche Kunst und Dekoration 34, 1914, 376 ill. [champagne glass] – Neuwirth Waltraud, [coll. cat.] Das Glas des Jugendstils. Österreichisches Museum für angewandte Kunst Wien. München 1973, 238, no. 111 ill. [champagne glass] – [exh. cat.] Josef Hoffmann Wien. Museum Bellerive. Zürich 1983, 87, 130, no. 168 ill. – Neuwirth Waltraud, [exh. cat.] Glas 1905–1925. Vom Jugendstil zum Art Déco. Österreichisches Museum für angewandte Kunst. Wien 1985, vol. 1, 78, no. 54 ill. [champagne glass] – Bröhan Torsten (pub.), Glaskunst der Moderne. München 1992, 162, no. 60 ill. [wine glass]

Josef Hoffmann
Wine Glass and Saucer
Champagne Glass, 1910/1912

Mold-blown and cut colorless
glass
Wine glass: h. 16.8 cm,
ø foot 8 cm, ø bowl 7.4 cm
Champagne glass: h. 18.7 cm,
ø foot 8.1 cm, ø 9.6 cm
Made by J. & L. Lobmeyr,
Vienna
Acc. no. 528/95-1,2

Koloman Moser

1868 Vienna – 1918 Vienna
1886–1892 studied at the Akademie der
Bildenden Künste in Vienna and
1892–1895 at the K.K. Kunstgewerbeschule Wien; was already at this time
illustrating for the journal "Wiener
Mode" and making ex libris for the
publisher Martin Gerlach. One of the
founders of the Vienna Secession in 1897;
planned in 1898 the stained glass
windows for the Secession building.
Numerous cover designs for the journal
"Ver Sacrum." As of 1899 teacher and
from 1900 to 1918 professor at the K.K.
Kunstgewerbeschule Wien. Founded
together with Josef Hoffmann the Wiener
Werkstätte in 1903 and was editor of
the associated journal "Hohe Warte."
Moser's work covered a broad spectrum
of furniture designs, graphics, textiles,
glass, leather, book covers, toys,
metalwares, ceramics, and leatherwork.

Koloman Moser's display cabinet, made by the company Jakob & Josef
Kohn in a limited quantity and first introduced to the public during the
winter exhibition 1901/02 at the Austrian Museum für Kunst und
Industrie (today Museum für angewandte Kunst), holds an outstanding
position in the history of furniture at the beginning of the 20th century.
It is the first formally convincing example of corpus furniture in the
bentwood technique. Using a system design worked out by Josef
Hoffmann, which is based on the use of angular rather than round bar
cross-sections, an extraordinary piece of furniture was created that
paradigmatically realizes in its successful unity of form and function the
aesthetic and theoretic ideas of modernism. JS

Sel. Lit.: [exh. cat.] Koloman Moser. Hochschule für angewandte Kunst. Wien 1979,
177 ill. – Ostergard Derek E. (pub.), Bent Wood and Metal Furniture 1850–1946.
New York 1987, 110 ill., 115 ill. – [exh. cat.] Torino 1902. Le Arti Decorative Internazionali
del Nuovo Secolo. Turin 1994, no. 143 ill. – [exh. cat.] Torino 1902. Die internationalen
dekorativen Künste des neuen Jahrhunderts. Museum für angewandte Kunst.
Gera 1995, 11 ill.

Koloman Moser
Display Cabinet, Model
1304/3140, c. 1901

Polished beech, mahogany-
colored stain; brass ball feet,
rivets, and hardware
H. 190 cm, w. 65 cm, d. 63 cm
Made by Jakob & Josef Kohn,
Vienna
Acc. no. 113/95

Bruno Paul

1874 Seifhennersdorf – 1968 Berlin
Studied 1886–1894 at the Kunstgewerbeschule Dresden, 1894–1897 at the Akademie für Bildende Künste in Munich.
Graphic work for the journals "Simplicissimus" and "Jugend." In 1898 one of the
founders of the Vereinigte Werkstätten
für Kunst im Handwerk, Munich. In 1907
founding member of the Deutscher
Werkbund and appointment as principal
of the school at the Kunstgewerbemuseum Berlin. 1924–1933 director of the
Vereinigte Staatsschulen für freie und
angewandte Kunst (state schools for fine
and applied arts) in Berlin. In 1933 private
studio in the Mark Brandenburg, lived in
Düsseldorf and Berlin after 1945.
Comprehensive design activities for the
Vereinigte Werkstätten für Kunst im
Handwerk, Munich – for example, the
"Typenmöbel" (standard furniture, 1908)
– as well as for the Deutsche Werkstätten
Dresden-Hellerau.

Bruno Paul
Coffee Maker on a Tray,
1904

Cast and polished brass,
pewter interior
H. 30 cm, ø tray 39 cm,
ø coffee maker 15.5 cm
Commissioned by Vereinigte
Werkstätten für Kunst im
Handwerk, Munich
Acc. no. 432/92

Around the turn of the century Bruno Paul had a significant part in
renewing art and the crafts in Munich. In 1898 he was one of the
founders of the Vereinigte Werkstätten für Kunst im Handwerk, almost
ten years later one of the founders of the Deutscher Werkbund, both
in Munich. The many-sidedness of Paul can be seen alone in the products
he designed for the Vereinigte Werkstätten, which included everything
from door handles to complete interiors. Amongst the metal works,
above all lighting fixtures, the coffee maker stands out as a particularly
stringent design in terms of craftsmanship and functionality. The simple
groove design reminds of the candelabra of around 1901, no documents
pertaining to the object can, however, be found in the archives of the
Vereinigte Werkstätten. But since all of Bruno Paul's metal works of these
years were commissioned by the Vereinigte Werkstätten, one can assume
that the same is true for this coffee maker. JS

Sel. Lit.: Dekorative Kunst vol. 14, 1906, 44 ill. – Ziffer Alfred, [exh. cat.] Bruno Paul.
Münchner Stadtmuseum. München 1992, 89, no. 183 ill. [further literature]

Peter Behrens

1868 Hamburg – 1940 Bremen
1886–1889 studied painting in Karlsruhe
and Düsseldorf. As of 1889 in Munich, in
1893 one of the founders of the Munich
Secession, in 1897 of the Vereinigte
Werkstätten für Kunst im Handwerk in
Munich. In 1899 appointment to the
artists' colony in Darmstadt. 1901–1902
course director at the Kunstschule in
Düsseldorf. In 1907 founding member of
the Deutscher Werkbund. 1907–1914
artistic advisor for the AEG in Berlin.
1922–1936 professor at the Meisterschule
für Architektur at the Vienna academy,
1936–1940 at the academy in Berlin.

Peter Behrens
Cover design for "Mittei-
lungen der Berliner
Elektricitaets-Werke," 1908

Two-color letterpress printing
H. 23.2 cm, w. 15.7 cm
Acc. no. 76/91

No doubt the most lasting impulse for industrial design in Germany in
the contemporary sense came from Peter Behrens and his work for the
AEG. The Allgemeine Elektricitaets-Gesellschaft commissioned Peter
Behrens in 1907 to develop a uniform company image, not only in terms
of the technical products of the company, but also of the graphics:
signet, letterhead, packaging, posters, and brochures for the company
advertising, or the periodicals represented here, were designed by
Behrens. He even designed the new factory buildings and workers'
housing developments. Thus the first "corporate identity" in the history
of design was created.

Just as successful was the re-designing of products, the ventilators,
kettles, arc lamps, etc. With the aesthetic translation and illustration of
the principles of function, Behrens founded a new tradition of industrial
functionalism that earned him the reputation of being the first industrial designer. JS

Sel. Lit.: [exh. cat.] Ein Dokument deutscher Kunst. Darmstadt 1901–1976. Vol. 2.
Darmstadt 1977, 181, 183 ill. – Buddensieg Tilmann, Industriekultur. Peter Behrens und
die AEG 1907–1914. Berlin 1979, D 196–197, no. G 1–3, D 199 ill. [further literature] –
Pinakothek der Moderne: eine Vision des Museums für Kunst, Architektur und Design
des 20. Jahrhunderts in München. Pub. Stiftung Pinakothek der Moderne. München/
New York 1995, 55 ill.

Mackay Hugh Baillie Scott

1865 Ramsgate/Isle of Man – 1945
London
Studied at the School of Art, Douglas, Isle
of Man. Worked at first as architect and
founded in 1885 together with C.R.
Ashbee the Guild of Handicraft. In 1897
interior design for the Neues Palais in
Darmstadt. Publications by the art author
H. Muthesius and the competition
"Haus eines Kunstfreundes" (1902) in
the journal "Innendekoration," allowed
Baillie Scott to reach a broad public
interested in the arts. Between 1900 and
1914 numerous furniture designs for
the Dresdner Werkstätten für Handwerkskunst, later called the Deutsche
Werkstätten.

Mackay H. Baillie Scott
Wardrobe, c. 1903

Wavy-grained birch with
intarsia, inlaid maple and
mother-of-pearl, mahogany
interior
Cornice with company signet
of 1901/02
H. 200 cm, w. 200 cm, d. 64 cm
Made by Dresdner Werk-
stätten für Handwerkskunst,
Dresden
Acc. no. 116/95

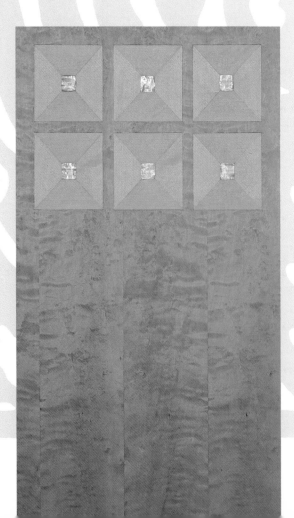

The English architect and designer Mackay H. Baillie Scott was one of the
first representatives of the Arts and Crafts Movement to also carry out
commissions in Germany, amongst others for Grand Duke Ernst Ludwig
von Hessen-Darmstadt (1897/98). His collaboration with Dresdner
Werkstätten, which can be proven as of 1902 but is hardly substantiated
by any objects, documents in a unique way the close relationship
between the English Arts and Crafts Movement and the reform program
of one of the most important German furniture manufacturers at the
beginning of the 20th century: Dresdner Werkstätten für Handwerkskunst established in 1898 (since 1907 Deutsche Werkstätten). Baillie Scott
designed a complete bedroom suite, which was made by the Dresdner
Werkstätten in two different versions, wavy-grained birch or oak. With its
emphasis on the decorative effect of the grain, its severe proportioning
of planes and the geometrically stylized intarsia ornamentation,
this wardrobe represents a particularly striking example of Japanese
influence. Without knowledge of Japanese design, the development of
modernism in this form would not have been possible. JS

Sel. Lit.: [co. cat.] Deutsche Werkstätten. Handgearbeitete Möbel. Dresden 1909,
190 ill. [dresser from the same series] – Arnold Klaus Peter, Vom Sofakissen zum Städtebau.
Die Geschichte der Deutschen Werkstätten und der Gartenstadt Hellerau. Dresden/Basel
1993, 54–55, 409, 457 [re Baillie Scott's works for the Deutsche Werkstätten]

Otto Wagner

1841 Penzing/Vienna – 1918 Vienna
Studied in 1857 at the Wiener Technische
Hochschule, in 1860 at the Berliner
Bauakademie and 1861–1863 at the
architecture school of the Akademie der
bildenden Künste in Vienna, where he
taught from 1894–1913. 1899–1905
member of the Vienna Secession.
Comprehensive architectural projects
such as in Vienna, for example the
stations of the city railroad (1894–1907),
the postal savings bank office building
(1904–1906), and the Steinhof Landes-,
Heil- und Pflegeanstalt (asylum) with
church. In addition to his buildings, he
planned as of 1890 interiors and
furniture. Wagner also designed textiles,
glass, silverware and wrought-iron work.

The architect and designer Otto Wagner belongs to the pioneers of
modern architecture and of design. With the interior design of his major
architectural work, the office of the Postsparkasse in Vienna (1904–1906,
1910–1912), he contributed decisively to the development of modern
furniture. The furniture designs for the Postsparkasse constitute at the
same time the new style of the Viennese avant-garde, which consciously
makes construction and function of furniture visible, dispenses with decor
in the traditional sense and also employs the most modern materials
(aluminum). The chairs, armchairs, stools, filing cabinets, and desks were
made by the two traditional Viennese bentwood companies, Thonet and
Kohn. While the desk was used only in the offices of the Postsparkasse,
the stool belonged to the furnishing of various, different types of rooms.
JS

Sel. Lit.: Mang Karl, Geschichte des modernen Möbels. Stuttgart 1978, 46 ill., 82–83 –
[exh. cat.] Gebogenes Holz. Künstlerhaus. Wien 1979, no. 56 ill. – Asenbaum Paul, Peter
Haiko, Herbert Lachmayer and Reiner Zettl, Otto Wagner. Möbel und Innenräume.
Salzburg/Wien 1984, 36–37, 208–212 ill. – [exh. cat.] Otto Wagner. Designs for Architecture.
Museum of Modern Art. Oxford 1985, no. 22, no. 26 ill. – Mundt Barbara, [coll. cat.]
Produktdesign 1900–1990. Kunstgewerbemuseum. Berlin 1991, 34–35 ill.

Otto Wagner
Desk and Stool of the
Viennese Postsparkasse
(Postal Savings Bank), c. 1904

Beechwood stained brown
and aluminum
Desk: h. 109 cm, w. 107 cm,
d. 66 cm
Stool: h. 47 cm, w. 42 cm,
d. 42 cm
Made by Gebr. Thonet, Vienna
Acc. no. 133/95, 134/95

Patrick Nordström

1870 Sweden – 1929 Islev
Studied 1889–1890 at the Svenska
Slöjdföreningens Skola (school of the arts
and crafts association), Göteborg, and
1894/1895 at the Tekniska Yrkesskolan
(trades school), Lund. Trained as
wood sculptor, he turned to ceramics
already in 1902. As of this time he
lived in Copenhagen and returned to
Sweden only in 1922. From 1912 to 1923
employed at the Royal Porcelain
Manufactory Copenhagen. Then his own
workshop in Islev.

In 1911 the Swedish sculptor and ceramist Patrick Nordström and the
oldest Danish porcelain manufacturer, the Royal Porcelain Manufactory
Copenhagen, began working together. What is unusual about this
collaboration is the fact that Nordström was commissioned to develop
stoneware techniques at a porcelain factory; this did not happen
anywhere else than in Copenhagen (Bing & Grøndahl, Royal Porcelain
Manufactory), if one disregards the porcelain-like Boettger stoneware in
Meissen. Thus the objects produced as unique pieces as of 1912 also
received work numbers, so that at least until the numbering stopped in
1917 all objects had been individually registered. Patrick Nordström's
works, which exerted a great influence on Danish and Swedish ceramics,
had in turn been inspired by two different sources: by French stoneware
of the close of the 19th century, which he had come to know during
a stay in Paris, and by East Asian ceramics, which in the end were of
decisive significance for both the French and Danish ceramists. JS

Center: Vase No. S 98, c. 1913

Cast stoneware, gray body;
matt brown foundation glaze,
matt gray-green overglaze,
around the neck glossy dark
blue glaze with small air
bubbles; bronze lid
H. 21 cm, max. ø 14 cm
Made by the Royal Porcelain
Manufactory Copenhagen
Acc. no. 169/93

Right: Vase No. S 2544,
c. 1914

Cast stoneware, gray body;
matt light brown glaze with
ivory-colored spots; bronze lid
Base: brushmark in under-
glaze blue
H. 21 cm, ø 15 cm
Made by the Royal Porcelain
Manufactory Copenhagen
Acc. No. 170/93

Patrick Nordström
Left: Vase, 1919

Cast stoneware, gray body;
brown speckled foundation
glaze, ochre overglaze;
bronze lid
Base: brushmark in under-
glaze blue
H. 14.5 cm, max. ø 13 cm
Made by the Royal Porcelain
Manufactory Copenhagen
Acc. no. 171/93

Bernard Essers
Cover Design for the Journal
"Wendingen," 1924

Series VI, no. 11/12.
Saantport: C.A. Mees
Woodcut, black
33 x 33 cm
Acc. no. 233/93

Bernard Essers

1893 Kraksaän (Dutch West Indies) –
1945 Doniawerstal
Studied at the Hendrik de Keyserteken-
school in Amsterdam and at the Royal
College of Arts, Kensington/London.
Met the painters R.N. Roland Holst and
Jan Toorop. Since 1919 worked for the
journal Wendingen in design. Illustrated
numerous books, e.g. "Een zwerver
verfield" and "Een zwerver verdwaald e
Saphia" by A. van Schendel, "Kunstenaar
en Samenleving" by C.J. Adama van
Scheltema, "Beirdre en de zonen van
Usnach" by A. Roland Holst.

Aside from "De Stijl", "Wendingen: Maanoblad voor Bauwen en Sieren"
(1918–1931) is the most important Dutch art and architecture journal
published between the two world wars. Similar to "De Stijl,"
which served as organ for the constructivist architects, "Wendingen"
was mouthpiece and a forum for discussion of the other, the more
expressionistic style, particularly of the so-called Amsterdam school and
the social reform movements associated with it. The theme issue
"Kristallen, wondervormen der natuur," with the cover design by Bernard
Esser shown here, reflects this style in a paradigmatic manner. With an
introduction on "Architectonische phantasieen in de wereld der
kristallen" by the architect H.Th. Wijdeveld, the moving spirit, publisher,
and chief editor of the journal, the issue revolves around one of the
leitmotifs of expressionistic architecture – compare, for instance,
Bruno Taut and his Berlin group Die gläserne Kette. While Wijdeveld
designed the pages of "Wendingen" in a very decorative style himself,
he let a variety of other artists – architects, painters, graphic artists,
designers, etc., including J.L.M. Lauweriks, H. Finsterlin, J. Toorop,
S. Jessurun de Mesquita, A.D. Copier, but also V. Huszár and E. Lissitzky –
design the covers.
The set of "Wendingen" journals which was acquired in 1993 thus represents a particularly significant addition to the collection from various
perspectives. CR

Sel. Lit.: Wendingen. Grafica e cultura in una rivista olandese del Novecento. Testo di
Giovanni Fanelli ... Mailand 1986, 128, ill. 55, 243 – Breuer Gerda, [exh. cat.] Wendingen
1918–1931. Amsterdamer Expressionismus. Museum Künstlerkolonie. Darmstadt
1992, 96–97, 111 – Broos Kees and Paul Hefting, Grafische Formgebung in den Niederlanden
20. Jahrhundert. Laren/Basel 1993, 72–75 [re. Wijdeveld and "Wendingen"]

The Wiener Werkstätte had been founded in 1903, 14 years previously, when in the summer of 1917 an independent artist workshop for ceramics was also installed. That this happened so late in time would primarily have had to do with the permanent financial distress of the Wiener Werkstätte and the political and economic situation. Due to World War I, almost exclusively women were employed in this production workshop.

The many-sided student of Hoffmann, Hilda Jesser, delivered works from the most varied areas of the crafts, as, for example, lace, embroidery, printed material and wallpaper, glass decor, porcelain, leatherwork, and commercial art. She designed only a few ceramic pieces, but these belonged to the most successful in the production. Jesser paid strict attention to the usability of her works, was very reserved in her use of color and decor and avoided all playfulness. Between 1921 and 1925 her ceramic models were produced more than 100 times; the jardiniere of Die Neue Sammlung, illustrated on the left, was produced, as one of the most successful models, more than 380 times in various decors and colors or glazes. JS

Sel. Lit.: [exh. cat.] Expressive Keramik der Wiener Werkstätte 1917–1930. Bayerische Vereinsbank. München 1992, 58–59, no. 26 ill. [identical shape, different glaze]

Hilda Schmid-Jesser

1894 Marburg – 1985 Vienna
First trained at the Wiener Frauenaka-demie (academy for women); 1912–1917 studied at the Kunstgewerbeschule Wien, under J. Hoffmann, et al. 1916–1922 member of the Wiener Werkstätte. 1922–1932 an assistant and 1935–1938 assistant professor at the Wiener Kunst-gewerbeschule; returned to teaching in the years from 1949 to 1967. Designed textiles, ceramics as well as numerous glass decors for Lobmeyr, Vienna.

Hilda Jesser
Right: Vase, Model No. 868, 1921
Left: Jardiniere, Model No. 872, 1921

Formed stoneware, reddish-brown body; yellow, green, red, and blue glaze
Blind-stamp on base: WW (ligature)
H. 25 cm, max. w. 12 cm
H. 13.5 cm, l. 30 cm, w. 16 cm
Made by Wiener Werkstätte, Vienna
Acc. no. 461/92 (jardiniere: acc. no. 62/27)

Jacques-Emile Ruhlmann

1879 Paris – 1933 Paris
After his father's death in 1907, took over
the family-owned interior design business. As of 1913 wall paper, carpets,
lighting fixtures, and furniture designed
by him are exhibited at the fall salon
in Paris. In 1919 he founded together with
the painting expert Pierre Laurent Les
Etablissements Ruhlmann et Laurent, a
very successful business for exclusive
interior design. In 1923 opened his own
workshop. The famous Exposition
Internationale des Arts Décoratifs et
Industriels Modernes in Paris in 1925 was
the international breakthrough for
Ruhlmann as a celebrated French
furniture designer.

The highlight of French art deco and at the same time a milestone in the
development of unit and combination furniture is the Bibliothèque of
the renowned actress Jeanne Renouardt. She acquired the furniture
exhibited at the Salon des Artistes Décorateurs for her newly built villa in
Saint Cloud near Paris. The exemplary, technically perfect execution is
characteristic of Ruhlmann's luxurious furniture, which made him the best
paid and most sought after furniture designer of art deco. The maharajah
of Indore, who was having his palace in Manik Bagh designed and
furnished by the best European artists of his time, also commissioned
Ruhlmann to make a second version of this piece of furniture, executed
in macassar wood. Due to the wood grain overlapping from piece to
piece, though, it was no longer possible to freely combine the individual
box elements. But it is exactly in this that the importance of this furniture
lies – aside from its outstanding significance for a certain style and its
utmost refinement.

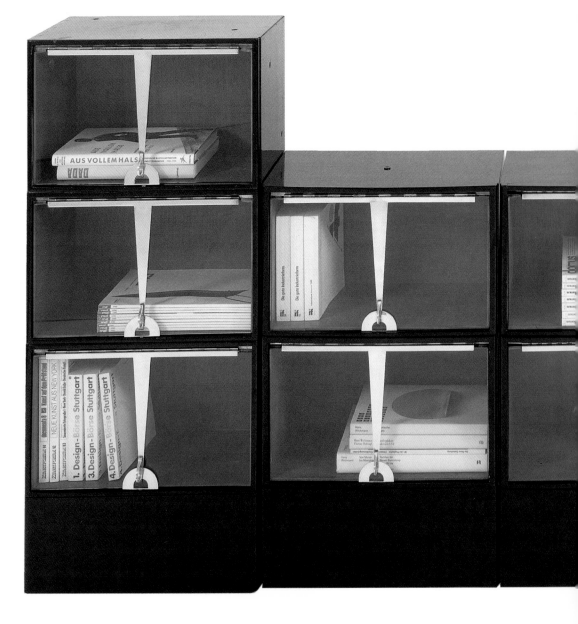

As combination furniture consisting of units that could be built-up and screwed together, the way of modern furniture – from wall cupboard to wall unit – was realized for the first time, and this by an ebonist standing in a century-old tradition. FH

Sel. Lit.: Camard Florence, Ruhlmann. Paris 1983, 74–75 ill. [the version made for the maharaja of Indore], 120 ill. [Salon des Artistes Décorateurs, 1929] – Pinakothek der Moderne: eine Vision des Museums für Kunst, Architektur und Design des 20. Jahrhunderts in München. Pub. Stiftung Pinakothek der Moderne. München/New York 1995, 120 ill. – Niggl Reto, Eckart Muthesius. International Style 1930. Der Palast des Maharadschas in Indore, Architektur und Interieur. Stuttgart 1996

Jacques-Emile Ruhlmann
Bookcase, 1928

Black lacquered and polished limewood, colorless glass, and chrome-plated metal
Several brands on back:
Ruhlmann
H. 134 cm, w. 235 cm,
d. 27.5 cm
Provenance: Jeanne Renouardt, Saint Cloud, France
Acc. no. 50/92

Functional elements such as joint frames, glass holding devices, and handles, designed as an entity, come to be a structuring ornament of the furniture. The principle of repetition within a row illustrates the system character. Due to the high technical quality, however, each unit also exists formally in itself.

Frank Lloyd Wright

1867 Richland Center, Wisconsin, USA –
1959 Phoenix, USA
Studied mechanical engineering
1885–1887 at the University of Wisconsin.
As of 1887 worked as architect for
Dankmar Adler and Louis Sullivan in
Chicago (1889–1892), et al. Around 1885
first furniture designs. Wright always
did the interior design of his buildings as
well, e.g. Imperial Hotel, Tokyo
(1915–1922). In 1904 he designed
for the first time worldwide metal office
chairs and desks that do not imitate
wood.

Frank Lloyd Wright
Pieces from a Coffee and
Dinner Service, 1916/1922

Cast porcelain, white body;
glazed; red, yellow, light
green, and light blue decor
Stamped on all pieces:
Noritake/N (in a laurel wreath)
NIPPON TOKI KAISHA/JAPAN/
1966 (or) HEINZ AND CO 1984/
Noritake (N in a laurel wreath)
Dinner plate: ø 26.9 cm
Dessert plate: ø 16.2 cm and
19.3 cm
Cup: h. 5.5 cm, ø 8.7 cm
Saucer: ø 13.5 cm
Commissioned by the Imperial
Hotel, Tokyo
Made by Noritake Nippon Toki
Kaisha, Japan
Acc. no. 151/93

The service by Frank Lloyd Wright in Die Neue Sammlung symbolizes in a nutshell, as it were, the manifold and extremely fruitful interaction between the various countries and continents in the first quarter of our century. The American architect and designer erected a few years after his first stay in Europe – giving European architecture an important impulse – one of his major works, the Hotel Imperial in Tokyo (1915–1922, torn down in 1968). Using an earthquake-proof construction principle, a building was created in which – based on the idea of an integral whole – every element of the furnishing and interior was coordinated with the building in total. Thus Wright designed the corresponding furniture, lighting fixtures, and other objects for the interior – even the hotel porcelain was based on his ideas. Although Wright otherwise hardly occupied himself with porcelain or ceramics, he created with this service a design that forms a synthesis of various cultural groups. The geometric decor of overlapping circles, which can also be seen in other works (e.g. glass windows for the Avery Coonley Playhouse of 1912 or even more directly in the murals for Midway Gardens in 1914), still clearly reflects the impressions his trip to Europe from 1909 to 1910 had made on him. One is reminded, for example, of Jutta Sika's coffee service for Josef Böck. At the same time the circle theme, which originally was also to be continued on the inside of the cups, reminds, precisely in this detail, of the so-called Nabeshima porcelain made in Japan in the 18th century. The first services delivered to the Hotel Imperial were still made of very fine and thus fragile porcelain. It was soon replaced by a more robust porcelain better suited to the hotel business. The service was so successful that, even though it was being made until the late 1960's, it went into renewed production again in 1984. CR/JS

Sel. Lit.: Hanks David A., The Decorative Designs of Frank Lloyd Wright. New York 1979, 134–135 ill. – Hanks David A., Frank Lloyd Wright. Preserving an Architectural Heritage. Decorative Designs from the Domino's Pizza Collection. New York 1989, 95 ill. – Rudoe Judy, [coll. cat.] Decorative Arts 1850–1950. British Museum. London 1991, 125, no. 317 ill. 107 – McCready Karen, Art Deco and Modernist Ceramics. London 1995, 128, no. 200 ill.

Jacques-Emile Ruhlmann

1879 Paris – 1933 Paris
After his father's death, in 1907 took over
the family-owned interior design business. As of 1913 wall paper, carpets,
lighting fixtures, and furniture designed
by him are exhibited at the fall salon
in Paris. In 1919 he founded together with
the painting expert Pierre Laurent Les
Etablissements Ruhlmann et Laurent, a
very successful business for exclusive
interior design. In 1923 opened his own
workshop. The famous Exposition
Internationale des Arts Décoratifs et
Industriels Modernes in Paris in 1925 was
the international breakthrough for
Ruhlmann as a celebrated French
furniture designer.

1925 – the year in which an exhibition took place in Paris, giving a whole
style its name: Exposition Internationale des Arts Décoratifs et Industriels
Modernes. In the same year Leon Moussinac published a collection of
woven and brocaded fabrics for furniture covers, a representative cross-
section of the French textile art of this time. Amongst the designers are
such famous names as Edouard Bénédictus, Maurice Dufrène, Raoul
Dufy, Paul Follot, René Herbst, André Mare, Louis Süe, and Jacques-Emile
Ruhlmann, just to mention the most important. Ruhlmann, whose designs
for the company Lampas are shown here, was the leading ebonist in
France. He designed not only furniture but also everything which
belonged to a complete interior. These furnishing textiles also prove, like
the other designs with their unusual, abstract decors, the outstanding
position of Ruhlmann at the peak of the French art deco designers. JS

Sel. Lit.: Garner Philippe, Möbel des 20. Jahrhunderts. München 1980, 74 ill.

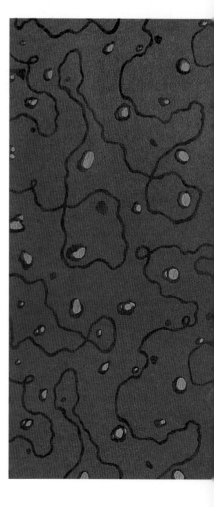

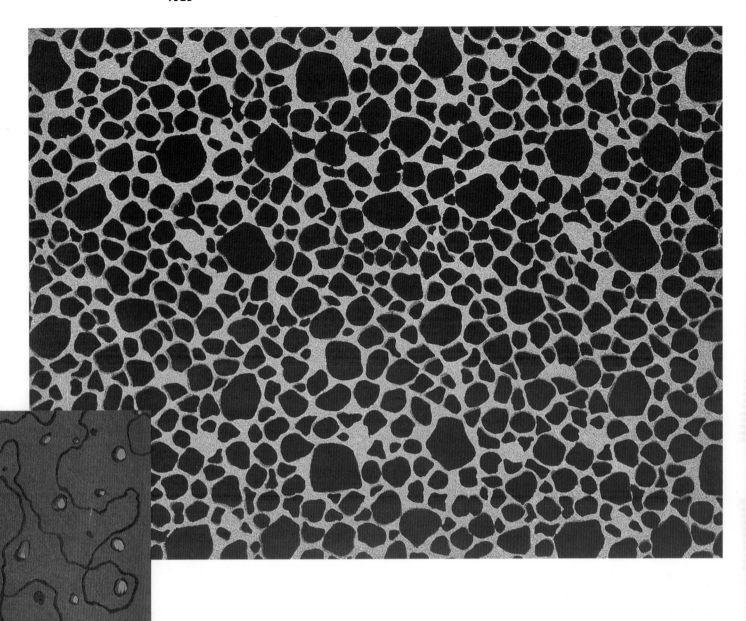

Jacques-Emile Ruhlmann
Designs for Furnishing Fabric,
before 1925

Collotype, color stenciled
32.2 x 25 cm
In: Leon Moussinac, Etoffes
d'Ameublement tissées et
brochées. Paris: Editions
Albert Lévy 1925
Acc. no. 639/93

Theodor Bogler

1897 Hofgeismar, Germany – 1968 Maria
Laach
1919–1920 studied at the Staatliches
Bauhaus Weimar under Johannes Itten
and Lyonel Feininger, in 1923 first designs
for the stoneware factories Velten-
Vordamm, in 1927 entered the Bene-
dictine abbey Maria Laach, in 1932
ordination to the priesthood, 1936–1968
collaboration with the Staatliche
Majolika-Manufaktur Karlsruhe, as of
1948 director of the Kunstwerkstätten
and art publisher of "Ars Liturgica," Maria
Laach, as of 1951 designs for various
ceramic manufacturers in Höhr-
Grenzhausen.

The combination tea pot of 1923 belongs to the earliest works of the
Bauhaus made for industry or for industrial mass production. The various
basic elements of the pot – the graduated body, spout, lid, handle – could
be partially pre-fabricated and combined in various ways, so that
standardized types with variation possibilities were created for easy mass
production. As they were never mass-produced, though, they remained
unique pieces.

Early on already Walter Gropius, the first director of the Bauhaus, called
the multiplication of ceramics the most important task of the experimental workshop of the Bauhaus, located in the traditional pottery town
Dornburg. Technical training was to be supplemented with time in a
porcelain factory, where the cutting of plaster forms for cast porcelain
vessels could be learned. Thus were not only the necessary skills for
the design of mass production ceramics transmitted, but also contacts to
industry, including to the Älteste Volkstedter Porzellanfabrik and to the
Harkortsche Steingutfabrik in Velten-Vordamm, established. The pottery
was thus the first Weimar Bauhaus workshop to collaborate with
industrial companies. JS

Sel. Lit.: Neue Arbeiten der Bauhauswerkstätten. Bauhausbücher 7. München 1925,
102 ill. – Hüter Karl-Heinz, Das Bauhaus in Weimar. Berlin/Ost 1976, 163, ill. 49 – [exh. cat.]
Keramik und Bauhaus. Bauhaus-Archiv. Berlin 1989, 89, no. 21 [further literature] –
Mundt Barbara, Produkt-Design 1900–1990. Berlin 1991, 54 ill.

Theodor Bogler
Combination Tea Pot, 1923

Cast and assembled stone-
ware, red-brown body,
matt black glaze, nickel silver
handle with wickerwork
H. 11.8 cm, ø 15 cm,
w. 22.5 cm
Made by Töpferwerkstatt
des Staatlichen Bauhauses
Weimar, Dornburg
Acc. no. 570/93

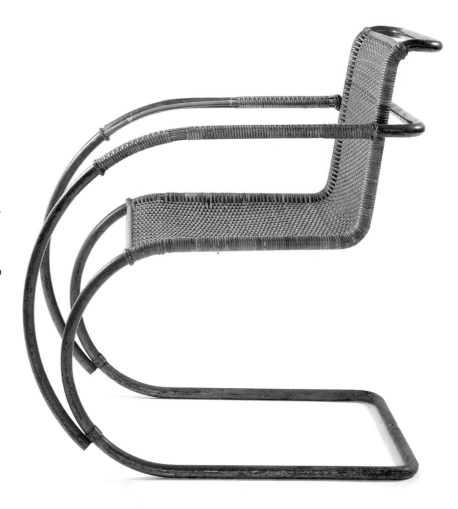

Ludwig Mies van der Rohe
Cantilevered Armchair MR 20,
1927

Red lacquered tubular steel
and cane
H. 78.5 cm, w. 47 cm, d. 74 cm
Made by Berliner Metall-
gewerbe Josef Müller, Berlin,
and Bamberg Werkstätten,
Berlin
Acc. no. 44/93

Ludwig Mies van der Rohe

1886 Aachen, Germany – 1969 Chicago
1897–1900 trained at the Aachener
Dombauschule (cathedral workshop
school). In 1905 moved to Berlin. Studied
until 1907 under Bruno Paul. 1908–1911
worked together with Le Corbusier
and Walter Gropius in the office of Peter
Behrens. 1930–1932 director of the
Bauhaus Dessau. In 1937 emigrated to
the USA. 1938–1952 director of the
department of architecture at the Illinois
Institute of Technology, Chicago.

The success and amount of publicity received by the Weißenhof development of the Stuttgart Werkbund exhibition, for which this chair was
designed in 1927, substantially contributed to the spread of tubular steel
furniture. It soon came to be a synonym for modern furniture construction. Although the momentous construction principle of the tubular steel
chair without back legs and thus freely suspended, stems not from
Mies van der Rohe – this role is claimed by the Dutch Mart Stam – it was
Mies van der Rohe who created the most balanced and harmonious form.
In addition he was the first to consequentially utilize the resilient
quality of tubular steel for a cantilevered chair, receiving a patent within
the same year. Because of the limited number of tubular steel chairs
still existing in their original state and conditioned by our historical view
defined by black and white photographs, as well as being influenced by
the production of chrome-plated tubular steel chairs in the post-war
aesthetics, it is today generally not known that the Weißenhof chair was
to begin with – even if only in a limited quantity – lacquered in various
colors (yellow, blue, red)! JS

Sel. Lit.: Ostergard Derek E. (pub.), Bent Wood and Metal Furniture 1850–1946. New York
1987, 275–276, no. 71 ill. – Mundt Barbara, [coll. cat.] Produktdesign 1900–1990. Kunstgewerbemuseum. Berlin 1991, 62 ill. [without armrests] – Möller Werner and Otakar Màcel,
Ein Stuhl macht Geschichte. München 1992, 27–28 ill.

Lena Bergner – later married to Hannes Meyer, who directed the Bauhaus as successor of Walter Gropius – studied weaving at the Bauhaus from 1926 to the spring of 1929 "with creative and practical participation on the 'Bauhaus textiles' for industry." This sketch, one of a series of four, might still have been made during the time Lena Bergner studied at the Bauhaus. Decisive for this assumption are the powerful colors and the pseudo-symmetric patterning with its irregularly distributed, horizontal stripes in various widths. None of the stripes stretch across the whole width of the design, they end in a straight cut towards the center or towards the edges, so that steps or stairs are created. This type of design reflecting the influence of Paul Klee is especially typical for the early Weimar Bauhaus. Bergner was a student in his course in 1927/28. After Hannes Meyer took over the directorship of the Bauhaus, the textile workshop changed dramatically. No longer do Paul Klee's theories or the use of optical elements such as triangles and stripes, which define this design, characterize the products of this workshop – texture replaced the dominance of color. The sketch, which could be acquired with other works from the estate, superbly supplements the textile department of Die Neue Sammlung, in which works of such women as Gunta Stölzl, Anni Albers, Otti Berger and other Bauhaus weavers can already be found. FH

Lena Meyer-Bergner

1906 Coburg, Germany – 1981 Bad Soden 1926–1929 studied at the Bauhaus majoring in weaving. 1929–1920 director of the Ostpreußische Handweberei in Königsberg. In 1931 travelled to Moscow with her husband Hannes Meyer, the successor of Walter Gropius at the Bauhaus. From March 1931 to June 1936 worked at the Moscow textile factory Dekorativkanj. 1937–1938 owned a carpet workshop in Genf. As of 1939 lived in Mexico with Hannes Meyer, after their return to Switzerland in 1949, collaborated on publications on the Bauhaus.

Lena Meyer-Bergner
Design for a Knotted Carpet,
c. 1927

Watercolor over pencil on
light paper
Sheet: 36 x 19 cm,
composition: 28 x 17.5 cm
Acc. no. 594/91-1,2,3,4

Anton Stankowski

1906 Gelsenkirchen, Germany – lives in
Stuttgart
1927–1928 training at the Essener
Folkwangschule under Wilhelm Poetter
and Max Burchartz majoring in interior
design, typography and photography;
in 1929 commercial artist in the Reklame-
Atelier Max Dalang in Zurich, in 1938
founded his own Grafisches Atelier in
Stuttgart, 1940–1948 military service and
prisoner of war, in 1964 guest lecturer
at the Hochschule für Gestaltung in Ulm,
in 1982 honorary guest at the Villa
Massimo in Rome, in 1983 retrospective
in Kassel, in 1983 founding of the
Stankowski-Stiftung, in 1991 Hans-
Molfenter-Preis.

Stankowski sees photography as "design of light." Thus photograms, montages, and light experiments belong to his repertory. Especially in the early thirties he was attempting to find a completely new way of seeing things, avoiding, though, an over-aestheticizing of the industrial product. In this, the medium of estrangement played a central role. The example illustrated here also shows that he was inspired by the ideas of László Moholy-Nagy who recommended the deliberate use of light-dark effects and unusual perspectives. The object here served as an excuse for perceptual-philosophical reflections, which were certainly also enriched by cognition of the natural sciences. Whether the subject is a metal coil or textiles seems secondary. The photographic staging is central, and this is Stankowski's main interest. Thus the product receives an aesthetic dimension which is located far beyond its thing quality and peaks in the dance of the spiral pirouette or in the multiplication and monumen-talization of a shadow play. The photograph, which came to our institution together with others from Stankowski's collection, superbly supplements Die Neue Sammlung with its numerous graphic works by an artist working integrally and across boundaries. EM

Sel. Lit.: [exh. cat.] Anton Stankowski. Vol. 2. Stuttgart 1991, 83, no. 64, 139 ill.

**Anton Stankowski
Photograph: Coil Spring with
Shadow, 1932**

**Black-and-white print made
later from the original
negative
Signed and dated on reverse
24 x 18 cm
Made by Atelier Stankowski,
Stuttgart
Acc. no. 387/95**

Hans Finsler
Photograph: Electric
Lightbulb, 1928

Black-and-white print made
later from the original
negative
Label on reverse: Staatliche
Galerie Moritzburg, Halle,
Hans-Finsler-Nachlaß (estate
of H.F.)
Image: 19 x 13.7 cm, sheet:
21.7 x 16 cm
Commissioned by Deutscher
Werkbund
Acc. no. 598/93

Hans Finsler

1891 Heilbronn, Germany – 1972 Zurich
1911–1915 studied architecture at the
technical college in Stuttgart and Munich,
1915–1921 studied art history in Munich
under Heinrich Wölfflin et al. and
in Berlin, until 1925 under Paul Frankl in
Halle/Saale. In 1923 first attempts at
photography. As of 1927 director of the
photography course at the Kunstgewerbeschule Burg Giebichenstein, in 1932
appointed to the Kunstgewerbeschule
Zurich, 1944–1955 president of the
Schweizer Werkbund, 1958 professor
emeritus, 1971 member of the Stiftung
für Photographie Schweiz.

The photography by Hans Finsler is dedicated to the beauty of apparently irrelevant things. Influenced by the "Sehschule" (seeing school) of Heinrich Wölfflin, under whom he had studied art history as of 1915, and in the end following his teacher Paul Frankl to Halle, Finsler came to photography autodidactically. His work in Halle and Zürich contributed enormously to the development of object photography which, free of all traditional values, follows the laws of the things themselves. In contrast to Renger-Patzsch who swore on the pure aesthetic of the surface, Finsler sought to penetrate the objects in order to retain their separate magical existence in the image. The photograph on hand was made for the book "Licht und Beleuchtung" by Wilhelm Lotz, published in 1928 as volume 6 of the Werkbund series "Bücher der Form." The lightbulb appears outside of time and space in its nacked presence, contrasted and supplemented by the image of its shadow. Light and dark are not only the essential components of its function, they also belong to the elements of photography. Thus the special characteristics of the object and the process-technical laws of the medium melt to a single unity in Finsler's work. EM

Sel. Lit.: [exh. cat.] Film und Foto. Stuttgart 1929, no. 208 ill. – Die Form no. 1, Jan. 1933, 25 ill. – [exh. cat.] Hans Finsler. Neue Wege der Fotografie. Staatliche Moritzburg, Halle. Leipzig 1991, 220, no. 196 ill.

France

For the synthetic products of the late 19th and early 20th century design hardly played a role yet. Plastics were originally used to replace other materials such as wood, for example, and in order to make the imitation perfect, were adapted to the respective current language of forms. As with all new materials the already existing and tested forms were used at first. The manifold possibilities which plastics opened up for design only began to be recognized in the mid-twenties, were used more broadly only in the years following, and have probably still not been exhausted. Stylized, abstract geometric forms belong to the stylistic characteristics of art deco as much as the lightning shaped zig-zags, schematic cascades, and sunrays which allude to the development of electricity and technical progress and which are easy to translate into plastic. The various art styles of the first quarter of the century, especially cubism and constructivism as in the case of the shoe racks, served as formal source of inspiration. With almost playful ease the designer seems to have adopted the language of forms. The result is an extraordinary ensemble rich in variations for individual shoe displays in window decorations. JS

Four Shoe Racks, c. 1930

Red and black plastic
H. 10–15.5 cm, l. 9–23.3 cm,
w. 6.9–9 cm or ø 10.6 cm
Made by Iseghen, France (?)
Acc. no. 497/93

Marguerite Friedländer-Wildenhain

1896 Lyon, France – 1985 Guerneville,
USA
1919–1926 student at the ceramic workshop of the Staatliches Bauhaus Weimar
in Dornburg/Saale. Between 1925 and
1933 director of the ceramic workshop
Burg Giebichenstein (Halle/Saale) together with G. Marcks and F. Wildenhain.
During this time numerous designs for the
Staatliche Porzellanmanufaktur Berlin,
e.g. Hallesche Form (1930) and Burg
Giebichenstein (1930). 1933–1940 set up
a pottery in Putten, the Netherlands.
Between 1940 and 1942 director of the
ceramic course at the College of Arts and
Crafts Oakland, California. 1942 own
workshop in Guerneville and 1948
founding of the ceramic school Pond Farm
Pottery.

At the time that Günther von Pechmann, the former director of Die Neue
Sammlung, took over the directorship of the Staatliche Porzellanmanufaktur in Berlin in 1929, the mass production of modern china was given
a decidedly new orientation. Von Pechmann had already during his
museum work in Munich made contact with the Kunstgewerbeschule
Burg Giebichenstein in Halle and had dedicated a special exhibition in Die
Neue Sammlung to this arts and crafts school in 1928. In the fall of 1929
von Pechmann turned to the arts and crafts school and commissioned
Marguerite Friedländer, who after attending the Bauhaus was in charge
of the ceramic, later the porcelain workshop of Burg Giebichenstein,
to make a modern, functional everyday service. After various services of
the so-called "Halle form" had been produced at first, Friedländer
designed the table service "Burg Giebichenstein" in the fall of the same
year. In doing so the combination of pieces contained in a dinner service
was thought through anew and adapted to the changed eating habits,
thus dispensing with such traditional items as candelabra, jugs, small
bowls, etc. The strictly geometric forms found their correspondence in
the decor: Fine grooves in relief, borrowed from the field of ceramics, are
subordinated to the whole and emphasize the geometric design of the
individual pieces. The integral unity of the service was achieved by
limiting the bowls and plates to two basic shapes which could then be
varied in size as desired. Such a reduction – in the number of pieces as
well – fulfilled the modern demand for variability and at the same time
the striving for the perfect shape. This also finds expression in the
catchword of the time: "Ewige Formen" (Wolfgang von Wersin: Eternal
Forms), the title of an exhibition of Die Neue Sammlung in the year 1930.
CR/JS

Sel. Lit.: Schneider Katja, Burg Giebichenstein. Weinheim 1992, vol. 1, 295 ff., vol. 2, 342,
no. 238 ill. – [exh. cat.] Burg Giebichenstein. Staatliche Galerie Moritzburg, Halle/
Badisches Landesmuseum. Karlsruhe 1993, 265, no. 311 ill. – [coll. cat.] Porzellan. Kunst und
Design 1889–1939. Bröhan-Museum. Berlin 1993, 252–254, no. 246 ill. [further literature]

Marguerite Friedländer-
Wildenhain
Pieces from the Dinner Service
Burg Giebichenstein, 1930

Cast porcelain, white body;
glazed
Each piece: blue sceptre mark
and brown-black stamp of
the castle
Bowl: H. 12.3 cm,
max. w. 29.5 cm
Sauce boat: h. 7.9 cm,
ø 15.3 cm
Platter: h. 44 x 33 cm
Plate: ø 24.6-26.7 cm
Made by Staatliche Porzellan-
manufaktur, Berlin
Acc. no. 457/90

Individual luxury with the most precious materials and most perfect forms
was before World War II possible only in Paris – a city with a long
tradition of internationalism and refinement. Only here could such an
undertaking as La Maison Desny, selling the most exclusive interior decors
around world, exist. Desny commissioned the most important artists of
the time to make designs that were then produced in highly specialized
workshops as unique pieces or in very small series. Aside from André
Masson, Alberto and Diego Giacometti, as well as Jean-Michel Frank
amongst others, Robert Mallet-Stevens also worked for La Maison Desny.
His unusual designs are characterized by a strictly geometric decor – a
style that the silver service in Die Neue Sammlung also demonstrates. This
required a particularly precise and fine workmanship of the valuable
materials. In the history of art deco silver this work undoubtedly
represents a fascinating highlight. JS

Sel. Lit.: Pinakothek der Moderne: eine Vision des Museums für Kunst, Architektur und
Design des 20. Jahrhunderts in München. Pub. Stiftung Pinakothek der Moderne.
München/New York 1995, 127 ill.

Robert Mallet-Stevens
Tea and Coffee Service,
c. 1930

Repoussé and polished silver,
partially gilded on the
interior; macassar wood
Stamped on each piece:
Desny, Paris, MADE IN FRANCE
H. 13.4 cm,
w. (with tray) 34.5 cm,
d. (with tray) 10.8 cm
Commissioned by La Maison
Desny, Paris
Acc. no. 53/91

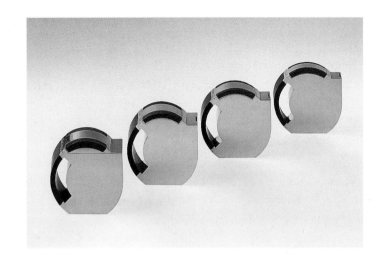

Robert Mallet-Stevens

1886 Paris – 1945 Paris
1905–1910 studied at the Ecole Spéciale
d'Architecture in Paris. In 1929 founding
member and president of the Union
des Artistes Modernes. Aside from
furniture and silver objects, also designed
film sets. Influenced by Japanese architecture, by Frank Lloyd Wright and
De Stijl, Mallet-Stevens was one of the
most important representatives of
modernism in France.

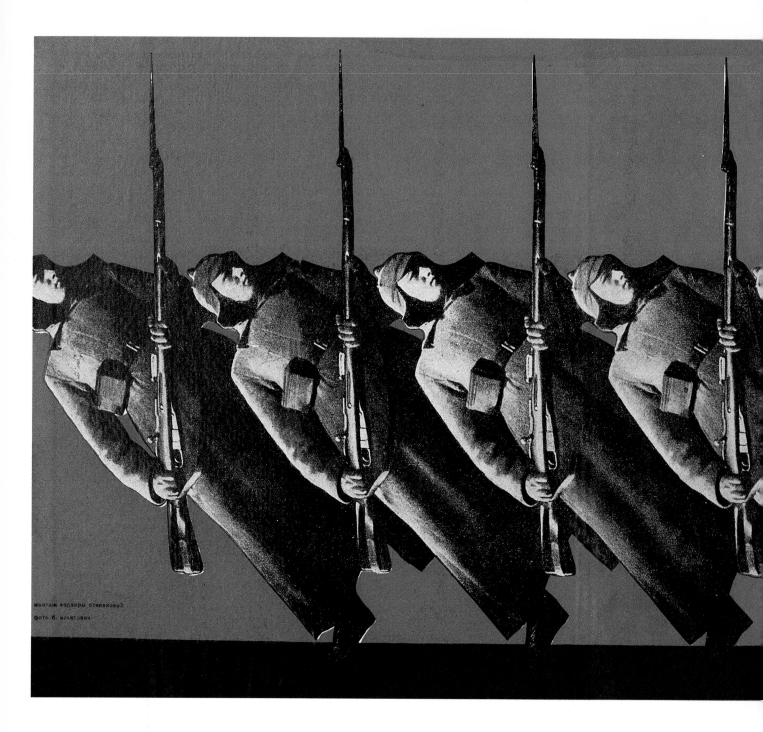

Two years after the suicide of Vladimir Majakovskij (1893–1930) a book on his agitprop posters was published entitled "Terrible Laughter" (also cited as Threatening or Cruel Laughter). The so-called Rosta windows were made from 1919 to 1921 for a ROSTA (Russian telegraph agency) campaign to inform broad sections of the public on the aims of communism: large broadsheet-like posters with colorful, stylized graphics and satirical texts. Varvara Stepanova, one of the outstanding protagonists of the Russian avant-garde, took on the book presentation and designed the cover of the publication. She structured the contents on pages of alternating width: pages of two columns as wide as the book between pages of single columns half as wide. The black-and-white poster reproductions are always in the outer column; the text is next to these in the inner column or on the narrow pages in between, so that the illustrations always remain visible next to the texts. For the signal red

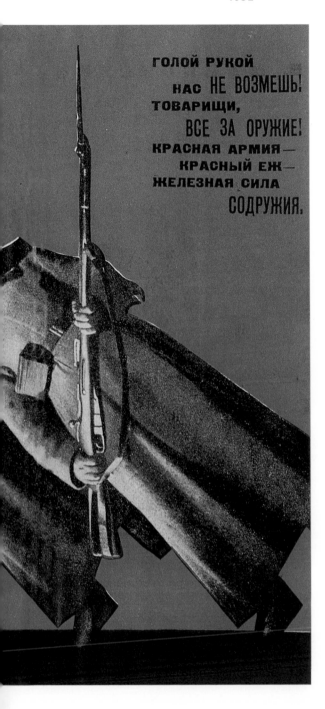

ГОЛОЙ РУКОЙ
НАС НЕ ВОЗМЕШЬ!
ТОВАРИЩИ,
ВСЕ ЗА ОРУЖИЕ!
КРАСНАЯ АРМИЯ—
КРАСНЫЙ ЕЖ—
ЖЕЛЕЗНАЯ СИЛА
СОДРУЖИЯ.

Varvara Fjodorovna Stepanova
Endpaper for V. Majakovskij.
Groznij smech, 1932

Moscow/Leningrad:
Gosudarstvennoe Izdatel'stvo
Chudozestvennoj Literatury
(State Publishing Company for
Literature on Art)
Photomontage, mixed media,
black, red
Double page: 24.3 x 43.5 cm
Acc. no. 317/92

Varvara Fedorovna Stepanova

1894 Kovno (Kaunas), Lithuania – 1958
Moscow
Studied in 1911 at the art school in
Kazan, where she met Rodchenko with
whom she lived and worked together
as of 1916; studied in Moscow under
I. Maskov and K. Juon at the Stroganov
Art School in 1913/1914. Also used
the pseudonyms "Varst" and "Agrarykh."
Worked as painter, textile designer,
graphic artist, and poet. 1921–1925
taught at the University for Social
Education in Moscow, 1924–1925 at the
textile department of VKHUTEMAS,
member of the group October, worked
for journals including "Kino-fot," "LEF,"
and "Novyi LEF."

endpapers Stepanova made a photographic montage of a Red Army
soldier with a rifle repeated five times. By placing the soldiers diagonally
the rifles end up in a vertical position. The montage of diagonals and
verticals, together with the horizontal band on the "ground," spans the
horizontal format of the book's double-page. The lines by Majakovskij
"To arms, comrades!" printed in the upper right corner, the rigid
parallelism of the uniforms, the staccato-like rhythm of the row, and the
tips of the bayonets pointing upwards five times lend the composition an
extraordinarily suggestive aura of threat and unstoppable dynamics,
referring to the aggressive pathos of the book's contents. It was a particular aspiration to acquire this outstanding work of modern book
art – still created before Stalinist restrictions limited or prohibited the
freedom of design of the Russian avant-garde – for our department
of graphic design. CR

Factory design BMW

The Bayerische Motorenwerke were already able to advertise their competitiveness with the "fastest motorbike in the world" in 1929. In a timespan of eight years Ernst Henne alone was able to break the speed record 76 times on BMW motorbikes. The most striking characteristic in the appearance of these machines, exemplary in terms of technology and construction, was the wedge-shaped double frame that came to be a symbol for the successful combination of technology, function and form. The Bayerische Motorenwerke, founded in 1916, had begun with the building of airplane engines and produced as of 1923 motorbikes as well. Over a period of just a few years several models were developed that were based on the principle of the opposed cylinder engine and cardan gears in a double tubular frame. Model R 52, introduced in 1928, was the most fully developed solution in terms of technology and design, and the basis for the world record machines driven by Henne. JS

Sel. Lit.: Pinakothek der Moderne: eine Vision des Museums für Kunst, Architektur und Design des 20. Jahrhunderts in München. Pub. Stiftung Pinakothek der Moderne. München/New York 1995, 121 ill.

Motorrad BMW R 52, 1928

Black lacquered metal and rubber
500 cc, 18 hp
L. 210 cm, max. w. 89 cm,
h. 95 cm
Made by Bayerische Motoren-
werke, Munich
On permanent loan from
BMW AG, Munich
Acc. no. L 569/93

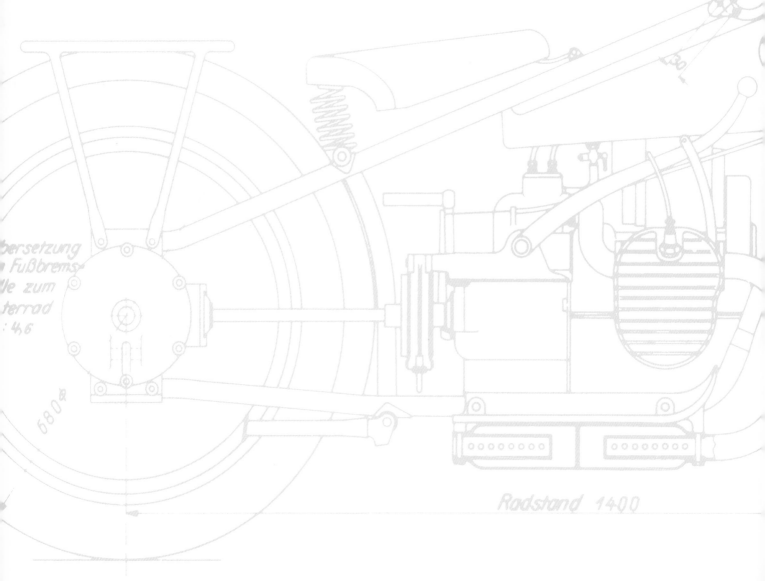

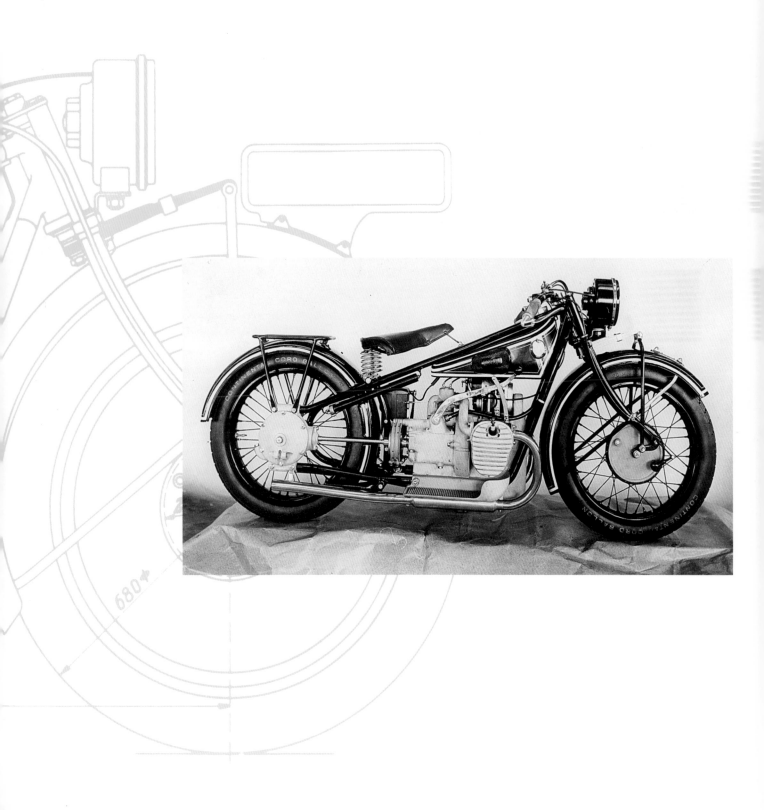

Marcel Breuer

1902 Pecs, Hungary – 1981 New York
Studied as of 1920 at the Bauhaus under
Gropius, director of the furniture
workshop there 1925–1928. During this
time he made his first tubular steel chairs.
Worked in Zurich, London, and in 1937 in
Cambridge, Massachusetts, together
with Gropius at the Graduate School of
Design, Harvard University. 1946–1976
architectural office in New York. Buildings
constructed according to his plans were
amongst others: the Unesco Building
in Paris (1953–1958) and the New York
Whitney Museum of American Art (1966).
Aside from numerous interiors Breuer
designed such furniture classics as the
"Wassily" armchair or the "Cesca" chair.

Only with Breuer's designs did aluminum, the "metal of modernism," find its way into furniture production. Previously the rigid, brittle, and relatively expensive material had been considered unsuitable to this purpose. Aluminum was used early on already, but only to cover smaller areas or as decorative elements, as, for example, in Otto Wagner's Postsparkasse furniture. On the basis of newly developed principles of construction and their convincing aesthetic translation, Marcel Breuer was able to utilize the advantages of aluminum – lightweight and rust-free – for furniture production. In November 1932 he had his "frames for resilient seating furniture" patented in Germany, later also in other countries. Thus he could protect his idea to produce resilient metal furniture of flat steel and aluminum – until then possible only in tubular steel. To begin with, this furniture was manufactured by Embru Rüti AG for the Swiss company Wohnbedarf AG in Zurich, later under license by Arnold in Schorndorf and Stylclair in Lyon. With five models supplied by Embru, including this lounge chair, Breuer participated at a competition of the large Parisian company Alliance Aluminium Ciel in 1933. The competition was intended to spurn on the continued development of aluminum furniture. His designs were awarded the first prize by each of two different juries – members were amongst others Le Corbusier, Gropius, and Giedion – independently of one another. The steel band constructions allowed several variations: thus the crossbars could be of aluminum, but also of wood; the width and distance between could be modified; in addition, upholstery for outdoor or indoor use was available. But inspite of the international recognition, aluminum furniture was not accorded sweeping financial success. It finally ended with the take over of the metal production for the armaments industry shortly before the begin of World War II. JS

Sel. Lit.: Wilk Christopher, [exh. cat.] Marcel Breuer. Furniture and Interiors. Museum of Modern Art. New York 1981, 125 ill. – Vegesack Alexander von, Deutsche Stahlmöbel. München 1986, 122–123 ill. – Ostergard Derek E. (pub.), Bentwood and Metal Furniture 1850–1940. New York 1987, 322, no. 109B ill. — Mahlau-Wiebking Arthur and Ruggero Trapeano, Schweizer Typenmöbel 1925–1935. Sigfried Giedion und die Wohnbedarf AG. Zürich 1989, 65 ill., 89, 93 ill., 140, 142 ill. – Thelin Birgit, Leicht ... Federnd... Unverwüstlich. In: [exh. cat.] Aluminium. Metall der Moderne. Kölnisches Stadtmuseum. Köln 1991, 166 ff. ill. – Droste Magdalena and Manfred Ludewig, [exh. cat.] Marcel Breuer. Bauhaus Archiv. Berlin 1992, 118–119 ill.

filling section

so goes from 'A' to 'H'

NOT ACCURATE

from 'B' to 'J'

low section. so welded or drown in one piece & cut from 'A' to 'B'

top face

3/4" thick

Scale full size

SECTION RE
Scale full size

Marcel Breuer
Lounge Chair Model 313,
1932–1934

Aluminum and black
lacquered wood
H. 75 cm, l. 140 cm, w. 54 cm
Made by Embru-Werke AG,
Rüti, Zurich
Acc. no. 174/94

F is a hardwood strap 1½ x ½

B

Scale full size

Scale ½" to 1'

Germany

In 1992 Die Neue Sammlung was able to acquire an unusual group of extremely attractive architectural models. Aside from the objects shown here, these included two models also made in the mid-thirties: the Chilehaus (this example of expressionistic architecture was built in 1922/24 according to the plans by Fritz Höger in Hamburg) as well as the Deutschlandhaus in Essen (Jakob Koerfer, 1928/29). The pieces presumably come from the Ore Mountains; even then the area had been internationally renowned for the production of wooden toys for a long time already. The inscription on the base of Café Kugelhaus, which was by the way realized for the exhibition "Die technische Stadt" in 1928, indicates that such complicated pieces were made as homework in the winter.

These models were not intended as so-called teaching models, i.e. models of buildings that served didactic purposes and were to fulfill either technical-constructive or artistic tasks. Nor were they meant as models for specific purposes by architects, since the emphasis is less in the representation of the construction and more on the general impression. Accuracy of detail was obviously not so important, instead the decorative aspect stood in the foreground. This is also supported by the scale used for the pieces, being neither standardized nor customary: e.g., Hannoverscher Anzeiger 1: 182, Deutschlandhaus 1: 138, Chilehaus 1: 167. Thus the models were apparently made without knowledge of the blue prints or actual sizes and on the basis of illustrations in the respective publications, which would explain the divergence from the built architecture. CR/JS

Architectural Models

Left: "Hannoverscher Anzei-
ger," Hannover (architect:
Fritz Höger, 1927/28), c. 1935
Light gray and silver-colored
lacquered wood
H. 22 cm, w. 25.4 cm, d. 10 cm
Acc. no. 109/92

Center: "Hochhaus," c. 1935
Light green lacquered wood
Inscription on reverse: ø siehe
unter Boden/Schraube zum/
festschrauben am/ Raster-
boden
H. 34.5 cm, w. 38 cm, d. 14.5 cm
Acc. no. 113/92

Right: "Café Kugelhaus,"
Dresden (architect: Peter
Birkholz, 1928), 1937
Light gray and yellow
lacquered wood
Inscription on base: 1/12–
18.12.37/77 Arbeitstd./
22 Anstreichstd./ 89 Std.
H. 21 cm, ø pedestal 13.3 cm,
ø 17.5 cm
Acc. no. 111/92

Walter Dorwin Teague

1883 Decatur, Indiana – 1960 Flemington,
New Jersey
Studied 1903–1907 at the Art Students
League in New York. As of 1911 free-lance
commercial artist. In 1926 opening of
an office for industrial design. Founded
in 1944 together with Dreyfuss and
Loewy the American Society of Industrial
Designers. Designed cameras, radios,
vehicles, railways, gas stations, etc. Main
representative of the streamlined form
in the USA.

With this object an almost thirty year collaboration between one of the most significant American industrial designers and the Polaroid Corporation began. Together with his son Walter Dorwin Teague jr. and Frank Del Giudice, Teague re-worked the design of a table lamp which Polaroid had put on the market the year before. A totally new lamp emerged out of the redesign, which technically and formally surpassed its predecessor by far and was even cheaper in production. One kept only the cellulose film that was responsible for the softly spreading light and that was now stretched "invisibly" under the reflector, while in the predecessor it still belonged to the front of the lamp. Teague transformed the massive box shape into an elegant streamlined form, whose cone of light was large enough to illuminate a newspaper page. JS

Sel. Lit.: Duncan Alistair, American Art Deco. München 1986, 71 ill. – Wilson Richard G., The Machine Age in America. New York 1986, 334 ill. – Eidelberg Martin (pub.), Design 1935–1965. What modern was. Le Musée des Arts Décoratifs de Montreal. New York 1981, 80 ill.

Walter Dorwin Teague
Table Lamp No. 114, 1939

Black-brown phenoplast
(Bakelite) and aluminum
H. 32 cm, w. 29.5 cm, d. 25 cm
Made by Polaroid Corp.,
Cambridge, Massachusetts
Acc. no. 153/93

Clarence Karstadt
Radio "Silvertone" Model
6111, 1938

Ivory-colored and black
plastic (phenoplast), and
ivory-colored lacquer
H. 16.5 cm, l. 30.5 cm,
w. 16.3 cm
Made by Sears Roebuck & Co.,
Philadelphia
Acc. no. 571/91

Clarence Karstadt

Biographical data not known.

"To tear down the boundaries between industry and art" was the goal of the exhibition "Machine Art," which took place at the Museum of Modern Art in New York in 1934 under Philip Johnson and whose subject was industrial design. It marks at the same time the fact that American industrial design had reached its first peak, and that it had in part surpassed Europe in terms of progressiveness. This is exemplified by such products as the radio designed by Clarence Karstadt in 1938. Not only was it one of the first models that had push buttons for the stations, making it much easier to use, the continued technical development had also led to ever smaller dimensions of the inner apparatus. This – in combination with the potentials of the yet new plastic – made it possible to realize small, compact casings in almost every conceivable form … in this case, the "futuristic," laconically cool radio set resembling a motor casing. The era of solid, furniture-like wooden boxes could actually have been past, if World War II had not interrupted this development. CR/JS

Sel. Lit.: Wilson Richard G., The Machine Age in America. New York 1986, 275 ill. [model 6110] – Collins Philip, Radios Redux. San Francisco 1991, 32, 107 ill.

England

As a 20th century material, plastics have left their mark on the history of modern industrial design. Named after the Belgian chemist Leo Hendrik Bakeland (1863–1944), Bakelite was the first fully synthetic material produced in Europe as of 1920 and came to be the generic term for the various plastics developed by and by, differing in their composition and in their characteristics. The salt and pepper shakers and the thermos jug do not, for instance, consist of Bakelite, but of Ureum, an aminoplast which was developed as of 1924 and served as a starting point for the later melamine. The production methods vary in part as well, thus Ureum is cast in the respective forms, while the phenoplast Bakelite is pressed. Aside from that is the mass production with a nearly unlimited number of pieces. Only this made it possible that plastics in the form of every type of functional object – from electrical plugs and radios to household appliances, office supplies and cameras down to ashtrays and toys – have become so much a part of our lives that we cannot imagine being without. After World War II the early plastics such as Bakelite or Ureum were rapidly replaced by newly developed ones such as ABS, etc. JS

Sel. Lit.: [exh. cat.] Kunststoff-Objekte 1860–1960. Sammlung Kölsch. Museum Folkwang etc. Essen 1983, 47, 51, no. 4.1458 and 4.1468 ill. – Cook Patrick and Catherine Slessor, Bakelite. London 1992, 109 and 114 ill.

Salt and Pepper Shakers, 1935

Yellow-orange and dark-green
speckled aminoplast (Ureum)
H. 12.8 cm, ø 3.8 cm
Made by BEF Product, England
Acc. no. 58/92, 318/92

Thermos Jug Model 65,
c. 1928

White and red aminoplast
(Ureum)
H. 26 cm, ø base 8.8 cm,
ø 11 cm
Made by Thermos Ltd.,
England
Acc. no. 117/95

Factory design Pratt & Whitney, USA

Of the two engine concepts dominating the first decades of motorized flying – the in-line motor with coolant and the air-cooled radial engine – the latter began to assert itself because of its lesser weight and simpler construction. At the tip of the development was the American company Pratt & Whitney that had constructed efficient 9-cylinder radial engines in 1928. Within the same year the then general director of BMW Franz Josef Popp visited Pratt & Whitney and initiated negotiations for the licenses for the two engine types Hornet and Wasp. BMW developed the BMW 132 series on the basis of these engines; they were built as a successful mass production version into airplanes such as, for example, the JU 52. That these radial engines had a high aesthetic appeal in addition to their technical qualities is shown by the fact that they were included in the exhibition "Art and the Machine Age" in 1936. Two Pratt & Whitney radial engines are illustrated in the catalog and are commented upon with the words: "abstract compositions arrived at without benefit of artist." JS

Sel. Lit.: Cheney Sheldon and Martha, Art and the Machine Age. 1936. Reprint, New York. 1992 – Wichmann Hans, Design contra Art Déco. München 1993, 84–85 ill.

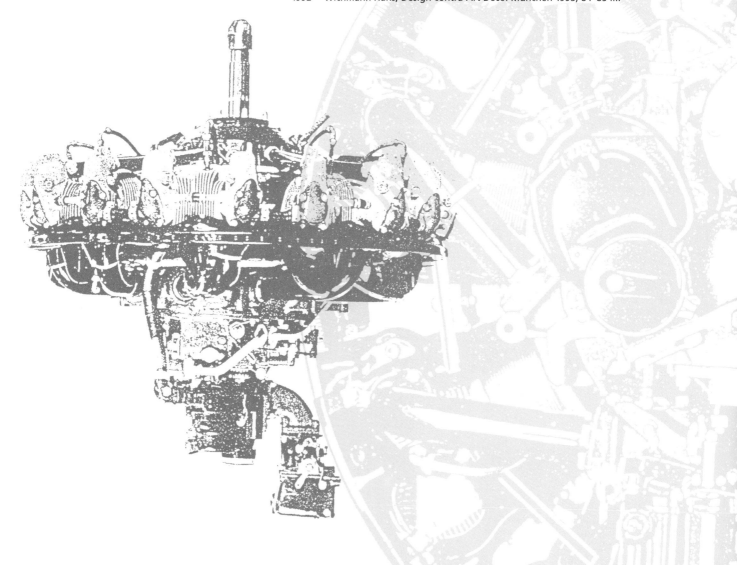

9-Cylinder Radial Engine
"Wasp Junior," Model R 985-
AN1, 1928 (basic design)

Metal
ø 120 cm, d. 100 cm
Made by Pratt & Whitney, USA
Restored and repaired by the
MTU Motoren- und Turbinen-
Union München GmbH
Acc. no. 584/93

Clarice Cliff

1899 Tunstall/Staffordshire – 1972
In 1912 apprenticeship in pottery under
Lingard Webster. 1916–1920 worked at
the ceramic manufactory A.J. Wilkinson
Ltd. (Royal Staffordshire Pottery, Burslem),
1924–1925 studied painting at the School
of Art, Burslem/Stoke-on-Trent, 1927
studied sculpture at the College of Art in
London. 1929–1935 production of the
successful "Bizarre" decor by the Newport Pottery, further decors followed, e.g.
"Fantasque" and "Biarritz," carried out
decor designs by freelance artists such as
Duncan Grant, Vanessa Bell, Graham
Sutherland, et al., artistic direction of
Newport Pottery until 1963, ended her
work as designer in 1965.

Associated with the name "Bizarre" is one of the most exceptional
accomplishments of English everyday ceramics of the 20th century. Clarice
Cliff wanted to give her new decor designs an unusual name so that
she would stand out amongst contemporary designers and manufacturers
and their products not only in terms of design, but also in terms of the
name. Connected with this was also a new type of advertising strategy:
Even before the "Bizarre" objects came on the market, the first ads were
already appearing. Decisive for the great success of these works was,
however, the enormous artistic potential of Cliff. At the beginning she
still used pre-fabricated pieces for her new and very colorful decors. But
very soon already these pieces no longer satisfied her artistic demands,
so that she began to design her own forms. She received inspiration from
the silver work of the French art deco that she knew from illustrations in
the journal "Mobilier et Décoration." Thus parts of the tea service
"Stamford" were based on a silver service by Jean Tétard. The dinner
service of the same name is, in contrast, Clarice Cliff's own creation. With
the reserved decor underlining the strictly geometric forms, this work
counts as one of her most convincing designs. JS

Sel. Lit.: Griffin Leonard, Louis K. and Susan Pear Meisel, Clarice Cliff. The Bizarre Affair.
London 1988, 31, 65–66 [drawing or cartoon]

Clarice Cliff
Pieces from the Dinner Service
"Stamford," 1930

Cast stoneware, gray body;
decor of stripes in various
colors
Stamped on base of each
piece: HAND PAINTED/Bizarre/
by Clarice Cliff/WILKINSON
LTD/ENGLAND

Tureen: H. 18.5 cm, w. 22.5 cm,
ø 18.8 cm
Sauce boat: H. 6.1 cm, w. 16.5
cm, ø 11.5 cm
Platters: H. 3.4-4.5 cm,
w. 31.2–41.8 cm,
d. 24–33.2 cm
Made by Wilkinson Ltd.,
Burslem, England
Acc. no. 26/92

Isamu Noguchi

1904 Los Angeles – 1988 New York
In 1917 began training as cabinet-maker
in Chigasaki, Japan; moved to the USA
in 1918, where he first studied sculpture
and then studied at the Columbia
University in New York from 1921 to
1924; in 1927 he went to Paris in order to
assist in Constantin Brancusi's studio,
before he finally settled as a sculptor in
New York in 1932; as of the late thirties
he designed numerous squares and
gardens; in the early forties he began to
design furniture for H. Miller and Knoll
Möbel, et al., as well as the famous Akari
lamps of handmade paper.

In the twenties and thirties the sculptor Isamu Noguchi devoted himself almost exclusively to portrait heads. In contrast to earlier works, which were completely different in material and style, he developed a standardized type of head for men and women, as if he were searching for a universal, infinitely reproducible archetype. With the set shown here, he then, in 1937, designed an object that looked like a stylized human head and could be mass-produced. He described his "Radio Nurse" as a "means to hear into the other rooms of the house, as a precautionary measure against kidnapping (as in the Lindbergh case, for example)." Its form with the horizontal slits reminds of Japanese Kendo masks. This illustrates its protective function, which was important for Noguchi's social consciousness. The design of this object represents the beginning of his interest in applied art, leading to designs for glasses, furniture, and lighting fixtures as well. Thus his tea table of 1946 came to be, for example, a symbol for the biomorphic and organic design of the late forties and fifties. JS

Sel. Lit.: Wilson Richard G., The Machine Age in America. New York 1986, 333 ill. – Grove Nancy, [exh. cat.] Isamu Noguchi. Portrait Sculpture. National Portrait Gallery. Washington 1989, 19–20, ill. 24 – [exh. cat.] Isamu Noguchi. Retrospective 1992. The National Museum of Modern Art, Tokio / The National Museum of Modern, Kyoto. Tokio 1992, 71, no. 27 ill.

Isamu Noguchi
Shortwave Set "Radio Nurse,"
1937

Black-brown phenoplast
(Bakelite)
H. 21 cm, w. 17 cm, d. 16 cm
Made by Zenith Radio Corp.,
Chicago
Acc. no. 152/93

Gerald Marcus Summers

1899 Alexandria, Egypt – 1967
1915 until 1916 apprenticeship in the
machine factory Ruston, Proctor & Co.
Ltd., Lincolnshire, England. 1916–1918
combatant. After the war was for
a short period of time a worker in Wales.
Returned to England in the twenties.
Manager at Marconi's Wireless Telegraph
Co. Ltd., London. 1931 founded the
firm Makers of Simple Furniture, also on
initiative of his wife Marjorie Amy
Butcher. The name of the firm, which had
to close down in 1940, was its program:
production of simply designed furniture
without ornamentation and meant
for daily use.

Gerald Summers no doubt belongs to the most significant English furniture designers before World War II. Beginning with a material used primarily in aircraft construction, he developed a new working method that made an exact rendering of his ideas on form possible. The individual layers of plywood were precisely cut, glued and in a still wet state pressed into a form. After drying, no work other than treating the surface was necessary. The armchair in Die Neue Sammlung, constructed of a single sheet of plywood, illustrates in an exemplary manner the convincing combination of a simple uniform material and efficient production method with outstanding design. Marcel Breuer as well as Alvar Aalto succeeded at about the same time in designing revolutionary plywood furniture. But the armchair by Summers – one of the earliest examples of this model, as can be seen by the lacquering – represents the most consequential and least compromising solution for such furniture.
JS

Sel. Lit.: Ostergard Derek E. (pub.), Bentwood and Metal Furniture 1815–1946. New York 1987, 318–319, no. 106 ill. – Deese Martha, Gerald Summers and Makers of Simple Furnitures. In: Journal of Design History 5, 1992, no. 3, 183 ff. ill.

Gerald M. Summers
Plywood Armchair, 1934

White lacquered plywood
H. 75 cm, w. 60.5 cm, l. 95 cm
Made by Makers of Simple
Furniture Ltd., London
Provenance: Architect
A. Grimmon, Amsterdam
Acc. no. 317/95

England

Plastic began to be used for toys in the twenties and after World War II increasingly replaced other materials, amongst which only wood could more or less hold its own. With the two illustrated examples, one can document not only the high quality of early plastic toys but also an important step in design: The streamlined look of the sports car, which can also be driven with a wind-up mechanism, is clearly influenced by contempory car design (e.g. the Cord sports car). The train, on the other hand, is much more than a miniaturized edition of a larger model – the simplified and stylized, in part angular, forms are proof of a conscious translation, which clearly show the maker's intentions in terms of design. JS

Sel. Lit.: [exh. cat.] Kunststoff-Objekte 1860–1960. Sammlung Kölsch. Museum Folkwang etc. Essen 1983, 26, no. 2.1311 ill. – Cook Patrick and Catherine Slessor, Bakelite. London 1992, 22 and 23 ill.

Toy Car, 1939

Black-brown phenoplast (Bakelite)
H. 8.5 cm, l. 34.5 cm,
w. 14.3 cm
Made by Codec, England
Acc. no. 54/92

Locomotive with Two Cars
"Chad Valley," 1940's

Marbled reddish-brown, red,
black and white phenoplast
(Bakelite) and metal
Loc.: h. 8.7 cm, l. 26.6 cm,
w. 9 cm
Car: h. 6.7 cm, l. 18 cm,
w. 9 cm
Made by Chad Valley,
Harborne, England
Acc. no. 55/92

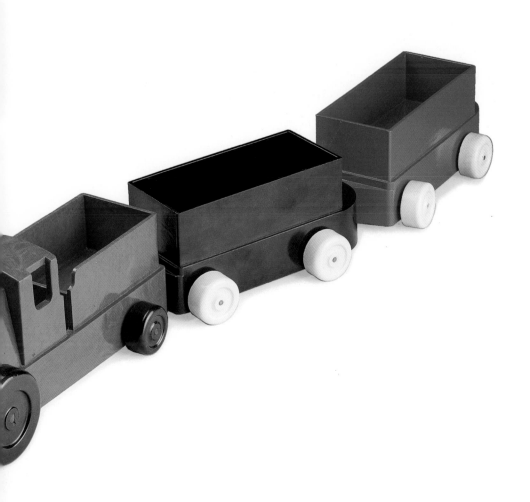

Jean Prouvé

1901 Paris – 1984 Nancy
Trained metal-craftsman, as of 1923 own
workshop in Nancy, first furniture
production using thin sheet-steel. In 1930
founded the company Les Ateliers Jean
Prouvé, collaboration with the architects
Tony Garnier, Eugène Beaudoin, and
Marcel Gabriel Lods. Active in the
Resistance until 1944. In 1955 founded
the company Les constructions Jean
Prouvé in Paris, designed metal furniture
together with Charlotte Perriand,
substantially contributed to the plans for
the Centre Georges Pompidou. Numerous
honors and prizes, including the Big
Architecture Prize of the City of Paris in
1982.

After the trained metalworker Jean Prouvé had opened his own studio
in Nancy in 1923 and had begun finishing metal furniture, he developed a
system of partitions which could be dismantled: Prouvé was convinced
that architecture could be industrially produced, and that there were
no basic differences between the construction of a piece of furniture and
of a house. Together with the architect Eugène Beaudouin and Marcel
Lods he realized at the end of the thirties his first buildings of metal,
including the Maison du Peuple in Clichy. The door elements of corrugated aluminum were created in that context. He designed the doors
together with other light metal structures, wall elements, supports, roofs,
and window frames on the principles of automotive and aircraft construction and mass-produced them in his factory in Maxéville, which he
opened in 1947. JS

Sel. Lit.: Huber Benedict and Jean-Claude Steinegger (pub.), Jean Prouvé. Architektur aus
der Fabrik. Zürich 1971, 118 ill. – [exh. cat.] Jean Prouvé. Meubles 1924–1953. Musée des
Arts Decoratifs. Bordeaux 1989, 15, 21 ill. – [exh. cat.] Jean Prouvé »constructeur«. Centre
Pompidou. Paris 1990, 167 ill. – Geest Jan van, Jean Prouvé. Köln 1991, 133–139 ill.
[variations]

1927

1940-45

Jean Prouvé
Door Element, c. 1948

Vertically corrugated alu-
minum sheet metal
H. 214 cm, w. 84 cm
Made by Les Ateliers Jean
Prouvé, Maxéville, France
Acc. no. 147/91

Factory design Fada

The company Fada, named after its founder Frank A. D'Andrea, is inextricably linked with the history of American radio design. The streamlined model, which came to be known under the name "Streamliner" or "Bullet," proved to be the most successful set. Produced as model 115 before World War II, it came back on the market with exactly the same shape, as model 1000, after the end of the war: civil radio production had been discontinued in the USA in 1941. The success of this radio was above all based on the casing's unusual synthetic material. This was a new type of plastic manufactured in the USA under the name Catalin. It stood out – in contrast to Bakelite, for example, which was available only in dark brown, green or red hues – for its various extraordinarily luminous as well as lighter colors. In addition it had qualities such as being heat-resistant, hard-wearing, neutral to taste and odors. Disadvantageous was the complicated production. Traditional plastics, which although pressed under high pressure and high temperature into expensive steel forms, could continue to be worked upon immediately after cooling down. Catalin was cast in inexpensive tin molds, but then the hardening process at about 80° took several days and surfaces had to be finished by grinding, waxing, and polishing. This made manufacturing so expensive that as of the late forties other cheaper, but also colorful, plastics were utilized for radio casings. The new plastics could not, though, adequately replace the luminous colors and surfaces of the "Catalin radios," reminding of onyx, marble, or opaque glass. JS

Sel. Lit.: Collins Philip, Radios. The golden age. San Francisco 1987, 64–66, 112 ill.

Radio Set Model 1000
"Streamliner," 1940
(prototype)

Yellow and red plastic
(Catalin)
H. 17 cm, w. 26.3 cm, d. 15 cm
Made by Fada Radio & Electronic Co. Inc., Long Island
City/New York
Acc. no. 199/92

The table lamp "Jumo" patented in France in 1945 illustrates the European counterpart to the streamlined American designs of the late thirties and forties (as they are represented in Die Neue Sammlung by a table lamp by Walter Dorwin Teague (see page 104, for example). Characteristic is the combination of a Bakelite base and a reflector with metal arm. Several joints allow the lamp's arm to be extended to various lengths and also make a smooth adjustment of the angle of the reflector possible. In contrast to traditional table and office lamps, the "Jumo" can be completely collapsed and thus also be used as a streamlined "paper weight." In addition to the version in dark brown Bakelite, the lamp was also available in a green or white plastic. JS

Sel. Lit.: DiNoto Andrea, Art Plastic. Designed for Living. New York 1984, 208–209 ill. – [exh. cat.] Lumières. Centre Georges Pompidou. Paris 1985, 168, no. 355 ill. – Koch André, Struck by Lighting. Rotterdam 1994, 59–60, no. 66 ill.

Factory design Jumo

Table Lamp "Jumo," 1945

Dark brown phenoplast
(Bakelite) and copper-colored
and chrome-colored metal
H. 44 cm or 13.5 cm (when
folded), w. 19 cm, l. 27.5 cm
Made by Jumo Brevete, Paris
Acc. no. 486/90

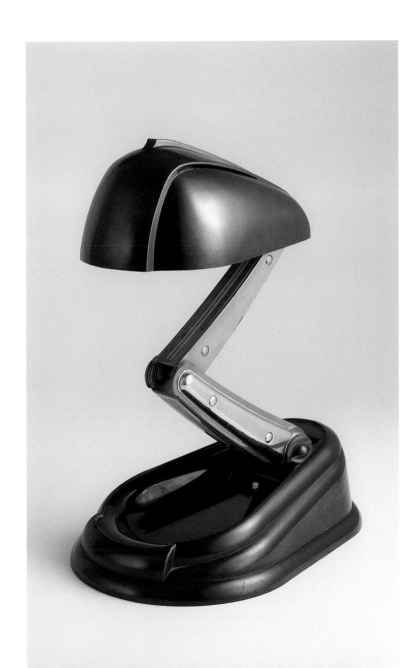

No other car manufacturer realized the streamlined form in mass-produced vehicles as radically as the Czechoslovak company Tatra in Nesselsdorf (Koprivnica). Under the direction of the Austrian designer Hans Ledwinka this unusual vehicle was designed on the basis of developments by Paul Jaray, a pioneer in aerodynamics. Its avant-gardistic streamlined form left its decisive mark on the history of modern design. Characteristic for the Tatra 87, which in contrast to the preceding model Tatra 77 was given an all-metal body, are the short front hood, a long drawn-out rear, air scoops situated between roof and hood and opening towards the front, side windows inclined towards the interior, as well as the three-piece windshield. The rear with its dorsal fin was considered sensational, the absent rear windows showing the form to its best advantage (a rear view was possible through the ventilation slits in the back hood). The drag coefficient of this consequently, aerodynamically designed body is not even remotely approached by many of today's vehicles. In the history of automotive design, which is certainly not lacking in variety, the Tatra 87 is a nearly unique manifestation. JS

Sel. Lit.: Scharbeck Wolfgang, Tatra. Die Geschichte der Tatra Automobile. Lübbecke 1989, 124 ill. – Margolius Ivan and John G. Henry, Tatra. The Legacy of Hans Ledwinka. Harrow 1990, 96 ill. – [exh. cat.] Stromlinienform. Museum für Gestaltung. Zürich 1992, 256–257 ill. – Pinakothek der Moderne: eine Vision des Museums für Kunst, Architektur und Design des 20. Jahrhunderts in München. Pub. Stiftung Pinakothek der Moderne. München/New York 1995, 139 ill.

1934

Hans Ledwinka

1878 Klosterneuburg, Austria – 1967
Munich
Studied at the Technische Fachschule für
Maschinenbau in Vienna. As of 1897
employed at the Nesselsdorfer Wagenbau
Fabriks-Gesellschaft (later called Tatra-
Werke). 1905–1945 technical director
of the company. Moved to Munich in 1954
after being a prisoner of war for many
years.

Hans Ledwinka
Tatra 87, 1934

Black lacquered metal
L. 474 cm, w. 167 cm,
h. 150 cm
Made by Tatra Werke, Nessels-
dorf, Czechoslovakia (1938)
Acc. no. 585/93

"Organic design" was the keyword for furniture design in the fifties. Charles and Ray Eames belonged to the most important pathbreakers. In 1940 Charles Eames had together with Eero Saarinen won the competition "Organic Design in Home Furnishings" of the Museum of Modern Art in New York. The realization of their design, gently curved shell chairs of plywood, for which the plywood would have had to be three-dimensionally deformed, failed due to the then still insufficient technology. The necessary prerequisites were only created in the course of the Second World War, especially through the advance of aircraft technology. By the end of the war, the development for several types of chairs ready for production had been concluded: instead of one-part seating shells, though, they were separately worked, convincingly comfortable chairs with armrests having an "organic" effect. Edward S. Evans in Venice, California, began the mass production of the plywood chairs, the first examples of which were delivered in the summer of 1946. Eames' original idea, to produce a shell of one piece, could only be realized as of 1950. The renewed starting point was a further competition announced in 1948 by the Museum of Modern Art entitled "International Competition for Low-Cost Furniture Design." For this the "Plastic Armchair" shown here was designed in several color variations; it was in every way revolutionary. For the first time seating furniture consisting of a shell of plastic without any covering, having little in common with the traditional armchair, was created. With the plastic shells developed by Eames, producible in various colors mostly in combination with metal supports, the USA gained the leading position in international furniture design after 1945. JS

Sel. Lit.: Neuhart John, Marylin Neuhart and Ray Eames, Eames design. New York 1989, 138–141 ill. – Eidelberg Martin (pub.), Design 1935–1965. What modern was. Le Musée des Arts Décoratifs de Montréal. New York 1991, 211–212 ill. – [exh. cat.] Interieur und Design in Deutschland 1945–1960. Kunstgewerbemuseum. Berlin 1993, 73, no. 46 ill. [further literature] – Kirkham Pat, Charles and Ray Eames. Cambridge/Massachusetts 1995, 231–236 ill.

Charles Eames

1907 St. Louis, Missouri – 1978 St. Louis, Missouri
Studied architecture at Washington University in St. Louis (1925–1927). In 1930 opened an architectural office together with Charles M. Gray. Worked at the Cranbrook Academy of Art 1938–1941. Worked at the office of Eliel Saarinen 1939–1940. On commission of the U.S. Navy, continued his experiments with formed plywood. Founded with his wife Ray the Plyformed Products Company in California. As of the fifties also exhibition and communication design.

Ray Eames

1913 Sacramento, California – 1988 Los Angeles
Studied painting at the May Friend Bennett School in Millbrook and as of 1933 at the School of Art under Hans Hofmann. In 1940 attended weaving courses at the Cranbrook Academy of Art Michigan. Married Charles Eames in 1941.

Charles and Ray Eames
Three Armchairs LAR
(Lounge Armchair Rod), 1948
(produced as of 1950)

White, red, or blue fiberglass-
reinforced polyester and
chrome-plated metal frame
H. 62 cm, w. 63 cm, d. 61 cm
Made by Herman Miller
Furniture Company, Zeeland,
Michigan
Acc. no. 10/95-1,2,3

Corradino D'Ascanio

1891 Popoli, Italy – 1981 Pisa
Studied mechanical engineering at the
polytechnic in Turin, was subsequently
appointed technical director of the
Società d'Aviazione Pomilio. After World
War I built up his own company together
with Veniero D'Annunzio, in 1926
founded another company in order to
realize Leonardo da Vinci's helicopter
designs, in 1930 broke several records for
altitude and flying time. As of 1934
designer of aircraft components at
Piaggio in Genoa; in 1945 the development of the scooter Vespa, later a
designer for helicopters, amongst other
things.

After World War II the Italian armaments factory Piaggio took up the
production of motor scooters. The first model, though, was called
Paperino, not Vespa, as one often reads, and was produced just as a
prototype in a series of about 100 pieces. The breakthrough success came
only with the Vespa. Already in 1945 Corradino d'Ascanio, who had
previously constructed aircraft components for Piaggio, took on the project and developed the first prototype of the Vespa. The bold and new
conception immediately aroused considerable attention. The unitized
body, front suspension, and single rear wheel suspension – the rear wheel
rests directly on the transmission output shaft of the engine mounted on
the side – are clearly derived from aircraft construction. In addition, the
traditional foot shift mechanism was replaced by a newly developed
twist-grip shift control, later taken over by almost all scooter and moped
manufacturers. The 98-cc engine Vespa went into production in 1946 and
immediately came to be the most popular means of transport – and not
only in Italy. A more powerful 125-cc version went onto the market in
1948 already, a 150-cc version in 1956. One million vehicles had been sold
by 1956 – to the present day it is over seven million.

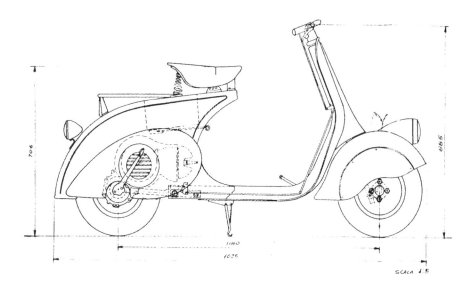

Various features from the first development phase can still be seen in this early example in Die Neue Sammlung. From the perspective of form development, this is above all the additive design principle, which characterizes most technical appliances up to and into the fifties: here, amongst other things, the still separate headlight, later integrated into the handlebars, or the "organically" rounded contrasting fender skirts. CR/JS

Sel. Lit.: Gregotti Vittorio, Il disegno del prodotto industriale. Italia 1860–1980. Mailand 1982, 283 ill. – Roos Peter, Vespa Stracciatella. Berlin 1985 – [exh. cat.] Italien: Design 1945 bis heute. Die Neue Sammlung. München 1988, 140 ill. – Noblet Jocelyn de (pub.), Industrial Design, Reflection of a Century. Paris 1993, 219 ill. – Rivola Luigi, La Leggendaria Vespa. Schindellegi 1994

Corradino D'Ascanio
Motor Scooter "Vespa 125,"
1951 (basic design 1945)

Dark gray lacquered metal
H. 94 cm, l. 168 cm, w. 80 cm
Made by Piaggio & C., Genoa
Acc. no. 549/95

Henning Koppel

1918 Copenhagen – 1981 Copenhagen
1936–1937 studied at the Kongelige
Danske Kunstakademi (Royal Danish
Academy of Fine Arts) in Copenhagen,
1938–1939 at the Académie Ranson in
Paris. Emigrated to Stockholm from
1940 to 1945. Worked as silver and
goldsmith for Svenskt Tenn and Orrefors.
Had a share in the Georg Jensen
Sølvesmedie as of 1945, in the Bing &
Grøndahl porcelain factory as of 1961.
Worked free-lance with Louis Poulsen
(in the areas lighting fixtures,
wristwatches), as of 1971 at the glass
manufacturer Orrefors. Numerous awards,
particularly for his metalwares, incl. gold
medals at the Milan triennials (1951,
1954, 1957); in 1963 International Design
Award.

For his unusual bowl, as well as for the pitcher designed a few years later, Henning Koppel received the gold medal of the IX. Triennale in Milan in 1951. Form and craftsmanship place these works at the peak of modern silversmithing. Originally trained as sculptor, Koppel belongs to the most important Scandinavian designers of the post-war period. As of 1945 he worked for the renowned Copenhagen silversmith Georg Jensen, as of 1961 for the porcelain manufacturer Bing & Grøndahl, as of 1971 for the Swedish glass manufacturer Orrefors. His designs led to a completely new design quality in Jensen's silver production, which decisively set itself off from the naturalistic decor elements of the Scandinavian silver objects of the early 20th century, but also from the geometric functional forms of the thirties. The example of the pitcher and bowl shows particularly clearly how Koppel translates utilitarian objects into abstract sculptural shapes that are created out of a play between rounded body and curvilinear contours with reflecting light on the smooth unadorned surfaces. JS

Sel. Lit.: Aloi Roberto, L'Arredamento Moderno. Mailand 1952, no. 150 ill. – Fifty Years of Danish Silver in the Georg Jensen Tradition. Kopenhagen 1954, [cover ill.] – Hiort Esbørn, Modern Danish Silver. Kopenhagen 1954, 96 – Møller Viggo Sten, Henning Koppel. Kopenhagen 1965, 11 ill. – [exh. cat.] Georg Jensen. Silversmithy. Renwick Gallery of National Collection of Fine Arts. Washington 1980, 19 – [exh. cat.] Henning Koppel. Kunstindustrimuseet. Kopenhagen 1982, 6 ill. – Bony Anne, Les Années 50. Paris 1982, 353 ill. – Design from Scandinavia 18, 1991, 7 ill. – Tätigkeitsbericht 1995. Danner-Stiftung. München 1995, 74 ill.

**Henning Koppel
Bowl No. 980, 1948**

**Repoussé and assembled
silver 925/100
Stamped on base on inside
of arch: DESSIN / HK (oblong
oval) / DENMARK GEORG
JENSEN (in dotted oblong
oval) STERLING / 980 / A
H. 16 cm, w. 40 cm, d. 38.5 cm
Commissioned by Georg
Jensen Sølvsmedie,
Copenhagen
On Permanent Loan from
the Benno und Therese
Danner'schen Kunstgewerbe-
stiftung, Munich
Acc. no. L 45/92**

Sel. Lit.: Fifty Years of Danish Silver in the Georg Jensen Tradition. Kopenhagen 1954,
50 ill. – Hiort Esbørn, Modern Danish Silver. Kopenhagen 1954, 97 – Karlsen Arne, Dansk
Brugskunst. Kopenhagen 1960, 2 ill. [drawing], 41–43 ill. – Møller Viggo Sten, Henning
Koppel. Kopenhagen 1965, 81 ill. [drawing] – [exh. cat.] Georg Jensen. Silversmithy.
Renwick Gallery of National Collection of Fine Arts. Washington 1980, no. 88 ill. – [exh. cat.]
Henning Koppel. Kunstindustrimuseet. Kopenhagen 1982, 8 ill. – [exh. cat.] Scandinavian
Modern Design 1880–1980. Cooper-Hewitt Museum. New York 1982, 24, 168–169 ill.
192 – Bony Anne, Les Années 50. Paris 1982, 357 ill. – Design from Scandinavia 18, 1991,
7 ill. – Tätigkeitsbericht 1995. Danner-Stiftung. München 1995, 74 ill.

Henning Koppel
Pitcher No. 992, 1952

Repoussé and assembled
silver 925/100
Stamped on base: DESSIN/HK
(in oblong oval)/DENMARK
GEORG JENSEN (in dotted
oblong oval) STERLING/992
H. 29 cm, l. 22 cm, w. 15 cm
Commissioned by Georg
Jensen Sølvsmedie, Copen-
hagen
On Permanent Loan from
the Benno und Therese
Danner'schen Kunstgewerbe-
stiftung, Munich
Acc. no. L 46/92

Le Corbusier (Charles Edouard Jeanneret)

1887 La Chaux-de-Fonds, Switzerland –
1965 Cap Martin, France
The architect, urban planner, architectural
theoretician, painter, and designer studied
under J. Hoffman in Vienna, A. Perret
in Paris, and P. Behrens in Berlin. With his
new principles of construction he
built, amongst other things, the Stuttgart
Weißenhof development (1926–1927),
erected the Unité d'Habitation in
Marseille (1947–1952), and the pilgrim-
age chapel in Ronchamp (1950–1954). As
of the forties he developed the Modulor
system of proportions.

Aside from his work as architect, architectural theoretician, and urban planner, Le Corbusier was a painter, sculptor, and graphic artist; in addition he designed furniture as well as, especially after 1945, tapestries and wall decoration (see also p. 136), posters and books. It does not surprise that this uomo universale, in whose integral view of the world the alleged boundaries between fine and applied arts are abolished, developed a comprehensive theory of proportion as had Polyclitus and Vitruvius in antiquity or Alberti and Leonardo in the Renaissance before him. Derived from the module, a classical unit of measurement (from Latin modulus: a little measure), Le Corbusier's "Modulor" is based on the golden section and the proportions of a person standing with raised hand: "the aim and object is the search for a harmony of measurement, especially as basis for architectural and industrial norms," as the dictionary of art formulates concisely. This canon, worked out between 1942 and 1948, was published in 1950 and 1955 in two volumes (Modulor 1 and 2), was translated and reprinted numerous times, and influenced modern architecture world wide. Le Corbusier applied his theory to his own designs for, for example, the Unité d'Habitation in Marseille and the parliament building in Chandigarh, India. Larger-than-life bas reliefs of the homme modulor at both buildings testify to this. Le Corbusier used his modulor, but without illustrating the person, for the cover design of the book shown here, "Modulor 2" with the subtitle "La Parole est aux Usagers." (A compilation of readers' letters and other responses to the first volume, examples for using the "mèthode Modulor," and other tables of proportions). The back cover explains: "La composition de la couverture a été faite au Modulor avec les séries 27 à 140 réduites au dixième." 140 is the measurement of the total width (and height), 27 the width of the column with the book's title; the remaining surface of the square is divided in 43 as the width of the column with further publishing information and 70 for the representation of the modulor system, within which the vertical, wave-like row of circular segments in the left half reflects the scale of proportion.
One will hardly find another work of book art which symbolizes so ambitiously and earnestly the diverse relationships and interactions between fine art, applied art, and architecture! CR

Sel. Lit.: Boesiger Willy, Le Corbusier. Œuvre complète 1946–1952. Zürich 1955, 182–189 ill. [Modulor 1] – [exh. cat.] Künstlerplakate. Frankreich/USA. Zweite Hälfte 20. Jahrhundert. Die Neue Sammlung. München/Basel 1990, 81 ff. ill. [further literature]

1955

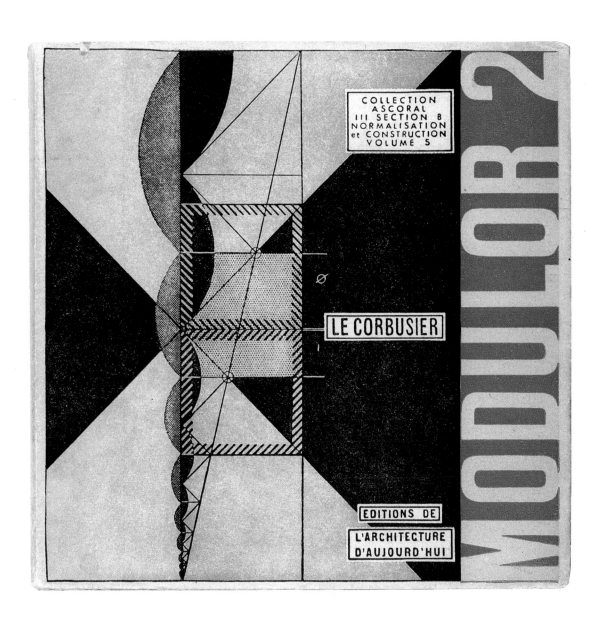

Le Corbusier
Cover for the Book
"Modulor 2," 1955

Boulogne: Editions de
l'architecture d'aujourd'hui
14.5 x 14.8 cm
Acc. no. 219/92

Achille Castiglioni

1918 Milan – lives in Milan
After receiving his degree in architecture
from the polytechnic in Milan in 1944, he
built up a design office in 1945 together
with his brothers Pier Giacomo and Livio,
who left the studio in 1952; in 1956
one of the founders of the ADI; as of 1969
assistant professor of industrial design
at the polytechnic in Turin, where he was
offered the chair of interior design in
1978; architect and industrial designer.

Pier Giacomo Castiglioni

1913 Milan – 1968 Milan
Received his degree in architecture from
the Milan polytechnic; worked at first
together with his brother Livio and later
with his younger brother Achille, as of
1945 in the same studio; specialized in
the area of lighting fixtures, also designed
furniture and technical equipment.

Achille and Pier Giacomo
Castiglioni
Table Lamp "Tubino," 1950

Plastic, aluminum, and
fluorescent tube
H. 30 cm, standing surface
31 x 26 cm, l. 70 cm
Made by Arredoluce, Monza,
as of 1971 by Flos, Brescia,
Italy
Acc. no. 185/94

Starting point for the design of the "Tubino" was the Castiglioni
brothers' idea of using a fluorescent tube as basic design element. Since
there were no fluorescent tubes of such small dimensions in Italy yet at
that time – one commercially available would have been dispropor-
tionately large for a desk lamp – these had to be at first imported from
the USA. A 6-watt tube with a diameter of 1.4 cm and a length of
22 cm, produced by General Electric, proved to be ideal for the translation of this design idea. To use it, one needed a starter and transformer
though; in order to not distort the uncompromising minimalistic design
of the extremely reduced tube and foot or arm with a cumbersome
box, Castiglioni detached these two functional elements from the actual
lighting fixture and installed them in a separate housing. He just as
elegantly solved the problem of supplying the tube with electricity by
leading the wires over the narrow reflector from one end of the tube
to the other. In order to adapt his lamp to changed norms and technical
renewals, Castiglioni reworked it once more, more than 20 years later:
the luminous power was increased by employing an 8-watt tube, the
starter was integrated in the tube-shaped casing, the transformer
replaced with a wire with integrated transformer, and the lamp now
consisted primarily of plastic. These technical changes did not effect the
design in any way; their being carried out, though, proves the progressiveness of the design. Even after two decades it was still considered
unspent and new. CR/JS

Sel. Lit.: Ferrari Paolo, Achille Castiglioni. Mailand 1984, 121, no. 363 ill.

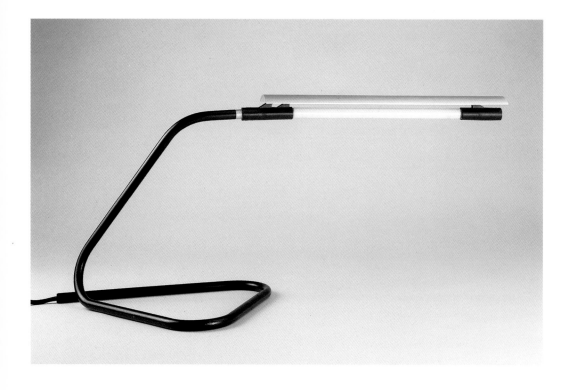

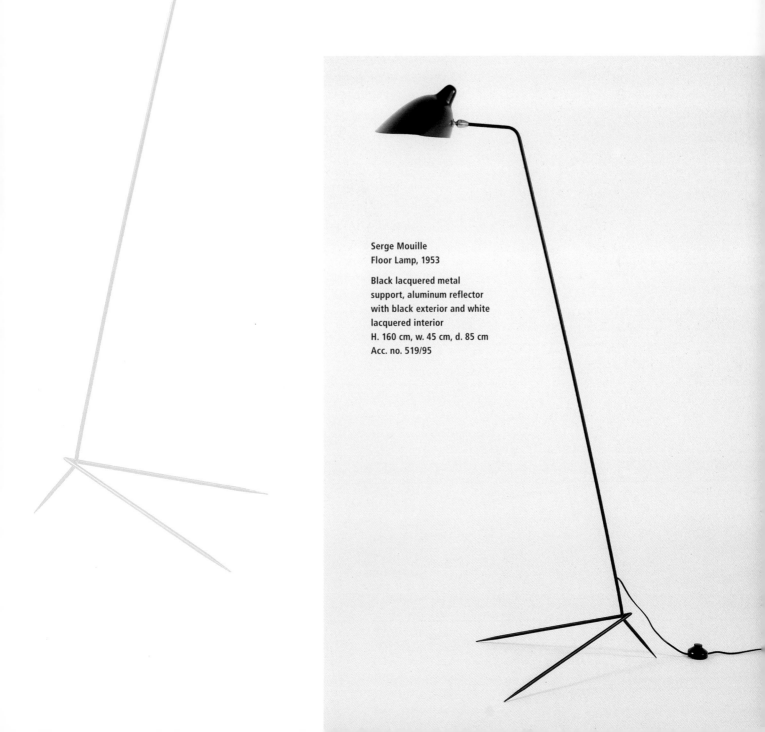

His artistic interest in light and space effects led the trained silversmith Serge Mouille to develop a series of most unusual lighting fixtures. Impulses and inspirations for this he drew from his collaboration with architects and designers such as Jean Prouvé, Louis Sognot, or Jacques Adnet, from whom he received his first commission for lighting fixtures. From 1953 to 1962 Mouille designed his first series, which included aside from simple floor lamps also ceiling and wall lamps with up to seven swivel arms or fixed arms; as "stabiles" or "mobiles" these works remind of Calder's metal sculptures. Mouille's love for the forms of nature, for snails, shells, insects, etc., left their traces in his mystically erotic light installations, whose shapes conjure up associations with heavenly bodies, spirals, kraken, eyes, and breasts. A new edition of some of these lighting fixtures, including the model of this floor lamp, was put out by Fab. Editions "Le regard d'Alan" in Paris in 1992. JS

Sel. Lit.: [exh. cat.] Jean Prouvé, Serge Mouille. Deux Maîtres du métal. New York 1985

Serge Mouille

1922 Paris – 1988
Trained as silversmith at the Ecole des Arts Appliqués in Paris, in 1937 worked in the studio of Gilbert Lacroix. As of 1953 successful designs for lighting fixtures and lamps, including "Œil" (1953), "Flammes" (1954) and "Saturn" (1958). In 1961 founded the SCM (Sociéte de Création de Modèles) in order to support young talents. Received in 1963 the gold medal of the Société d'Encouragement à l'Art et à l'Industrie as well as the medal of the City of Paris; in 1955 was awarded the Charles Plumet prize; numerous exhibitions and honors.

Serge Mouille
Floor Lamp, 1953

Black lacquered metal support, aluminum reflector with black exterior and white lacquered interior
H. 160 cm, w. 45 cm, d. 85 cm
Acc. no. 519/95

Dino Martens
Vase from the Series
"Oriente," between 1952
and 1954

Multi-colored glass
H. 24 cm, max. w. 24 cm
Made by Vetri Decorativi Rag.
Aureliano Toso, Murano
Acc. no. 730/94

Dino Martens

1894 Venice – 1970 Venice
Attended the Accademia di Belle Arti,
Venice, majoring in painting; graduated in
1936, while combatant in the Italian-
Ethiopian war, from the Academy of
Asmara, Ethiopia. Participated as painter
at the biennials in Venice 1924–1930.
Moved in the mid-twenties to Murano.
Worked there at the S.A.L.I.R. (Studio Ars
Labor Industrie Riunite). Worked as
designer at Salviati & Co. and in 1932 at
Andrea Rioda. As of 1944 artistic director
at Vetri Decorativi Rag. Aureliano Toso,
between 1959 and 1962 worked there
free-lance.

Due to the collaboration with the painter Dino Martens beginning in
1944, the manufacturing plant Vetri Decorativi Rag. Aureliano Toso,
established in 1938, developed to be one of the most important glass
workshops of the post-war period. Dino Martens had a feeling for
bizarre, painterly forms and glass decors, which stood in decisive contrast
to the Murano tradition. In order to carry out his new ideas, Martens
had to first of all develop new glass making techniques. In 1950 he began
with various experiments from which in the end the series he entitled
"Oriente" was created. In this Martens often worked with luminously
colored, primarily opaque, pieces of glass and often with the star-shaped
Murrina (millefiori) of black and white glass canes, so characteristic for
Murano. By fusing these pieces with the clear glass matrix, strongly
colored, abstract, splotchy decors were created that in combination with
the unusual, often playful seeming, forms mark a turning point in the
development of Venetian glass art. JS

Sel. Lit.: Barovier Marina, Rosa Barovier Mentasti and Attilia Dorigato, Il vetro di Murano
alle Biennali 1895–1972. Mailand 1995, 174, no. 111 ill. [comparable object]

After the pathbreaking designs of Aalto, Breuer, and Summers in the thirties or those of Charles and Ray Eames in the forties, a further development in the area of plywood furniture was not imaginable. But Charlotte Perriand, who for many years collaborated with Le Corbusier, proves the opposite with the stackable chair shown here, especially through its – apparent – simplicity, which in combination with the black lacquering draws on the principles of Japanese aesthetics.

After having worked as industrial design advisor in Tokyo on invitation of the Japanese government from 1940 to 1943, she was able to draw on these experiences in 1955, when she took over the design of the exhibition "Synthesis of Art," organized by the Japanese department store Takashimaya. Le Corbusier also participated with wall hangings and Léger with wall ceramics. The chair designed by Charlotte Perriand on this occasion and produced in Japan in a small number of pieces – later sold by the Gallery Steph Simon in Paris – stands paradigmatically for the motto of the exhibition as a perfect synthesis between the Eastern feeling for form and Western technique. JS

Sel. Lit.: Frey Gilbert, Das moderne Sitzmöbel von 1850 bis heute. Teufen 1970, 99 ill. – [exh. cat.] Charlotte Perriand. Un Art de Vivre. Musée des Arts Décoratifs. Paris 1985, 49, 50, 54 ill. – [exh. cat.] Europa nach der Flut. Kunst 1945–1965. Fundación "la Caixa", Barcelona/Künstlerhaus Wien. Barcelona 1995, 425, no. 17 ill., 471, no. 120 – L'Architecture d'Aujourd'Hui, 1996, no. 303, 108 ill.

Charlotte Perriand
Stackable Chair, 1955

Black lacquered plywood
H. 66 cm, w. 45 cm, d. 51 cm
Commissioned by
Takashimaya, Tokyo
Acc. no. 8/95

Charlotte Perriand

1903 Paris – lives in Paris
1920–1925 studied design at the Ecole
l'Union Centrale des Arts Décoratifs in
Paris, 1927–1937 developed, in collaboration with Le Corbusier and Pierre
Jeanneret, the "interior equipment of
a dwelling" and numerous revolutionary
furniture pieces as, for example, the
"Chaise Longue" or the "Grand Comfort"
of 1928/29; in addition, her own productions. After 1937 architect of winter sport
centers, 1938–1945 industrial design
advisor in Tokyo for the Japanese government, since 1946 again working in Paris
as designer and architect.

Dieter Rams

1932 Wiesbaden – lives in Kronberg/
Taunus, Germany
Studied at the Werkkunstschule
Wiesbaden (diploma in 1953). Worked
1953–1955 at the architectural office of
Otto Apel. Working since 1955 at Braun
AG, since 1961 as head of design. As
of 1981 professor of industrial design at
the Hamburger Hochschule für Bildende
Kunst. Since 1988 general representative
of the Braun AG. Head of the Rat für
Formgebung (Council for Design).

Dieter Rams
Combination Radio and
Record Player "Studio 2,"
1959

Light gray and aluminum-
colored metal, acrylic glass,
and dark gray plastic
Receiver CE 11: H. 11 cm,
w. 20 cm, d. 33.5 cm
Amplifier CV 11: H. 1.5 cm,
w. 20 cm, d. 32 cm
Record Player CS 11:
H. 16.5 cm, w. 40 cm, d. 32 cm
Made by Braun AG,
Frankfurt/Main
Acc. no. 704/94

The set represents an early example of the famous "Braun Line," which
came to epitomize German design characterized by functional aesthetic
in the second half of the century. Rams writes on the new design
principle of "Studio 2," with which Braun came to pave the way for high
fidelity equipment in Germany, in 1995: "We designed the functional
units – record player, amplifier, radio – as a single piece of equipment.
The building blocks had the same dimensions. Thus they could be
arranged next to or on top of one another. One could, another
advantage of the building block concept, buy the units individually
and put together a stereo system piece by piece. ... We were particularly
concerned to make the product graphics – the writing on the controls –
clear and easy to understand. For this we used the then still new
serigraphy technique." Studio 2 is not only the first Braun hi-fi system, it
is one of the first hi-fi systems altogether. JS

Sel. Lit.: Burkhardt François and Inez Franksen (pub.), Design: Dieter Rams et. Berlin 1980,
130, no. 26 ill. – Pinakothek der Moderne: eine Vision des Museums für Kunst, Architektur und Design des 20. Jahrhunderts in München. Pub. Stiftung Pinakothek der
Moderne. München/New York 1995, 174 ill. – Klatt Jo and Günter Staeffler (pub.), Braun
+ Design Collection. Bad Oeynhausen 1995 (2nd edition), 70, 72 ill. – Rams Dieter, Weniger,
aber besser. Hamburg 1995, 31–33 ill.

The floor lamp "Luminator" by the Castiglioni brothers is as radical and new, and ahead of the stylistic language of their times, as their desk lamp "Tubino" created just a few years earlier (see page 132). The extremely reduced design unites function and form to a new entity in a surprising manner. The basic design element is a metal tube whose diameter is large enough to hold the socket for the pressed glass reflector lamp. Three thin metal rods serve as legs; these can be removed and transported on the inside of the tube. One could hardly imagine a more minimalistic design. The progressiveness of the "Luminator," which was already in the year of its design honored with the Compasso d'Oro award, is also testified to with its recent reedition. JS

Sel. Lit.: Ferrari Paolo, Achille Castiglioni. Mailand 1984, 48–49 ill. – Eidelberg Martin (pub.), Design 1935–1965. What modern was. Le Musée des Arts Décoratifs de Montréal. New York 1991, 217–218 ill. – Castiglioni Piero, Chiara Baldacci and Giuseppe Biondo, Lux. Italia 1930–1990. Mailand 1991, 47 ill.

Achille Castiglioni

1918 Milan – lives in Milan
After receiving his degree in architecture from the polytechnic in Milan in 1944, he built up a design office in 1945 together with his brothers Pier Giacomo and Livio, who left the studio in 1952; in 1956 one of the founders of the ADI; as of 1969 assistant professor of industrial design at the polytechnic in Turin, where he was offered the chair of interior design in 1978; architect and industrial designer.

Pier Giacomo Castiglioni

1913 Milan – 1968 Milan
Received his degree in architecture from the Milan polytechnic; worked at first together with his brother Livio and later with his younger brother Achille, as of 1945 in the same studio; specialized in the area of lighting fixtures, also designed furniture and technical equipment.

Achille and Pier Giacomo Castiglioni
Floor Lamp Model B 9
"Luminator," 1955

Black lacquered metal
H. 175 cm
Made by Gilardi & Barzaghi, Milan, and Flos S.p.A., Brescia, Italy (re-edition)
Acc. no. 509/95

Vladimir Kagan

1927 Worms, Germany – lives in New York
Moved to the USA in 1938; studied
architecture at the Columbia University
in New York; in the late forties Kagan
began to design furniture; he opened his
first showroom in New York in 1949.
With the founding of the Vladimir Kagan
Design Group he also took over the production of his designs. Since the cessation
of production, he has in recent years
concentrated himself exclusively on the
design of furniture, carried out by
various firms. Aside from teaching at the
New York Parsons School of Design, he
has held numerous lectures on modern
architecture and furniture design.

The immigrant Kagan was one of the numerous designers, who in trans-
posing non-American ideas of design – but responding to American
conditions – nevertheless had an essential influence on the success of
American design in the post-war period. Originally a woodwork specialist
in his father's business, he turned after a short period of time to other
materials as well and opened in 1949 a first showroom in New York. Here
such prominent clients as Marilyn Monroe or Xavier Cougart soon
presented themselves. Later he worked as design consultant for General
Electric, Walt Disney, General Motors, and others.
Vladimir Kagan's designs can be subsumed under the generic term, the
so-called, "organic" design that not only in the USA characterized the
fifties so lastingly. The bold curvilinearity of the armchair and above all
the biomorphic aluminum frame, which also characterizes the stool, have
a sculptural quality. The perfect execution of the organically formed,
cast aluminum parts illustrates Kagan's sublime handling of materials and
techniques. With his lavish finishing and unusually designed furniture,
Kagan, whose works are still for the most part unknown in Europe, is one
of the most remarkable American furniture designers of the post-war
period. JS

Vladimir Kagan
Armchair No. 500 and Stool
No. 504 "Tri-symetric," 1958

Polished aluminum and red
leather
Armchair: h. 81.5 cm,
h.s. 32 cm, w. 55 cm, d. 72 cm
Stool: h. 33 cm, w. 53.5 cm,
d. 48 cm
Made by The Vladimir Kagan
Design Group Inc., New York
Acc. no. 118/95, 119/95

Willi Moegle
Photograph: Set of Goblets
No. 1012, c. 1957

Black and white print on Agfa-
Lupex
Image: 21.3 x 16.5 cm,
sheet: 22.5 x 17 cm
On reverse: company stamp
and studio sticker
Commissioned by Vereinigte
Farbenglaswerke AG, Zwiesel
Acc. no. 542/94

Willi Moegle

1897 Stuttgart – 1989 Leinfelden,
Germany
1911–1915 trained as chemigrapher in
Stuttgart, in 1919 studied graphics at
the Stuttgarter Kunstgewerbeschule
under Ernst Schneidler, as of 1927 free-
lance photographer in Stuttgart. In 1944
his studio was bombed out, in 1950
re-established; major areas of work were
product photographs, primarily for
porcelain, glass, and furniture
manufacturers. As of 1950 member of
the Gesellschaft Deutscher Lichtbildner, as
of 1954 member of the Deutsche Gesellschaft für Photographie (German
Society for Photography), in 1969 one of
the founders of the Bund Freischaffender
Foto-Designer. At the beginning of the
seventies he retired; Hansi Müller-Schorp,
his colleague of many years, took over
the management of the studio.

Hardly anyone else has so lastingly characterized the image of product photography like Willi Moegle. It was the time of the German economic miracle, in which not only a host of new products were created, but also the credo of "good form" – replacing the "eternal forms" of the twenties – was propagated. Moegle's major area of work lay in product photographs for porcelain and glass manufacturers or furniture firms. Thus this photograph of the award-winning set by Heinrich Löffelhardt was originally intended just for the company brochure: its task was simply to illustrate the various glasses in this set and their adherence to a generic form.

Schooled by the pathbreaking functional aesthetics of the pre-war period, Moegle focused on the essential, the "willfulness of the objects," which he unpretentiously stage- managed. Moegle had dedicated himself to the principle of simplicity and modesty. The simpler and more matter-of-fact the form of the objects appeared to be, the more successful he considered the shot. This stands in contrast to the amount of set-up work required: subtle light direction and stage-like placement of his "object portraits." These stylistic devices show a link with the ideas of the Bauhaus photographers, especially László and Lucia Moholy-Nagy. As a member of the Gesellschaft Deutscher Lichtbildner (Society of German Photographers) and one of the founders of the Bund Freischaffender Foto-Designer (BFF: Association of Free-lance Photographic Designers) Moegle set standards in product photography. At the same time he was, not only due to his date of birth, a link between the periods before and after World War II and the very different approaches used in this area. EM

George Nelson

1908 Hartford, Connecticut – 1986 New
York
Studied architecture at the Yale University
School of Fine Arts. 1935–1941 co-
publisher of the journal "Architectural
Forum," 1944–1949 sole publisher.
1936–1941 partner of W. Hamby, New
York, in the area architecture and interior
design. In 1944 Nelson designed, together
with Henry Wright, the storage wall
concept, which found much acclaim and
led in 1945 to the collaboration with
Hermann Miller Corp. For this company,
of which he was director of design
1946–1972, he made numerous designs
for furniture, clocks, and plastic dishes
(around 1953). In 1947 founded the
architectural office George Nelson,
specializing in industrial design, in 1968
typewriter "Editor 2" for Olivetti.

George Nelson (Assoc.)
Wall Clock Model 4755, 1947

White lacquered metal and
black lacquered wood
ø 47.5 cm, d. 6.5 cm
Made by Howard Miller Clock
Company, Zeeland, Michigan
Acc. no. 385/92

In 1947 the design office of George Nelson began developing a new clock
series for the Howard Miller Clock Company. The final finishing of designs
lay in the hands of Nelson's colleague Irving Harper. According to his
own statement, he was responsible for clock design at Nelson's up to the
late fifties. In an interview with Nelson, however, the Japanese- American
sculptor and designer Isamu Noguchi was named as the primary designer
(cf. Eidelberg). What was decidedly new in this clock series is the lack
of a traditional clock face with an indication of the hours. The visible wall
behind the star-shaped wooden rays, which as hour markers extend far
beyond the compact cylindrical metal case, functions as an integrated
background. The clock thus appears to be part of the wall or architecture
and is not just any wall object. For this reason, the clocks with their
unusual outlines could be used particularly well for their optical effect, as
accentuating elements, in the design of entire walls. JS

Sel. Lit.: Greenberg Cara, Mid-Century Modern. New York 1984, 29 ill. [there d. 1949] –
Eidelberg Martin (pub.), Design 1935–1965. What modern was. Le Musée des Arts Décoratifs
de Montréal. New York 1991, 254–255 [a variation of model 4755]

In Italy the rapid development of clock technology – from mechanical to electro-mechanical right down to electronic or quartz works – had, to begin with, no radical consequences for the design. Only at the end of the fifties did a far- reaching change set in. Designers increasingly turned their attention to table clocks in particular – meanwhile a typical industrial product. One of the earliest examples is the clock "Section" designed by Mangiarotti and Morassutti, which was produced in three different versions. New were, amongst other things, the unusual casings and the inclination of the clock face, which was supposed to make reading the time easier, also the absence of push-buttons or other control elements on the exterior – even the alarm clock version could be turned off by just lightly pressing the cover. Beginning with "Section," clock design in Italy received new impulses, which led to a series of unusual works by renowned designers such as Joe Colombo, Rodolfo Bonetto or Gino Valle, and others. JS

Sel. Lit.: Gregotti Vittorio, Il disegno del prodotto industriale. Italia 1860–1980. Mailand 1982, 342 ill. [there dated 1963] – Hiesinger Kathryn B., [exh. cat.] Design since 1945. Philadelphia Museum of Art. London 1983, 90 ill. [there dated 1962] – Bona Enrico D., Mangiarotti. Genua 1988, 26 ill. [there dated 1956]

Angelo Mangiarotti

1921 Milan – lives in Milan
1945–1948 studied architecture at the Milan polytechnic. 1953–1954 guest lecturer at the department of design, Illinois Institute of Technology; between 1955 and 1960 worked closely with Bruno Morassutti. One of the founders of the Association of Industrial Design (ADI); lectured in various countries. His major areas of work are construction of furniture and furniture systems, but he also designed technical equipment; numerous works for the firms Cassina, Knoll, and Artemide.

Bruno Morassutti

1920 Padua
Studied architecture in Venice until 1947, 1949–1950 worked at the office of Frank Lloyd Wright in Taliesin (Scottsdale, Arizona). 1955–1960 collaboration with Angelo Mangiarotti, in 1968 founded an office in Milan with Mario Memoli, Giovanna Gussoni, and Gabriella Benevento. His major architectural works include the church of Baranzate di Bollato (1957), residential buildings in Milan, a villa in Sorrento (1962), and many more.

Angelo Mangiarotti and Bruno Morassutti Table Clocks "Section," 1956–1960

White or red, and clear plastic and metal
H. 8.5–24 cm,
max. w. 10–13 cm
Made by Le Porte-Echappement Universel SA, La Chaux-de-Fonds, Switzerland
Acc. no. 251/92 (left), 136/82 (center), 380/95 (right)

Antonio Da Ros

1936 Venice – lives in Italy
Studied at the Istituto Statale d'Arte
Carmini in Venice. Taught as professor of
architecture. After a short period as
ceramic designer, he came to Cenedese in
1958, soon thereafter taking over the
artistic direction.

Glass from Murano became famous due to its technical perfection and extraordinary artistic quality early on already. But the decades after World War II, characterized by their new spirit and élan, also represent an extremely fruitful period in Venetian glass art. Aside from the longestablished glass workshops, who realized new ideas and forms with young designers, a few new firms were established as well. Amongst these the Vetreria Gino Cenedese, founded in 1946, stands out. From the beginning it attracted such important artists as Alfredo Barbini, Riccardo Licata, Fulvio Bianconi, or Napoleone Martinuzzi. At the time that Antonio Da Ros took over the artistic directorship, he initiated a new orientation in design. Characteristic for this is the group of "Sassi" (stones): heavy thick-walled vases, to which the two pieces in Die Neue Sammlung as particularly convincing examples also belong. In the vetro sommerso technique – that is, the layering (cf. casing or flashing) of glass in several different colors – one could achieve diverse forms and color combinations, which enriched Venetian glass art by another facet. JS

Antonio Da Ros
Two Vases "Coppa Ollandese"
and "AD Grande," 1959

Light green, brown-green,
light blue, and clear glass in
the vetro sommerso technique
AD Grande: h. 30.5 cm,
l. 16.5 cm, w. 7 cm
Coppa Ollandese: h. 14 cm,
l. 26 cm, w. 7.5 cm
Made by Vetreria Gino
Cenedese, Murano
Acc. no. 477/90, 476/90

Arne Jacobsen

1902 Copenhagen – 1971 Copenhagen
After training as bricklayer, studied
architecture at the Copenhagen academy.
1927–1930 worked at the architectural
office of Paul Holsoe. In 1930 he founded
his own architecture and design studio.
AS of 1956 professor at the Royal Danish
Academy of Fine Arts. Jacobsen worked
as architect, interior designer, and
designer of furniture, lamps, ceramics,
metal and glass, as well as textiles.
See also page 223.

As the most important Scandinavian designer, Arne Jacobsen influenced European furniture design decisively with his organic, symbolic forms in the fifties. By using native woods, plywood, and leather – as well as industrially produced materials such as cast aluminum and fiberglass-reinforced plastics – he consciously and clearly made a point against the, in his view, irresponsible use of precious exotic woods, which were at that time characteristic for large parts of the Scandinavian furniture industry. One of Jacobsen's most spectacular works was created in connection with the building and furnishing of the SAS Hotel designed by him in Copenhagen: the "Egg," a unique interpretation of a wing chair with integrated armrests. The oval form, unusual for a piece of furniture, required new production methods of utmost precision in order to give the upholstery and cover an exact fit. JS

Sel. Lit.: Kastholm Jørgen, Arne Jacobsen. Kopenhagen 1968, 56–57 ill. – [exh. cat.] Scandinavian Modern Design 1880–1980. Cooper-Hewitt Museum. New York 1982, 181 ill. – Hiesinger Kathryn B., [exh. cat.] Design since 1945. Philadelphia Museum of Art. London 1983, 127 ill. – Fiell Peter and Charlotte, Die modernen Klassiker. Schaffhausen 1991, 70, 78 , no. 57 ill. – Tøjner Poul Erik and Kjeld Vindum, [exh. cat.] Arne Jacobsen. Architect & Designer. Design Museum London, Die Neue Sammlung München, Dansk Design Center. Kopenhagen 1994, 78–79 ill.

Arne Jacobsen
Armchair "Egg," 1957

Fiberglass-reinforced plastic,
cast aluminum, and orange
fabric cover
H. 106 cm, w. 87 cm, d. 78 cm
Made by Fritz Hansen,
Copenhagen
Acc. no. 220/93

Isamu Noguchi

1904 Los Angeles – 1988 New York
In 1917 began training as cabinet-maker
in Chigasaki, Japan; moved to the USA in
1918, where he first studied sculpture and
then studied at the Columbia University
in New York from 1921 to 1924; in 1927
he went to Paris in order to assist in
Constantin Brancusi's studio, before he
finally settled as a sculptor in New York in
1932; as of the late thirties he designed
numerous squares and gardens; in the
early forties he began to design furniture
for H. Miller and Knoll Möbel, et al.,
as well as the famous Akari lamps of
handmade paper.

His many years of making sculptures lit from within – for example,
"Red Lunar Fist" of 1944 – seem to have predestined Isamu Noguchi to
designing lighting fixtures. Thus he accepted the invitation of the
Japanese city of Gifu, a center for making the traditional paper lanterns,
to bring new impulses to this important branch of industry. Noguchi
changed two things immediately. He banned the painted decorations,
not customary in the beginning, from the lamp shades; the old lanterns
produced in Gifu had been unadorned. In addition, he replaced the
candles with light bulbs, so that the lanterns previously used only for
festive occasions could also be utilized on a daily basis. The traditional
material of the lamp shades, paper made of the bark of the mulberry
tree, he retained. Noguchi called his lamps "Akari," a word that can be
translated as moon, sun, or light, having several meanings at once. From
1951 up to the seventies always new versions of the often bizarrely
shaped "Akari" were created. In 1962 Noguchi used fluorescent tubes for
the first time and thus developed a new type of floor lamp. With his
"Akari" – luminous sculptures in the room – Noguchi created a synthesis
of art and design, an extraordinary example of the strong Japanese
traditions that continue to live on and that already at the beginning of
modernism had so decisively left their mark on the West. JS

Isamu Noguchi
Floor Lamp, c. 1960

Black lacquered metal,
wood, and paper
H. c. 150 cm, w. 120 cm
Made by Ozeki & Co. Ltd.,
Gifu, Japan
Acc. no. 201/94

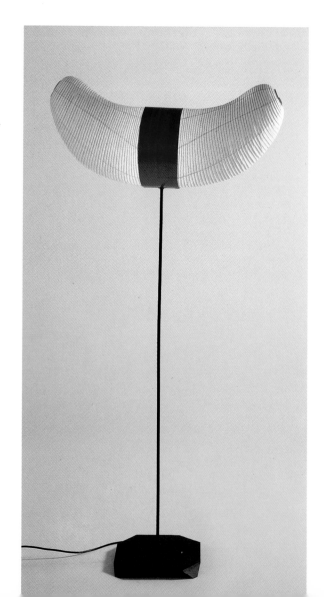

Verner Panton's career as international furniture designer began in 1958 with his first big commission, the renovation of the large garden café "Komigen" (Come Again) in the Langesø Park on Fünen. For the interior, he designed a chair in the shape of a cone standing on its tip, which has gone down in design history as the Cone Chair or Ice Cream Cone Chair. Percy von Halling-Koch founded his own company (Plus-linje) for the production of the chair. Panton collaborated with Plus-linje up to 1962. During this time, aside from numerous experiments, various versions of the Ice Cream Cone Chair were created: the chair with heart-shaped back was used in 1960 for the furnishing of the restaurant "Astoria" in Trondheim; it was also very popular as a wire netting chair; the version with the square shape was, in contrast, produced only in a limited number of pieces. The Ice Cream Cone Chair is a unique phenomena in its time: it seems to anticipate the furniture influenced by pop art about ten years later. JS

Sel. Lit.: Kaiser Niels-Jørgen and Henrik Sten Møller, Verner Panton. Kopenhagen 1987, [n.p.] ill. – Fiell Peter and Charlotte, Die modernen Klassiker. Schaffhausen 1991, 70, 78–79, no. 58 ill. [Cone Chair] – [exh. cat.] Interieur und Design in Deutschland 1945–1960. Kunstgewerbemuseum. Berlin 1993, 76, no. 55 ill. [Cone Chair; wire netting version]

Verner Panton

1926 Gamtofte, Denmark – lives in Binningen, Switzerland
Studied architecture at the Technische Hochschule in Odense from 1944 to 1947, then until 1951 at the Royal Academy of Fine Arts in Copenhagen. Worked from 1950 to 1952 at the office of Arne Jacobsen; after extensive travels for the purposes of study, he opened an architecture and design office in Copenhagen, since 1963 he lives in Binningen, Switzerland. Aside from architectural projects he designed, amongst other things, furniture, lamps, textiles, and complete interior environments. Panton received numerous awards, incl. the International Design Award in 1963 and 1968.

Center: Armchair "Cone Chair," 1958

Partially chrome-plated metal frame, foam upholstery with orange-colored fabric cover
H. 84 cm, w. 58.5 cm, d. 60 cm
Made by Plus-linje A/S, Copenhagen
Acc. no. 383/92

Verner Panton
Left: Armchair, 1960

Partially chrome-plated metal frame, foam upholstery with violet fabric cover
H. 76 cm, w. 80 cm, d. 66 cm
Made by Plus-linje A/S, Copenhagen
Acc. no. 162/94

Right: Armchair "Heart," 1960

Partially chrome-plated metal frame, foam upholstery with red fabric cover
H. 89.5 cm, w. 100 cm, d. 72 cm
Made by Plus-linje A/S, Copenhagen
Acc. no. 382/92

Verner Panton

1926 Gamtofte, Denmark – lives in
Binningen, Switzerland
Studied architecture at the Technische
Hochschule in Odense from 1944 to 1947,
then until 1951 at the Royal Academy
of Fine Arts in Copenhagen. Worked from
1950 to 1952 at the office of Arne
Jacobsen; after extensive travels for the
purposes of study, he opened an architecture and design office in Copenhagen,
since 1963 he lives in Binningen,
Switzerland. Aside from architectural
projects he designed, amongst other
things, furniture, lamps, textiles, and
complete interior environments. Panton
received numerous awards, incl. the
International Design Award in 1963 and
1968.

The widely distributed chair made of a single material and in a single cast
has a long history: the idea of making a chair all in one piece without
back legs lay in the air, as had decades earlier the idea of a cantilevered
tubular steel chair. Designers from different countries attempted to
realize this idea. In the late fifties Panton succeeded in finding firms first
in Denmark who were prepared to support his experiments with various
materials, especially with acrylic and fiberglass-reinforced plastic as
well as with rigid foam. But the breakthrough came only during the
collaboration with Vitra: As of 1963 Panton and Manfred Diebold, the
plastics expert of the company, developed on the basis of plaster models
first prototypes of fiberglass-reinforced polyester. In 1967 the chair
was finally ready to go into production. The first examples were made
of deformed and then lacquered Baydur (rigid polyurethane foam);
as of 1970 one used Luran-S, a plastic reinforced without fiberglass, and
malleable only by being heated in an injection-molding process.
Today the chair is being produced of PUR structural integral foam. One
precursor, amongst others, is Rietveld's Zig-Zag chair; Panton himself
designed a precursor model of wood. With this stackable chair, Panton
realized the goal, formulated by Eero Saarinen years before, of
producing furniture completely of plastic. JS

Sel. Lit.: Eidelberg Martin (pub.), Design 1935–1965. What modern was. Le Musée des Arts
Décoratifs de Montréal. New York 1991, 314–316 ill.

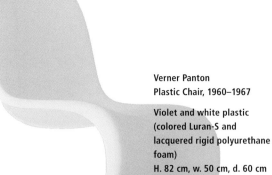

Verner Panton
Plastic Chair, 1960–1967

Violet and white plastic
(colored Luran-S and
lacquered rigid polyurethane
foam)
H. 82 cm, w. 50 cm, d. 60 cm
Made by Vitra GmbH, Basel,
for Herman Miller
International, New York
Acc. no. 718/94, 113/96

Cesare Leonardi

1935 Italy – lives in Italy
Studied architecture at the University of
Florence; since 1962 he runs, together
with Franca Stagi, a studio specialized in
architecture and urban development
in Modena; in addition joint designs for
furniture, lamps, and plastic objects.

Franca Stagi

1937 Italy – lives in Italy
Studied at the polytechnic in Milan;
in 1962 she became partner in Cesare
Leonardi's design office in Modena.

At the beginning of the sixties a decisive change took place in Italian furniture design. The producers recognized that they had to invest in research and new technology in order to keep pace with developments in Great Britain and in the USA. With the development of the injection-mold process the Italian industry made an important contribution to the furniture production of our century. The armchair by Cesare Leonardi and Franca Stagi is an early example of this new production method's application, making the realization of even such unusual and complex designs possible in series. Starting point for the design concept was the idea of making an armchair out of a circular band. By "pushing in" the back portion, a backrest was created whose curving transitions to the seating surface simultaneously create armrests. Comfortable sitting was achieved by the springy effect of the cantilevered tubular steel frame. A few years later Pierre Pauling again took up the basic idea of a chair consisting of a single band and developed his own "Ribbon" armchair (see page 165). JS

Sel. Lit.: Hatje Gerd and Elke Kaspar (pub.), Neue Möbel. Vol. 9. Stuttgart 1969, 34, no. 89 ill. – Katz Sylvia, Classic Plastics. From Bakelite to High-Tech. London 1984, 110 ill. – Fiell Peter and Charlotte, Die modernen Klassiker. Schaffhausen 1991, 90, 105, no. 63 ill. – Fiell Peter and Charlotte, Modern Chairs. Köln 1993, 90 ill.

**Cesare Leonardi and
Franca Stagi
Armchair Model CL9 "Ribbon
Chair," 1961**

White lacquered fiberglass-
reinforced polyester and
chrome-plated tubular steel
H. 64 cm, w. c. 100 cm,
d. 70 cm
Made by Bernini, Milan
(1961–1969), and Elco, Venice
(as of 1969)
Acc. no. 489/95

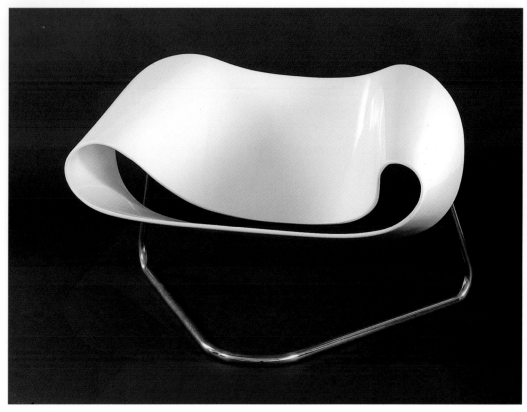

Eero Aarnio

1932 Helsinki – lives in Helsinki
1954–1957 studied at the Institute for
Applied Arts in Helsinki. In 1962 founded
his own studio in Helsinki, in the sixties
designed plastic furniture. Works primarily
as furniture and interior designer, but
also as graphic artist and photographer.
In 1968 Aarnio received the American
Industrial Design Prize.

The ball chair is one of the best known symbols of the space age, which began in 1961 with Juri Gagarin orbiting the earth and reached its temporary climax with the first landing on the moon. In a series of films and television shows the armchair could be admired as the essence of modernism. One was infatuated with the fantastic possibilities of the future. The seemingly worn-out paths of classical furniture design were left behind in favor of playful futuristic ideas, which Aarnio's armchair particularly well embodies. The sphere – the absolute and most perfect geometric body – isolates the user from his environment: The person seated there can, so to speak, create his own microcosm in his "space capsule." JS

Sel. Lit.: Hiesinger Kathryn B., [exh. cat.] Design since 1945. Philadelphia Museum of Art. London 1983, 121 ill. – Eidelberg Martin (pub.), Design 1935–1965. What modern was. Le Musée des Arts Décoratifs de Montréal. New York 1991, 316–318 – [exh. cat.] Möbel aus Kunststoff. Vitra Design Museum. Weil am Rhein 1990, 22–23 ill. – Fiell Peter and Charlotte, Die modernen Klassiker. Schaffhausen 1991, 94, 107 ill. – Fiell Peter and Charlotte, Modern Chairs. Köln 1993, 93 ill. – Hiesinger Kathryn B. and George H. Marcus, Landmarks of Twentieth-Century Design. New York 1993, 229 ill.

Eero Aarnio
Ball Chair, 1963–1965

Red fiberglass-reinforced
plastic, red lacquered metal,
and foam upholstery with
black fabric cover
H. 120 cm, w. 105 cm,
d. 100 cm
Made by Asko Oy, Lahti,
Finland
Acc. no. 134/94

David Gammon

Biographical data not known.

"Pure technology" was the design principle underlying this unusual piece, which allows an almost complete view of the functions and mechanisms of the individual power and control elements. Due to the shapes and arrangements of the individual elements, the covering housing could be reduced to a convincingly rigorous minimum. How far this design was ahead of its times, can be seen in the readoption of similar principles in the late seventies and eighties. One of the outstanding technical characteristics of the "Transcriptor" is the high precision of its synchronization, which almost completely eliminates swaying. This was achieved with a liquid in a container below the turntable, rotating at the same speed. The piece proves in an impressive manner that technical construction and aesthetic quality do not have to be mutually exclusive. Thus the "Transcriptor" stands in the classical English tradition of scientific technical instrument construction. JS

Sel. Lit.: [coll. cat.] The Museum of Modern Art. New York 1984, 453, no. 753 ill. – Pinakothek der Moderne: eine Vision des Museums für Kunst, Architektur und Design des 20. Jahrhunderts in München. Pub. Stiftung Pinakothek der Moderne. München/New York 1995, 194 ill.

David Gammon
Record Player "Transcriptor,"
1964

Aluminum, gilded brass, black
lacquered plywood, and
colorless acrylic glass
H. 18.2 cm, w. 44 cm,
d. 53.4 cm
Made by Transcriptors Ltd.,
Boreham Wood, England
Acc. no. 139/94

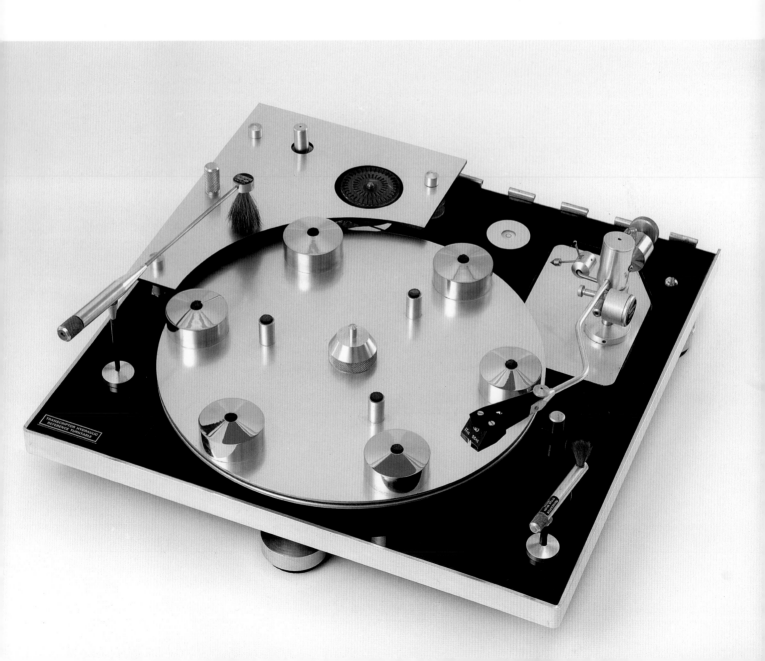

From the surrealist painter Roberto Sebastian Matta stems the design
for this unconventional seating system, which makes the flexible furnishing of an interior possible, indeed demands it: The individual sculptural
elements could be distributed in the room as desired or be compactly
stacked as "object." Sculpture and furniture in one, "Malitte" was one of
the earliest conceptions to totally negate the forms and structures of
traditional seating furniture.

New was not only the material, polyurethane foam, but also the construction, which dispenses with a frame. Matta attempted to find shapes
that made it possible to use all of the material without any waste;
that is how the four different seating elements and the round, differently
colored center piece, which could be used as a stool, emerged. JS

Sel. Lit.: [exh. cat.] Italy: The New Domestic Landscape. The Museum of Modern Art.
New York 1972, 115 ill. – Hiesinger Kathryn B., [exh. cat.] Design since 1945. Philadelphia
Museum of Art. London 1983, 129 ill. – Eidelberg Martin (pub.), Design 1935–1965. What
modern was. Le Musée des Arts Décoratifs de Montréal. New York 1991, 334–335 ill. –
Hiesinger Kathryn B. and George H. Marcus, Landmarks of Twentieth-Century Design. New
York 1993, 240, no. 130 ill. – Kjellberg Pierre, Le Mobilier du XXe Siècle. Paris 1994, 419–420
ill.

Roberto Sebastian Matta

1911 Santiago de Chile – lives in Paris
Graduated from the University of Chile in
architecture in 1931; 1934–1935 worked
at the office of Le Corbusier. Enthusiastic
about the surrealists, he decided to
devote himself to painting and later also
to sculpture. After a longer period of time
in New York, he settled in Rome and
Paris. In the sixties Matta was commissioned, amongst other architects and
designers, to design furniture for the
firm Gavina; as a result "Malitte" was
created.

Roberto Sebastian Matta
Seating System "Malitte,"
1966

Polyurethane foam with blue
and violet fabric cover
H. 160 cm, w. 160 cm, d. 65 cm
(when stacked)
Made by Gavina, Foligno, Italy
(1966–1968), and Knoll
International, New York
(1968–1974)
Acc. no. 217/95

Yonel Lébovici
Table Lamp "Satellite," 1965

Chrome-plated metal and
colorless acrylic glass (PMMA)
H. 41 cm, w. 40 cm,
max. d. 26.5 cm
Made by Yonel Lébovici, Paris
Acc. no. 205/95

Yonel Lébovici

1937 – lives in Paris
Designer of furniture, lighting fixtures,
and glass, usually carrying out the
production himself. Works for Jansen,
Cardin, the Club Mediterranée, and
Lancel.

The French designer Yonel Lébovici contributed important impulses to
the design of lighting fixtures. The object represented here, produced in
a small edition of 20 pieces, reflects the space age euphoria that was
so inpiring for the sixties, while his light sculptures created in the form of
safety pins or electrical plugs just a few years later can be seen in the
context of pop art. But Lébovici does not restrict himself simply to a game
of forms: In "Satellite" the acrylic glass surrounding the lamp shines from
within, so to speak, and thus contributes indirectly and diffusely to
the lighting of the room. At the same time the glass plates reflect some
of the light, emerging much brighter at the cut edges, the rays focused
by the plate's thickness. This principle is used today in countless
advertising and text panels. FH

Sel. Lit.: [exh. cat.] Lumières. Centre Georges Pompidou. Paris 1985, 155, no. 253 ill.

Nani Prina

1938 Milan – lives in Milan
Studied at the polytechnic in Milan.
Architect, industrial and graphic designer.
Works in the area of industrial design
since 1968; amongst other things, much
theoretical work on plastic, designs
of plastic. Works for the firms Molteni,
Cassina, Bazzani, and Roller, et al.
Member of the ADI (Associazione per il
Disegno Industriale).

Furniture design of the late sixties is characterized by the tendency to sculptural objects. Exemplary for this is Nani Prina's sofa, whose description "Sculpture" clearly points in this direction.
While in these objects functionality, i.e. particularly the useability and comfortableness, often takes second place to aesthetics, Prina's sofa fulfills both criteria in an exemplary manner. Nani Prina, who is also very interested in the theoretical aspects of design, designed together with Vittorio Parigi, amongst other things, an extraordinary desk of plastic, also in Die Neue Sammlung (Acc. no. 521/95). JS

Sel. Lit.: Bangert Albrecht, Italienisches Möbeldesign. München 1989, 99 ill.

Nani Prina
Sofa "Sculpture," 1968

Polyurethane foam, metal
frame, and black fabric cover
H. 72 cm, w. 144 cm, d. 79 cm
Made by Sormani,
Arosio/Como, Italy
Acc. no. 118/91

Sculptural furniture with object chararcter is typical for the Anglo-American as well as the Franco-Italian design scene in the late sixties. It stands in strong contrast to the quieter functional approach to design practiced in Germany and Scandinavia at the same time. The armchair designed in 1965 can be placed at the beginning of this development. Paulin developed a method that made it possible to produce upholstery furniture, even such new sculptural seating objects as the "Ribbon," solely by industrial means. A tubular steel frame fabricated in the basic shape of the piece of furniture was covered with a rubber cover, onto which the foam upholstery could be fastened. Stretch fabric covers fit even the most unusual forms. The design principle of a seating surface formed of a single twisted band, can be compared to the armchair of the same name by Leonardi and Stagi (see page 154) but not the material and production method. Paulin's pedestal solution also goes far beyond earlier Italian design: The rectangular base has been optically so reduced that nothing distracts from the sculptural quality of this work. Paulin's "Ribbon Chair" received the International Design Award (A.I.D.) in Chicago in 1969. JS

Sel. Lit.: Fiell Peter and Charlotte, Die modernen Klassiker. Schaffhausen 1991, no. 72 ill.

Pierre Paulin

1927 Paris – lives in Paris
Studied at the Ecole Nationale Supérieure des Arts Décoratifs in Paris. Since the late fifties designs for furniture. In 1968 commissioned by the Musée du Louvre to design the seating for visitors, in 1969 by the French president, the private rooms in the Elysée palace. In 1975 founded the firm ADSA + Partners. In 1983 again works for the Elysée palace.

Pierre Paulin
Armchair Model No. 582
"Ribbon," 1965

Tubular steel frame, foam upholstery with red jersey cover, and white lacquered wooden pedestal
H. 68 cm, w. 100 cm, d. 75 cm
Made by Artifort, Maastricht
Acc. no. 372/95

Pierre Paulin

1927 Paris – lives in Paris
Studied at the Ecole Nationale Supérieure
des Arts Décoratifs in Paris. Since the late
fifties designs for furniture. In 1968
commissioned by the Musée du Louvre to
design the seating for visitors, in 1969 by
the French president, the private rooms
in the Elysée palace. In 1975 founded the
firm ADSA + Partners. In 1983 again
works for the Elysée palace.

In this work Paulin is even more radical than in his "Ribbon Chair"
designed just shortly before. He rejects legs or base completely now: like
a wave-shaped object this "piece of seating furniture" sits directly on the
floor. Again the manufacturing methods developed by Paulin, in
connection with the stretch fabric, allow such independent forms. The
name "Langue" or "Tongue" characterizes not only the appearance of
the armchair, but also signals that a human organ enormously enlarged
and torn completely out of context can be adapted to the shape of a
piece of furniture! One is reminded of the films of the period with their
preference for almost surreal close-ups of body parts, but also of the
"Lips Sofa" by Salvadore Dali (1936), which significantly enough returned
to production in Italy in 1971 ("Bocca," Gufram). Thus Paulin's "Tongue"
reflects a position, characterized by the pop culture of the sixties, that
convincingly combines ergonomic principles with sculptural values. CR/JS

Sel. Lit.: Fiell Peter and Charlotte, Modern Chairs. Köln 1993, 101 ill.

Pierre Paulin
Armchair Model No. 577
"Tongue," 1967

Tubular steel frame, foam
upholstery with jersey cover
H. 61 cm, w. 90 cm, d. 90 cm
Made by Artifort, Maastricht
Acc. no. 234/94

The "Dondolo" by Cesare Leonardi and Franca Stagi is considered the outstanding example of plastic furniture that exhausts the technical potential and aesthetic qualities of this material to its fullest extent. The realization of the boldly curved form, appearing nearly weightless, was only made possible by the longitudinal rib structure that gave the material the strength to hold up to even large weights. With this solution one was able to increase the load-bearing capacity without any other reinforcement by, for example, metal and at the same time to retain the lightness of the object, the thinness of the material, and thus the extraordinary shape of the design. JS

Sel. Lit.: Hatje Gerd and Elke Kaspar (pub.), Neue Möbel. Vol. 9. Stuttgart 1969, 34, no. 89 ill. – [exh. cat.] Italy: The New Domestic Landscape. The Museum of Modern Art. New York 1972, 26–27 ill. – Hiesinger Kathryn B., [exh. cat.] Design since 1945. Philadelphia Museum of Art. London 1983, 129 ill. – Hiesinger Kathryn B. and George H. Marcus, Landmarks of Twentieth-Century Design. New York 1993, 240–241, no. 311 ill. – Kjellberg Pierre, Le Mobilier du XXe Siècle. Paris 1994, 379–380 ill.

Cesare Leonardi

1935 Italy – lives in Italy
Studied architecture at the University of Florence; since 1962 he runs, together with Franca Stagi, a studio specialized in architecture and urban development in Modena; in addition joint designs for furniture, lamps, and plastic objects.

Franca Stagi

1937 Italy – lives in Italy
Studied at the polytechnic in Milan; in 1962 she became partner in Cesare Leonardi's design office in Modena.

Cesare Leonardi and
Franca Stagi
Rocking Chair "Dondolo,"
1967

White lacquered fiberglass-
reinforced plastic
H. 75 cm, w. 40 cm, l. 174 cm
Made by Elco, Venice
(1967–1970)
Acc. no. 290/92

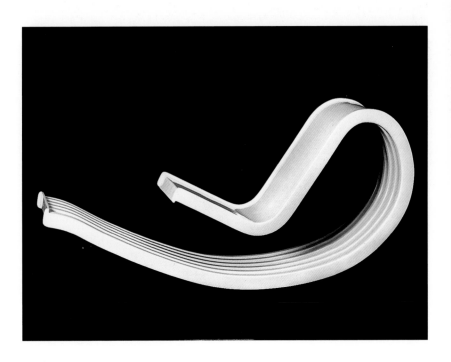

Vico Magistretti
Table Lamp "Telegono," 1968

**Plastic (red ABS plastic, white
polypropylene)**
H. 40 cm, w. 26.6 cm, d. 24 cm
**Made by Artemide, Pregnano
Milanese, Italy**
Acc. no. 114/95

Vico Magistretti

1920 Milan – lives in Milan
Studied architecture at the Milan
polytechnic until 1945, later under
Ernesto Rogers in Lausanne. His own
office in Milan, works as architect, urban
planner, and designer. Magistretti has
taught at architectural schools in Venice,
Florence, Barcelona, Vienna, and Toronto.
Since 1980 visiting professor at the
Royal College in London. Designed,
amongst other things, furniture and
lamps.

Vico Magistretti's interest in the spherical shape, a leitmotif of the sixties,
resulted in various solutions for lighting fixtures. Magistretti built on the
principle of his smaller table lamp "Eclisse", created just shortly before,
and consisting of a reflector casing with two hemi-spherical shells turning
towards one another on a vertical axis. For the "Telegono" he used a
casing with a second half-sphere reflector inside, rotating on the
horizontal axis. Thus the effect of the light could be altered. The material
is also different: instead of metal Magistretti now uses plastic. Not only is
it and its processing cheaper, as well as being light, but due to the various
colors in which the basic material is available, lacquering can be
dispensed with. Apart from that, one can manufacture a larger number
of pieces. The design came very close to the ideals of the late sixties:
creating well-designed, inexpensive objects for as broad and mobile a
public as possible. JS

Sel. Lit.: [exh. cat.] Lumières. Centre Georges Pompidou. Paris 1985, 154, no. 250 ill. – Pasca
Vanni, Vico Magistretti. Designer. Berlin 1991, 36 ill., 122 [there dated 1966] – [exh. cat.]
L'Utopie du tout Plastique. Fondation pour l'Architecture. Brüssel 1994, 50 ill. [there dated
1969] – domus 1995, no. 775, 72, no. 2 ill.

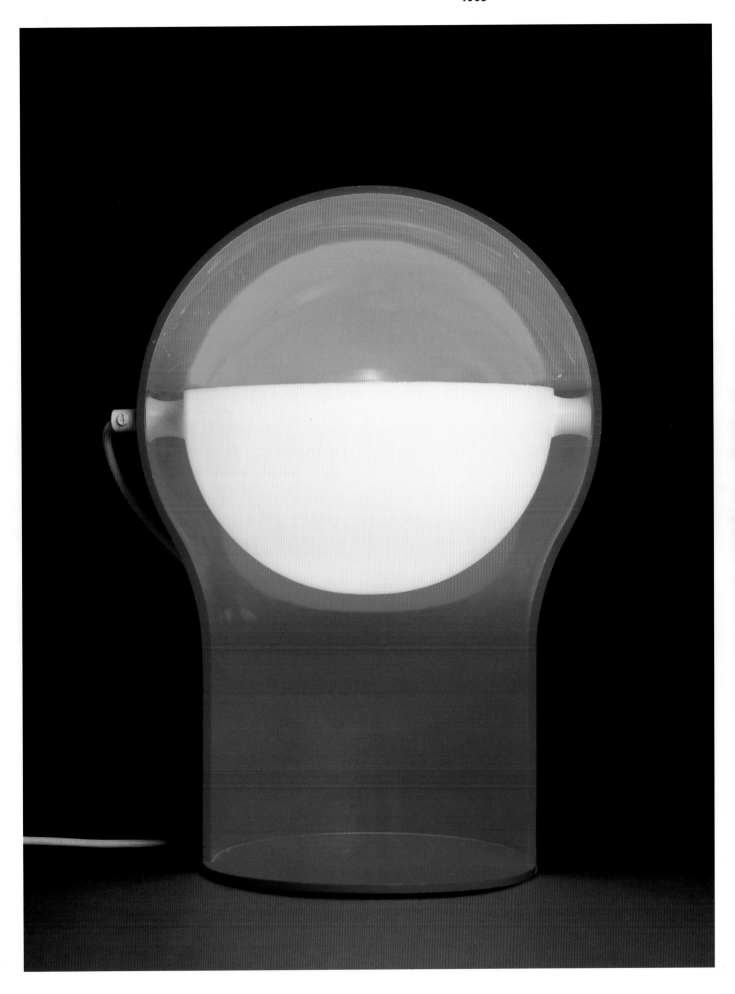

"Today one must be able to present furnishing that exists independently of architectonic prerequisites. It must be so flexible and capable of being integrated, that it qualifies for present-day as well as future conceptions of interiors." With these words – in which associations are conjured up of the, for that time typical, belief in the possibility of a completely different type of room conception in the future, for which one has to remain open – Joe Colombo explained the concept behind his designs. The aspect of multi-functionalism with open structures and variable uses always played an essential role in this, as can already be seen, for example, in his "Additional Living System" developed before "Tubo." The former consists of a series of elements that can be freely combined: several pillow-like cushions in various sizes that, connected with metal clasps, make armchairs, stools, or even beds. With "Tubo" Colombo took another decisive step forward, though, and not only because of the use of the new, seemingly transitory, wet-look leather. Stripping off all reminiscences of previous seating furniture, he dissolved the "armchair" into four tubes of various diameters, which can, in a playful manner, be variously put together. Held together only by simple clasps, which hardly distract, the tubes give the impression of continuous rotating movement and permanent instability: the German "Möbel" and the Italian "mobile" (meaning furniture) come from "mobile." Taken apart, the tubes can be stacked inside one another and carried away in a light linen bag! CR/JS

Joe Cesare Colombo

1930 Milan – 1971 Milan
Studied at the Academy of Fine Arts Brera until 1949, 1950–1954 in the faculty of architecture at the polytechnic in Milan. From 1951 to 1955 he worked primarily as painter and sculptor, incl. in the group Movimento Nucleare, in subsequent years as architect and designer. In 1962 he opened his own studio in Milan. Colombo worked as architect and interior designer, in addition, he designed furniture, lamps, a kitchen system, and appliances. His achievements have been honored with numerous international awards and exhibitions.

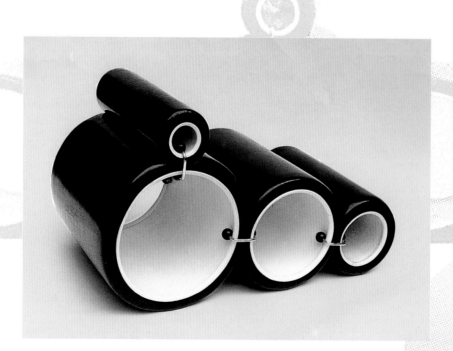

Joe Colombo
Armchair "Tubo" or "Tube
Chair," 1969

White plastic and foam
upholstery with red wet-look
leather
ø 50 cm, 39 cm, 29 cm, 18 cm,
w. 60 cm
Made by Flexform, Milan
Acc. no. 30/91

Factory Design Matsushita

The rapidly advancing technological development in radio construction since the mid-fifties – replacing the tube with a transistor, ever stronger miniaturization on the equipment's interior – also led to a change in the design of the exteriors, particularly in the sixties. While German and Italian designers such as, for example, Dieter Rams, Richard Sapper, or Mario Bellini pursued a line focusing on clarity and functionalism, unconventional forms inspired by the "craziness" of pop art were being created in Japan, an industrial nation shaking off traditions and striving for progress, around 1970. An extreme example of this tendency is the Matsushita radio, which, equipped with a swivel joint, could be worn on the arm like a bracelet and accompanied the flower power generation – a type of proto-walkmann. The second source of inspiration in Japan – as in the West – was space travel and thus inspired science fiction fantasies: spherical television and radio sets suggesting helmets of astronauts, as in the Weltron 2001 shown here, whose name refers to the movie "2001: A Space Odyssey" by Stanley Kubrick (1968), or UFO-like shapes as in the Weltron 2005 system. CR/JS

Sel. Lit.: Woodham Jonathan M., Twentieth Century Ornament. New York 1990, 237 ill. [radios] – [exh. cat.] L'Utopie du tout Plastique. 1960–1973. Fondation pour l'Architecture. Brüssel 1994, 123 ill. [Weltron sets]

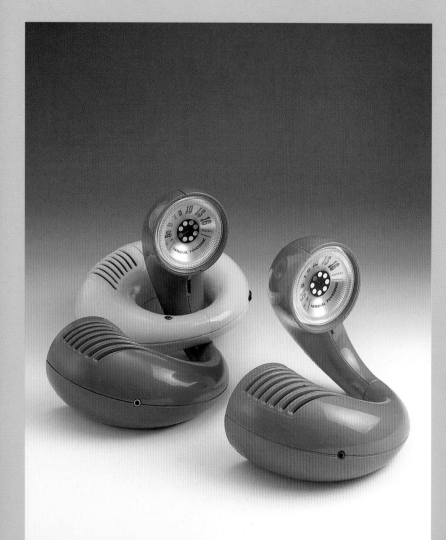

Radios, Model R-72S, c. 1969

Orange or blue or yellow
plastic
H. 7 cm, ø 15 cm
Made by Matsushita Electric
Industrial Co. Ltd., Japan
Acc. no. N 114/90-1,2

Combination Record and
Cassette Player Weltron 2005
Stereo System, c. 1970

White and black plastic,
colorless acrylic glass
(PMMA), and aluminum
pedestal
H. 70 cm, ø 58 cm
Made by Weltron, Japan
Acc. no. 165/93

Factory Design Weltron

Radio and Cassette Recorder
Model 2001, c. 1970

White and black plastic,
colorless acrylic glass (PMMA)
H. 30 cm, w. 27 cm, d. 27 cm
Made by Weltron, Japan
Acc. no. 429/90

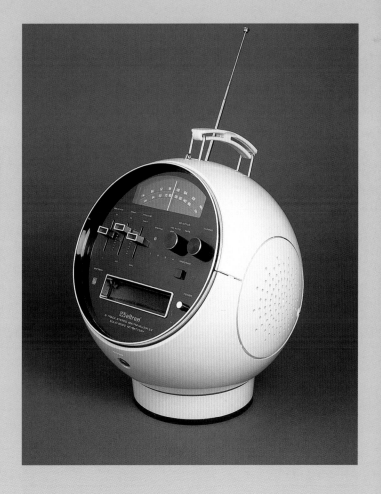

Maurice Calka

1921 – lives in Paris
Studied at the Ecole Nationale des Beaux
Arts in Paris, from which he graduated
with the Grand Prix de Rome. Later he
lectured at the same institution. Calka
became well-known in the seventies
primarily for his cast polyester desks such
as "P.D.G." (1969) and "Boomerang"
(1970), which he designed for the Société
Leleu-Deshays.

Curved like a boomerang, but instead of being dark as wood like the
Australian weapon, it is snow white and thus as immaterial, so to speak,
as the thoughts inspired at it; like a piece of throwing wood made all
of one piece, on all sides rounded, polished, smooth, and without edges:
that describes the desk made in only a few examples and designed by
Maurice Calka in 1970. The design of a sculptor: the three-dimensional
forms leave no doubt.
Calka, professor at the Ecole Nationale des Beaux-Arts in Paris, worked
with the most varied materials such as wood, metal, and stone, but also
with plastic. For his softly curvilinear furniture he utilized above all
polyester resin, which allowed various colors and the greatest freedom
of form. In 1969 he made his first design for a desk, awarded the Rome
Prize. A chair was solidly integrated within its form. For the
"Boomerang," Calka further developed this shape and improved it in
that he now – for practical reasons – abandoned the permanently
attached chair. Thus a most unique piece of furniture was created, which
although clearly marked by the spirit of the times, represents a perfect
synthesis between sculpture and furniture design. CR/JS

Sel. Lit.: Hatje Gerd and Elke Kaspar (pub.), Neue Möbel, Vol. 10. Stuttgart 1971, 103
ill. – DiNoto Andrea, Art Plastic. New York 1984, 166–167 ill. [with variations] – [exh. cat.]
L'Utopie du tout Plastique. Fondation pour l'Architecture. Brüssel 1994, 78–79 ill. –
Kjellberg Pierre, Le Mobilier du XXe Siècle. Paris 1994, 110 ill.

Maurice Calka
Desk "Boomerang," 1970

White lacquered fiberglass-
reinforced plastic
Inscription right: CREATION M.
CALKA
H. 75 cm, w. c. 185 cm,
d. c. 115 cm
Made by Leleu-Deshays, Paris
Acc. no. 680/93

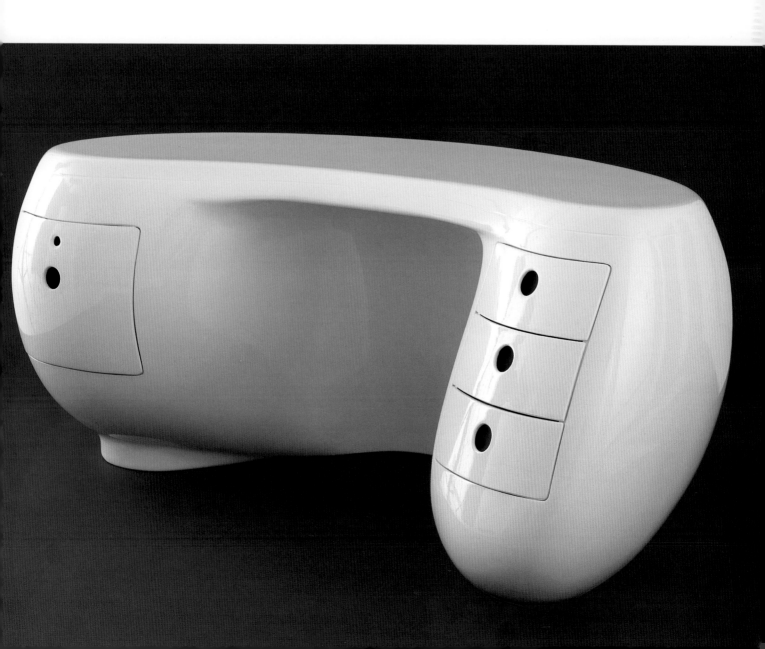

Frank Owen Gehry
(Frank Goldberg)

1929 Toronto – lives in Santa Monica,
California
Studied at the University of Southern
California and at the Harvard Graduate
School of Design. In 1962 founded an
architectural office in Los Angeles.
From 1972 to 1973 and 1988 to 1989
assistant professor at the University of
Southern California. In 1974 architectural
project together with Claes Oldenburg
for the biennial in Venice. Had a formative
influence on a new, experimental
architectural style with designs such as
his house in Santa Monica, California
(1977–1979). In 1979 designed the
Vitra Design Museum in Weil am Rhein.
Since 1969 Gehry also works in the
area of furniture design, preferably with
corrugated cardboard.

Long before the wave of "ecological design," Frank O. Gehry had made
corrugated cardboard furniture. The pieces from the series "Easy Edges"
were conceived of in 1972 as low-cost products. They were, however,
so successful that Gehry had the production stopped after three months,
because he feared that his rise as popular furniture designer would
prevent him from being able to prove his skill as architect. Only in 1980
did he turn to this material again. "Little Beaver" was created, the name
reflecting the fact that the unfinished edges look as if a beaver had
gnawed at them. In order to make the "art quality" of this armchair clear
and unambiguous, the edition was limited from the very beginning:
the "commodity" was listed in the catalog of the manufacturer as
"object"! JS

Sel. Lit.: Fiell Peter and Charlotte, Die modernen Klassiker. Schaffhausen 1991, 136, 143,
no. 109 ill. – Dormer Peter, Design since 1945. London 1993, 147, no. 124 ill. – Kjellberg
Pierre, Le Mobilier du XXe Siècle. Paris 1994, 266 ill.

**Frank O. Gehry
Armchair with Stool "Little
Beaver," 1980 (model)**

**Laminated corrugated
cardboard
Armchair: h. 85 cm,
w. 83.5 cm, d. 100 cm
Stool: h. 46 cm, w. 49 cm,
d. 61 cm
Made by Vitra GmbH,
Weil am Rhein, Germany
Acc. no. 551/95**

Gaetano Pesce
Chair "Dalila due," 1980

**Polyurethane foam coated
with black epoxy-resin
H. 75 cm, w. 53 cm, d. 61 cm
Made by Cassina S.p.A.,
Milan
Acc. no. 115/95**

Gaetano Pesce

1939 La Spezia, Italy – lives in New York
Studied architecture and industrial design
in Venice. In 1959 one of the founders
of the group N in Padua. Opened his own
studio together with Milena Vettore. In
1971 one of the founders of the society
Bracciodiferro, for the production of
experimental objects. In 1975 chair in
architecture and urban planning in
Strasbourg. Since 1983 Pesce lives in New
York. Has taught at various universities
in the USA, Milan, and Hong Kong.

The chair belongs together with two other chairs and the table
"Sansone" to a series of furniture pieces, whose names play on the Old
Testament theme of "Samson and Delilah." Pesce sees in this story, which
ends with the destruction of the columns of the tempel of the Philis-
tines, a "parabel for the necessity to free oneself of social, political, and
economic doctrines. The "Sansone" contradicts every prerequisite of
industrial standardization, because the worker decides during the production which shape the table top will have – the mold is flexible and
neither really round nor square nor rectangular – and which combination
of colors it will have" (according to Fiell). It is similar with the "Dalila"
chair, whose soft, anthropomorphic shape results from the liquid
consistency of the heated polyurethane and thus is left up to a certain
degree of chance. JS

Sel. Lit.: Bangert Albrecht, Italienisches Möbeldesign. München 1989, 116–117 ill. [Dalila tre]
– Vanlaethem France, Gaetano Pesce. Archaisches Design. München 1989, 77–78 ill., cover
ill. – [exh. cat.] Möbel aus Kunststoff. Vitra Design Museum. Weil am Rhein 1990, 38–39 ill.
[Dalila tre] – Fiell Peter and Charlotte, Die modernen Klassiker. Schaffhausen 1991, 136,
143, no. 110 ill.

Ettore Sottsass, Jr.

1917 Innsbruck, Austria – lives in Milan
Studied architecture at the polytechnic in
Turin until 1939. In 1947 opened his own
studio and began free-lance work in the
areas of architecture, painting, ceramics,
jewelry, furniture, tapestry, and industrial
design. In 1956 Sottsass worked at
George Nelson's in New York. 1958–1980
design consultant for the firm Olivetti.
In 1975 one of the founding members of
the group Global Tools, 1978–1979
worked for Alchimia. In 1980 founded the
studio Sottsass Associati. In 1981 Sottass
started the group Memphis, which had
a decisive impact on design development
in the following decade.

Ettore Sottsass
Table "Le Strutture Tremano"
from the Bau. Haus Collection
of Alchimia, 1979

Wood covered with white
Abet Print laminate, metal
lacquered in various colors,
and crystal glass
H. 115 cm, top: 50 x 50 cm
Made by Belux AG, Wohlen,
Switzerland
Acc. no. 644/93

The most radical turning point in recent design history took place in
Italy at the end of the seventies/beginning of the eighties, when the
attempt was made to break with the traditional values of design:
function and aesthetics. The goal of the designer groups Memphis and
Alchimia was formulated by Mendini, the theoretician of the new
movement: "The main characteristic is perhaps the idea of the objects,
not in their functional context, which is, so to speak, matter-of-course,
but the idea of a ritual and relative expressiveness. It has to do with
the relationship between person and object." Exemplary for this could
be these objects, which were shown in an exhibition with the purposely
misleading name "Bau. Haus" by Alchimia. With such designs De Lucchi
and Sottsass decisively distance themselves from the harmony of
the Italian "Bel Design," which had so lastingly dominated the seventies.
The movement set off by Alchimia and Memphis, although early on
already recognized as being not workable on a long-term basis, nevertheless lastingly left its mark on the design image of publishing.
The combination of banality and irony, of historical citation and fashionable attitude, accomodates the need for an aestheticizing art object and
at the same time received, through the small edition, the aura of the
unique. With that the split between a crafts-oriented unique object and
industrial design in the actual sense, had been completed. FH/JS

Michele de Lucchi

1951 Ferrara – lives in Milan
Studied architecture at the art college in
Florence 1969–1975. 1976–1977 assistant
at the faculty of architecture at the art
college in Florence, in 1976 opened his
first office in Florence; in the following
year moved to Milan; in 1978 first designs
for the design group Alchimia; works
since 1979 for Olivetti. In 1981 one of the
founders of the group Memphis, for
which he made numerous designs until
1987; in 1986 opened his Milan studio.
De Lucchi works as architect as well
as designer – everything from product
and graphic design to exhibition design.
Has taught at the Domus Academy in
Milan and at the Cranbrook Academy of
Art near Detroit, USA.

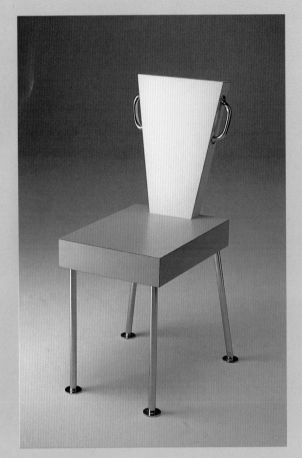

Ettore Sottsass
Chair "Seggiolina da Pranzo"
from the Bau. Haus Collection
of Alchimia, 1980

Wood covered with blue or
yellow Abet Print laminate
and chrome-plated metal
H. 84 cm, w. 41 cm, d. 48 cm
Made by Belux AG, Wohlen,
Switzerland
Acc. no. 177/94

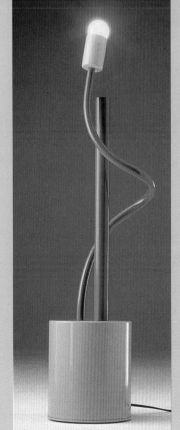

Michele De Lucchi
Lamp "Sinerpica" from the
Bau. Haus Collection of
Alchimia, 1979

Metal lacquered in various
colors
H. 75 cm, ø 17 cm
Made by Belux AG, Wohlen,
Switzerland
Acc. no. 614/93

Sottsass Associati

Founded in 1980 by Ettore Sottsass together with Marco Zanini, Aldo Cibic, and Matteo Thun. The group worked in the areas of architecture, interior design, graphics, and industrial design. Some of the most important commissions of the last few years are works for Fiorucci (interior design), Esprit (shops and corporate identity) and Alessi (since 1983 corporate identity).

Even with such a relatively banal object as the telephone, Ettore Sottsass' creative potential, which has made him one of the most important designers of the day, emerges. Whereas the design of telephones was characterized for a long time primarily by the curvilinear ergonomic line, Sottsass turned this tradition upside down in that he created a severe rectangular shape for the receiver, on which the individual areas of function are set off by bright colors. Corresponding to the unconventional design approach, the name chosen for this telephone is "Enorme," which literally translated means "deviating from the norm." More prophetic would have been, however, the description "constituting a norm," since not much later – parallel with the increasing popularity of the cordless telephone – the design, if not the colors, was adapted ever more often by other manufacturers. JS

Sel. Lit.: Burney Jan, Ettore Sottsass. London 1991, 168 ill. – [exh. cat.] Internationaler Designpreis des Landes Baden-Württemberg 1991. Stuttgart 1991, 84 ill. – Höger Hans, Ettore Sottsass jun. Tübingen/Berlin 1993, 62, no. 106 ill.

Sottsass Associati (Ettore
Sottsass, Marco Zanini, Marco
Susani)
Telephone "Enorme," 1986

Dark gray, red, and yellow
plastic and dark gray
aluminum
H. 19.5 cm, w. 5.4 cm,
d. 4.8 cm
Made by Brondi Telefonia
S.p.A., Settimo, Italy
Acc. no. 210/93

Christian Coigny

1946 Lausanne – lives in Lutry, Switzerland
Studied at the Schule für Photographie in Vevey, Switzerland, 1967–1968, since 1969 free-lance photographer in the area of advertising and fashion, e.g. "Vogue." Since 1976 studio in Lausanne, in 1979 the first exhibition of his own works. In 1981 the second prize for color photography at the triennial in Fribourg, Switzerland. Numerous publications and campaigns, e.g. American Express; in 1987 begins the Vitra series, which was exhibited in Lausanne, Rotterdam, and Munich.

The frequently honored advertising campaign Personalities impressively documents and communicates, with in the meantime about 115 subjects, the furniture manufacturer's company philosophy. He outlines his concept with the key words "creativity and diversity." We meet highly qualified representatives of very diverse professions seated on furniture of the Vitra production line. In doing so, the photographer has understood how to allow the personality of his opposite sufficient room for self-representation. The product takes second place to the expressive power of the portrait and serves as prop for his staging. The chair functions more or less as stage and reflects the respective position of the protagonist. In this case it is the famous fashion designer Issey Miyake on the metal chair designed by Shiro Kuramata in 1986. The geometric severity of the body's contours corresponds to the hard metal and the distinct silhouette of the piece of furniture. The dynamic play of light and shade suggests a tension-filled drama that belongs to the stage direction of the whole series and lends the sequences of the theatrum mundi its suspense. For this reason, Coigny's single shot endures, even without the interpreting commentary that normally accompanies advertising photography. EM

Christian Coigny
Photograph: Issey Miyake on the Armchair "How High the Moon," c. 1987

Black and white print
42 x 29.5 cm
Commissioned by Vitra International, Basel
Acc. no. 144/94

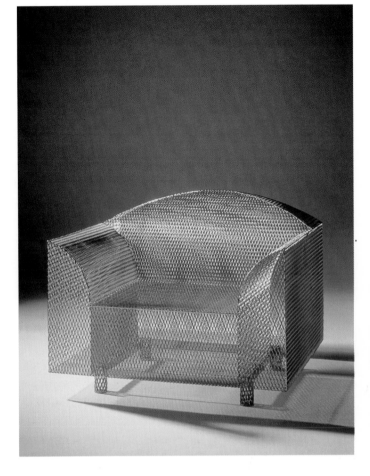

Shiro Kuramata

1934 Tokyo – 1991 Tokyo
Was trained in woodcraft at the Tokyo
Municipal Polytechnic High School before
studying in the Department of Living
Design, Kuwasa Institute of Design, Tokyo.
In 1965 founded his own design studio.
Designs for Memphis, Vitra, etc. Interior
designs for Seibu, Esprit, and Issey
Miyake.

Shiro Kuramata
Armchair "How High the
Moon," 1986

Nickel-plated steel mesh
H. 72 cm, w. 95 cm, d. 82.5 cm
Made by Vitra GmbH,
Weil am Rhein, Germany
Acc. no. 550/95

In experimenting with standard industrial materials such as expanded
metal mesh, terrazzo, corrugated aluminum, etc., Shiro Kuramata arrived
at very unusual designs; often he was the first to use these materials
for interior design. Kuramata began working with expanded metal mesh
while furnishing the Esprit boutique in Hong Kong in 1984. In 1985 he
again employed this material for the Issey Miyake boutique in the Seibu
building in Tokyo. The sophisticated game reached a new high one year
later in the design named after Duke Ellington's jazz title "How High
the Moon." The transparency and immateriality of the steel mesh stands
in provocative contrast to the shape based on the proportions and
outlines of a traditional, bulky upholstered armchair. The hardness of the
material contradicts the softness and comfortableness that this shape
would actually lead one to expect. JS

Sel. Lit.: Fiell Peter and Charlotte, Modern Chairs. Köln 1993, 122 ill. – Hiesinger Kathryn B.
and George H. Marcus, Landmarks of Twentieth-Century Design. New York/London/
Paris 1993, 300, no. 392 ill. – Kjellberg Pierre, Le Mobilier du XXe Siècle. Paris 1994, 349–350
ill. – Hiesinger Kathryn B. and Felice Fischer, [exh. cat.] Japanese Design. Philadelphia
Museum of Art. New York 1995, 162–163, no. 186 ill.

Taku Satoh

1955 Tokyo – lives in Tokyo
Studied design at the Tokyo National
University of Fine Arts and Music until
1981. After working at the agency
Dentsu, founded Taku Satoh Design Office
Inc. Graphic and product design for such
companies as Nikka Whiskey, Max Factor,
Parco, Morinago, and Kanebo. Numerous
awards and exhibitions.

fec. = fecit: "he/she made (it)" can often be seen after the signature of artists on works of art. In the present case, the self-assured testimony to authorship does without the artist's signature. It is the name of a Japanese cosmetic line and stands, in the true sense of the word, in the focal point of the packaging, playing on the company's name: Factor (Latin: manufacturer, creator, originator). In the same way that the word logo is an understatement, the product design is based on the principle of the severest possible reduction and abstraction in order to raise "fec." above the mass of competing cosmetics. There are no extravagant shapes or ornaments, no "gold" as status symbol, no colors to catch the eye. Instead the palette is restricted to a matt black (hinge and interior of the case, the tinted paper of the unlacquered collapsible box) and the moonshine of aluminum (the shell of the case, the screw top of the make-up bottle), as well as white for the small square label with delicate black lower case letters on the box. In addition there is an emphasis on basic geometric shapes in the outlines: the rectangle of the boxes, the tall oval of the bottle, the perfect circular shape of the containers. The powder compacts and eye-shadow containers represent a particularly successful, unusual solution to this type of packaging. The problem is "accomodating" the hinge, which usually detracts from the shape as a whole inspite of attempts to hide it. Satoh's design in fact emphasizes the hinge: isolated by a different color, material, and surface treatment, it has been accentuated – similar to precious furniture mountings – as a functional decorative element. Satoh utilizes for this an extraordinarily precisely formed finger hinge. The joint lies far outside the circular outline in order to not disturb it; the long "fingers" reach exactly into the curvature of the case's shell; their bevelled ends intimate an imaginary inner circle, in whose center the name of the make – like the artist's stamp on Japanese woodcuts – is imprinted as an important element in the composition. Without any outer splendour the impression of extreme preciousness and noblesse is awakened. The elegant restraint may remind of the packaging of Chanel, but its means to entice – clever surface treatment tempting to the touch, veiling and suggestion – place these new works in the long tradition of the highly refined Japanese art of packaging. CR

Sel. Lit.: [exh. cat.] Taku Satoh. Neo Ornamentalism. Axis Gallery. [n.p.] 1990, [n.p.] ill. – Pedersen B. Martin (pub.), Graphis Design 92. Zürich 1991, 227, ill. 576.

Taku Satoh
Packaging for the Cosmetic
Line "fec.," 1986

Brushed aluminum and black
plastic
Compact: H. 2.4 cm, ø 7.3 cm
Eye-shadow container:
H. 2.0, ø 6.9 cm
Commissioned by Max Factor,
Tokyo
Acc. no. 35/93

Gaetano Pesce

1939 La Spezia, Italy – lives in New York
Studied architecture and industrial design
in Venice. In 1959 one of the founders
of the group N in Padua. Opened his own
studio together with Milena Vettore. In
1971 one of the founders of the society
Bracciodiferro, for the production of
experimental objects. In 1975 chair in
architecture and urban planning in
Strasbourg. Since 1983 Pesce lives in New
York. Has taught at various universities
in the USA, Milan, and Hong Kong.

Through his experiments with innovative production techniques and
materials, particularly plastic, Pesce came upon a material that had
already been used by the Scythians in antiquity: felt. For the "Feltri" he
developed a new method in order to make the soft material a structural
part of a piece of furniture. Thus he soaked the felt in polyester resin,
using more resin for the lower part of the armchair than for the top,
so that it would not be completely rigid and could be easily given a
collar-like shape. The lower part was hardened in a form, sprayed with
color, decorated with laces, and finally upholstered with a quilted
blanket. Pesce describes the experimental approach to his work in this
way: "Many people say the future will be more complex. I don't believe
that. Instead, we will have shorter production runs, not millions of
copies but 3000 or 4000. Technologies must therefore be cheap ... Feltri
represents this idea very well. To make 10 copies of it is the same price as
to make a million." JS

Sel. Lit.: Isozaki Arata (pub.), Das internationale Design-Jahrbuch 1988/89. München 1988,
25 ill. – Fischer Volker (pub.), Design heute. München 1988, 65, no. 136 ill. – Vanlaethem
France, Gaetano Pesce. Archaisches Design. München 1989, 100–103 ill. – [exh. cat.] Elegant
Techniques. Italian Furniture Design 1980–1992. Chicago Cultural Center. Mailand 1992,
76–77 ill. – Hiesinger Kathryn B. and George H. Marcus, Landmarks of Twentieth-Century
Design. New York 1993, 298–299 ill. – Pinakothek der Moderne: eine Vision des Museums
für Kunst, Architektur und Design des 20. Jahrhunderts in München. Pub. Stiftung
Pinakothek der Moderne. München/New York 1995, 238 ill.

Gaetano Pesce
Armchair "Feltri," 1987

Light blue and brown felt
soaked in polyester resin, and
red fabric
H. 127.5 cm, w. 116 cm,
d. 76 cm
Made by Cassina, Meda near
Milan
Acc. no. 124/95

Andy Warhol (1931–1987), an impassioned collector (of clocks as well), designed this watch as one of his last works. It stands at the beginning of the Movado art collection series and is followed in subsequent years by chronometers by Yaakov Agam, Arman, and James Rosenquist, some of which are also in Die Neue Sammlung.

The company, established in 1881, had since 1961 been producing the watch with the "single dot" dial that the American Nathan George Horwitt had designed in 1947 already. Its prototype of 1959, influenced by the theories of the Bauhaus, was acquired by the Museum of Modern Art and Brooklyn Museum in New York and thus became famous under the name "Museum Watch." At the beginning of the eighties Gerry Grinberg, chairman of the board of the North American Watch Corporation (since 1983 parent company of Movado) suggested to Andy Warhol to design a watch for a limited edition production – a project that the artist only carried out four years later, though. From the very beginning he intended a watch with several faces – in keeping with his principle of reducing the traditional understanding of art, the concept of the original and of the boundaries between trivial objects and art works, to absurdum, through serial variations in his works, for example. After experiments with round and square shapes or painted images for the watchfaces, Warhol selected a rectangular shape for the five casings. They wrap around the wrist like an expanding bracelet. For the watchfaces he used black and white photographs in horizontal as well as vertical formats from a series of shots he took of buildings in Manhattan. By using horizontal formats that make reading the time difficult, he provoked an irritation of our normal means of perception, at the same time causing a constant alternation between the function of the watch to measure time and its function as jewelry. Its jewelry character is countered by the banality of the amateurish shots and the restriction to the non-colors black and white. The red hand on the second "image level" sets the only accent, instead of Warhol's usual graphic manipulations, so to speak. The name of the watch plays with the ambiguity of the word "times": time, the times or the circumstances of the times (as in the newspaper name New York Times) but also the "times" in multiplication, and thus refers at once to the author and to the idea of the design: "Andy Warhol times five." CR

Andy Warhol

1928 Pittsburgh – 1987 New York
Studied at the Carnegie Institute of
Technology, Pittsburgh, 1945–1949.
Moved to New York, at first working as
commercial artist and set-designer.
As of about 1962 he preferred serigraphy
as an artistic medium in which banal subjects of the everyday world found their
translation, usually in multiples. Founder
of the legendary Factory; also worked
as underground movie director and
photographer and is considered one of
the leading figures in pop art.

Andy Warhol
Watch "Andy Warhol Times/5," 1987

Black-brown metal and colorless glass
Edition of 250 (AP 13/15)
L. 22 cm, w. 2.5 cm
Made by Movado Watch Co., Grenchen,
Switzerland (came on the market in
1988)
Acc. no. L 481/95

Marc Newson

1962 Sydney, Australia – lives in Australia
Studied jewelry design at the College
of Art, Sydney, until 1984. Newson
became renowned with his Lockheed
Lounge in 1985. First exhibition in Sydney
in 1986. Visited Tokyo in 1987 and made
designs for the Japanese firm Idée, for
which he designed cane chairs in 1990. In
the same year design of the black Pod
watch. Worked for the Italian companies
Cappelini, Flos, Moroso (TV chair and TV
table), for OWO, France, and Shiseido,
Japan, amongst others.

The designs of the Australian designer Marc Newson often combine
organic forms with bright colors. Newson used the compact form of a
human body as basis for the "Embryo Chair," which is well-shaped, but
remains in the end an abstract torso. This stands in contrast to the
"organic" design of the post-war period, characterized by, for example,
the exactly matched outlines of a seated person in the chairs of Charles
and Ray Eames, or by a skeleton-like structure in Carlo Mollino's furniture. Nelson takes the volume of the body as starting point, achieving
a formal alignment between user and object. Newson describes his
unique language of forms as "pod-design." With the natural shape of the
husk, an organic counterpoint to geometrically defined volumes such
as cone, cylinder, etc., is created. The Japanese manufacturer Idée was the
first to recognize the design potential of this young Australian. Already
in 1987 Newson developed the idea of an "Insect Chair" and the "Super
Guppy" lamp. In the following year he designed the "Embryo Chair" for
the Powerhouse Museum in Sydney, one of his most striking works. JS

Sel. Lit.: [exh. cat.] 13 nach Memphis. Museum für Kunsthandwerk Frankfurt a.M.
München/New York 1995, 130, ill. 13, 192, no. 13

Marc Newson
Armchair MN-05 "Embryo
Chair," 1988

Aluminum, foam upholstery,
and black neoprene cover
H. 84 cm, d. 70 cm, w. 80 cm
Made by Idée, Tokyo
Acc. no. 407/94

The so-called W.W. Stool stems from the fanciful concept of an office ensemble, designed by Philippe Starck for the film director Wim Wenders and produced by Vitra in a small series. Usable as stool or as an aid to standing, it is more the sculptural than the functional aspect that predominates. Corresponding to Starck's conviction that aesthetics are an essential function of a piece of furniture, this design is characterized by its unique zoomorphic shape. JS

Sel. Lit.: Boissière Olivier, Philippe Starck. Köln 1991, 57 ill., cover ill. – Šipek Borek (pub.), Das Internationale Design Jahrbuch 1993/94. München 1993, 82 ill. – [exh. cat.] 13 nach Memphis. Museum für Kunsthandwerk Frankfurt a.M. München/New York 1995, 160 ill.

Philippe Starck

1949 Paris – lives in Paris
Studied at the Ecole Nissim de Camondo
1965–1967. Founded a firm for inflatable
houses in 1969; 1971–1972 art
décorateur at Pierre Cardin. Founded the
firm Starck Product in 1979. As of 1973
he designed various bars, restaurants
(e.g. Café Costes, Paris, 1984), hotels,
and the offices as well as private rooms
of the French president in the Elysée
palace (1982). In 1986 his design office
was expanded to include architecture
and industrial design. Numerous awards;
taught at the Domus Academy in
Milan in 1986 and at the Ecole des Arts
Décoratifs in Paris in 1987.

Philippe Starck
W.W. Stool, 1990

Aluminum with emerald-
colored lacquer
H. 96 cm, w. 53.5 cm, d. 53 cm
Made by Vitra GmbH,
Weil am Rhein, Germany
Acc. no. 176/93

Mario Bellini

1935 Milan – lives in Milan
Graduated in architecture from the Milan
polytechnic in 1959. Opened his own
office in Milan in 1962; since 1963
consulting designer for Olivetti. Founded
Environmedia, an organisation for
environmental research, and the group
Habitat Workshop. Received numerous
awards for his designs. Was professor at
the Institut for Industrial Design in Venice
from 1962 to 1965, also professor of
industrial design at the Hochschule für
angewandte Kunst, Vienna, from 1982 to
1983, and at the Domus Academy, Milan,
1983–1985. Since 1986 publisher of the
journal domus. Bellini designed, amongst
other things, furniture, lamps, office
equipment, radio and TV sets, as well as
cassette recorders.

Mario Bellini and Hagai
Shvadron
Notebook Model PT-XT-20
"Quaderno," 1991

Dark gray plastic housing
H. 3.5 cm, l. 21 cm, d. 15 cm
Made by Olivetti S.p.A., Ivrea,
Italy
Acc. no. 490/92

In the history of Industrial Design the Olivetti firm, established in 1908,
holds an outstanding position. After first attempts in the thirties, it was
primarily after World War II that innovative designers were commissioned
to design not only the products, primarily office equipment, but also the
total company image from factory buildings to interior design right down
to advertising. Many of these, to begin with not yet well-known,
designers achieved their reputation due to their work for Olivetti. That
is also true for the architect Mario Bellini, who has worked for Olivetti as
consulting designer for computers, typewriters, and photocopiers since
1963. Amazing is the high standard of design that Bellini has maintained
in the nineties as well, as can be seen in the extremely light and very
small notebook "Quaderno," which marks the beginning of Olivetti's
production of portable computers. JS

Sel. Lit.: [exh. cat.] if. Industrie Forum Design. Hannover 1993, 138–139 ill. – Arad Ron
(pub.), Das Internationale Design Jahrbuch 1994/95. München 1994, 176, no. 6 ill.

In the rapid development in the area of computer hardware, whose components show hardly any decisive differences in capacity, businesses are increasingly counting on design to improve their chances against competitors on the market. The French enterprise électronique d2, established since 1989, commissioned a series of designers to fashion hardware housing. It is typical that this task was not given to designers who are known for their objective functional designs or for integration in a comprehensive system, but to Philippe Starck and later Neil Poulton, designers who work very intensely with the concept of the emotional. Starck attempts to play down the "black box effect," i.e. the technical process no longer understood by the user. Thus the block shape of the housing is loosened up by arching it, the indicator element on the front receives the shape of an eye. With these tricks, he attempts not only to take away the user's fear of an anonymous, so to speak, technical piece of equipment, but also to awaken associations of the familiar, such as the "magical eye" of the tuning indicators on radio sets in the fifties. FH

Sel. Lit.: Boissière Olivier, Philippe Starck. Köln 1991, 149 ill.

Philippe Starck

1949 Paris – lives in Paris
Studied at the Ecole Nissim de Camondo 1965–1967. Founded a firm for inflatable houses in 1969; 1971–1972 art décorateur at Pierre Cardin. Founded the firm Starck Product in 1979. As of 1973 he designed various bars, restaurants (e.g. Café Costes, Paris, 1984), hotels, and the offices as well as private rooms of the French president in the Elysée palace (1982). In 1986 his design office was expanded to include architecture and industrial design. Numerous awards; taught at the Domus Academy in Milan in 1986 and at the Ecole des Arts Décoratifs in Paris in 1987.

Philippe Starck
Hard Disk K1, 1991

Black plastic (ABS)
H. 4.8 cm, w. 14.5 cm, d. 25 cm
Made by Electronique d2,
Paris
Acc. no. 368/93

David Lewis

1939 London – lives in Copenhagen
Studied in the Department of Industrial
Design at the Central School of Art,
London. Since the early sixties works as
designer for Bang & Olufsen, amongst
others. Opened his own office at the
beginning of the seventies, later was
head of the department of design at Bang
& Olufsen. Lewis designed, amongst other
things, sporting equipment, screw pro-
pellers, as well as hi-fi equipment, and
television sets.

Reducing hi-fi towers – which have become ever more complicated and thus also more confusing to use in the seventies and eighties – to forms as simple but as striking as possible in terms of disposition and han-dling has, so to speak, become the hallmark of the Danish enterprise Bang & Olufsen and their designers. In the specific use of material, color, and surface treatment, integrating such tactile qualities as warm and cold, rough and smooth surfaces, a product was created that com-municates competence through form. JS

Sel. Lit.: [exh. cat.] if. Industrie Forum Design. Hannover 1991, 23 ill. – Putman Andrée (pub.), Das Internationale Design Jahrbuch 1992/93. München 1992, 213 ill. – Pinakothek der Moderne: eine Vision des Museums für Kunst, Architektur und Design des 20. Jahr-hunderts in München. Pub. Stiftung Pinakothek der Moderne. München/New York 1995, 244 ill.

David Lewis
Audio System "Beosystem
2500," 1990

Black-gray and silver-colored
metal, black-gray plastic,
smoked glass, and cobalt blue
fabric
H. 36 cm, w. 83 cm, d. 16 cm
Made by Bang & Olufsen A/S,
Struer, Denmark
Acc. no. 125/95

Rodney Kinsman

1943 England – lives in London
Studied at the Central School of Art,
London. Diploma in furniture design.
Founded OMK Design Ltd. together with
Jerzy Olejnik and Bryan Morrison with
emphasis on furniture design. Designs
above all furnishings for English airports,
amongst others, the seating system for
the London airport Gatwick together with
Peter Glynn-Smith in 1981.

**Rodney Kinsman
Seating System "Sevilla,"
1991**

**Cast aluminum, partly
lacquered in dark gray
H. 56 cm, l. 244 cm, d. 35 cm
Made by OMK Design Ltd.,
London
Acc. no. 46/93**

The seating system "Sevilla" was created for the furnishing of the English
pavilion at the world exhibition EXPO 92 in Sevilla. Rodney Kinsman's
design of an aerodynamic seat addition was to correspond with the
functional aesthetic architecture by Nicholas Grimshaw. The concept of
the seat is based on a construction of cast aluminum formed pieces that
interlock. The individual seating elements are pushed onto a beam,
where they are held by, or anchored to, an upright and joint. Thus
further fastenings are not necessary in assembling the convex-shaped
aluminum benches. The furniture system represents one of the most
convincing designs for furnishing public spaces like, for example, train
stations or airports, and is also suited for exterior use. JS

Sel. Lit.: md (moebel interior design) 38, 1992, no. 10, 90–91 ill.

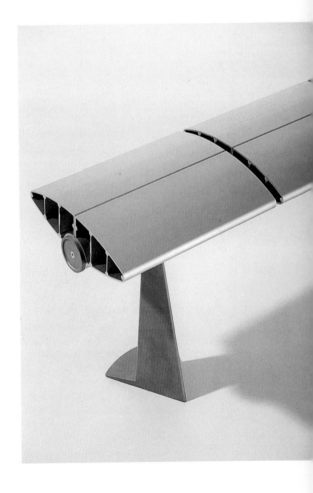

Harald Schaale

1952 Altdöbern, Brandenburg, Germany –
lives in Berlin
Graduated from the university with a
diploma in mathematical modelling and
data processing in industry and commerce
in 1981. In the same year began to work
at the Institut für Forschung und Entwicklung von Sportgeräten (FES) in East
Berlin with emphasis on development
and construction of racing bicycles. Since
1994 director of the institute.

The black bicycles of the German team were the mysterious sensation in
Barcelona in 1992 – and promptly won the Olympic gold medal in the
100-km team race!
Developed and designed by young designers from the former German
Democratic Republic, whose total design profession had just before
been pityingly, ironically smiled at as being "SED design" (SED being the
abbreviation for "Schönes Einheits-Design," i.e. beautiful standard
design, as well as for the East German political party "Sozialistische Ein-
heitspartei Deutschlands." Trans.). These racing bikes are exemplary
for combining the most modern technology with innovative form design.
New, particularly light and resistant materials as well as changes in the
angle of inclination led to the further perfecting of a transport
vehicle individually tailored to the human being, a vehicle that will gain
ever more importance in future. JS

Sel. Lit.: [exh. cat.] Der Nutzen der Dinge. Neues deutsches Industriedesign aus dem
Museum für Kunst und Gewerbe Hamburg. Shanghai Arbeiterkulturpalast. Hamburg 1993,
76–77 ill. – [exh. cat.] Design Positionen Deutschland. Design Center. Stuttgart n.d., 112
ill. – [exh. cat.] Exempla '96. Internationale Handwerksmesse. München 1996, 44–46 ill.

Harald Schaale
Street Racing Bicycle 89-1,
1992

Polyester resin, black carbon,
aramid, and glass fibers
H. 100 cm, l. 162 cm, d. 35 cm
Made by the Institut für
Forschung und Entwicklung
von Sportgeräten e.V. (FES:
Institute for Research and
Development of Sports
Equipment), Berlin
Gift of the Bund Deutscher
Radfahrer (Association of
German Cyclists) through Willi
Daume
Acc. no. 536/94

Jim Gentes

1957 Pawtucket, Rhode Island – lives in
Santa Cruz, California
Studied industrial design at the San Jose
State University, California 1976–1979.
Founded Giro Sport Design Inc. in Santa
Cruz in 1985. His bicycle helmet Giro
Ventoux (1992) received an award for
highest design quality (Design-
Innovationen '93) from the Design
Zentrum Nordrhein Westfalen.

Jim Gentes
(Giro Sport Design Inc.)
Bicycle Helmet "Giro
Ventoux," 1992

Metallic blue plastic and
polystyrene
H. 14 cm, l. 29 cm, w. 22 cm
Made by Giro Ireland Ltd.,
London
Acc. no. 493/93

Since founding his firm Giro Sport Design, Jim Gentes has been developing and designing bicycle helmets. Aside from safety and protection, it
is primarily the factors aeronynamics, comfort, and looks that Gentes tries
to optimize. Futuristic drop-shaped helmets of fiberglass showed up for
the first time in larger numbers at the 1984 Olympics – not for reasons
of safety, but in order to win the battle against the wind. Building on the
tests made in wind-tunnels to this purpose, Gentes developed his first
helmets. In this connection other problems, such as too much weight and
the build-up of heat, were also solved: by using the specially processed
and formed foam material, he achieved a reduction in weight, by an
ingenious system of air passages, the desired cooling effect. With "Giro
Ventoux" a limit in terms of material and finishing technology has
probably been reached for the time being. The relationship weight to
stability is fully exhausted in this helmet weighing only 200 grams. 13
openings on the outside and broadened passages on the inside direct the
air over and around the head without jeopardizing the stability. In an
exemplary manner Jim Gentes' design combines a sensational appearance
with aerodynamics, safety, and comfort. JS

Sel. Lit.: Zec Peter (pub.), Design-Innovationen Jahrbuch '93. Design Zentrum Nordrhein
Westfalen. Essen 1993, 52–53 ill.

With Plutonite the glasses manufacturer Oakley used an, optically speaking, unique material developed in space research. It is not only supposed to block all UV and blue light rays 100%, it is also supposed to be so robust that it can withstand a shot from a 12 calibre shotgun at a distance of 14 meters – therefore also protecting the eyes from fragments of rock and ice, etc., while skiing, climbing, and in other similar situations. The unusual shape of the shield is based on morphological research and studies. On the basis of the research results, one was able to exactly define the human angle of vision and conceive of glasses that offer an almost complete protection against sunrays falling in from every possible angle. At the same time the maximum field of vision, which is free of distortion even along the edges, was created. This is particularly important, as the product name suggests, during winter sports in glacier and snow regions with their blinding light. From the combination of the most modern material, newest scientific findings, and extraordinary design, a new aesthetic was created that lastingly determines our view of the present. CR/JS

Factory Design
Sunglasses "Sub Zero,"
1993/1994

Plutonite and plastic (Virgin-
Serilium)
H. 5.4 cm, w. 14.3 cm,
d. 14.5 cm
Made by Oakley Inc., Irvine,
California
Acc. no. 137/95

"He uses type the way a painter uses paint – to create emotions, to express ideas." That is how the photographer Albert Watson described the working method of David Carson. Since some years he is considered one of the most diverse and forward-looking protagonists of that new direction in graphic design that is characterized by the technical possibilities of computers, attacked by Otl Aicher, for example, as the "end of typography." In place of the means of classical typography now came complexity, ambiguity, and graphic richness; instead of functionalism and ratio: expression, emotion, temporality, deconstruction.

While Carson considers the visual and written material delivered him for his lay-out work for journals as simply the raw material for his two-page compositions, which can be manipulated by dismemberment, distortion, overlayering, placing it upside down, printing in mirror writing, jumps in size, change of type, etc., he left the photographs of Albert Watson in the lay-out of "Cyclops" – the first book publication of his comprehensive œuvre – untouched. The legends to the illustrations – of approximately 40 different types – were matched, so to speak, to the individual photographs in terms of expression and contents. Sometimes the motifs of photographs having a white, shadowless background and no border appear to stand freely in space – here Carson places the legend directly onto the ground of the image, but always in context to the motif. Some illustrations are framed in black, for example, those which suggest details from contact prints; some illustrations Carson has "fixed" with broadly brushed or, as if rolled out, underlayers in black paint.

The cover graphics show this. In its design Carson rejected the photograph usually used for books on photography: The frame remains empty – reserved for the title, which is continued on the lower bar of the frame. The positive-negative effects play on the medium of black and white photography, i.e. the contents of the book. Watson's works are reproduced in a complicated process (Agfa CristalRaster technology for producing the film, quadratone printing) that approximates the tonal values of the photographs as no other reproduction technique.

Carson transfers design devices from film and video to the print medium, consciously negates typographic rules and uses the most modern technologies uncompromisingly, while retaining a highly sensitive feel for composition. He hits the sensorium of a whole generation, whose seeing habits have undergone a lasting change after the flood of visual stimulation in the last decades. CR

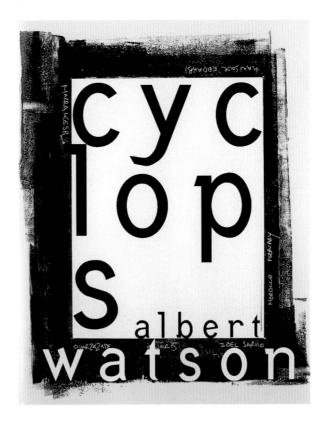

David Carson
Cover of the Photography
Book "Cyclops: Albert
Watson," 1994

Edited and produced by
Callaway Editions. Boston,
New York, Toronto, London:
Little, Brown and Company
(A Bulfinch Press Book)
Quadratone print
36.3 x 28.7 cm
Acc. no. 564/95

David Carson

1956 Corpus Christi, Texas – lives in San
Diego, California
As professional surfer amongst the
world's eight best in 1970; studied
sociology until 1977, as of 1980 studied
graphics at the San Diego State University, 1982–1987 taught sociology at
the Torrey Pines High School, Del Mar. In
1983 took a graphics course in
Rapperswil, Switzerland, under Hans
Rudolf Lutz, amongst others. Subsequently art director and designer for
the journals Transworld Skateboarding,
Musician, Beach Culture, Surfer, and Ray
Gun (1992–1995); as of 1993 he designed
campaigns for Nike, Pepsi, Sony, Levi's,
Chevrolet, Nations Bank, amongst others,
1994–1995 television advertising spots
for American Express, Coca-Cola, Sega,
etc. See also page 229f.

Donors 1990–1995

Abloy Oy, Joensuu (Finland)

Acerbis International S.p.A, Bergamo (Italy)

Advantest (Europe), Munich

Michael Aicham, Buxheim

Otl Aicher, Rotis

Alessi S.p.A., Crusinallo (Italy)

Algorithme, Paris (France)

Amat Muebles Para Collectividades S.A., Martorell/Barcelona (Spain)

Christian Anderegg, Ulisbach/Toggenburg (Switzerland)

Andreu World S.A., Alaquas/Valencia (Spain)

Apple Computer Inc., Cupertino, CA (USA)

Apple Computer GmbH, Ismaning

Robert Appleton, Hartford, Conn. (USA)

Makio Araki, Kobe (Japan)

Per Arnoldi, Copenhagen (Denmark)

Artemide S.p.A., Milan (Italy)

Porzellanfabrik Arzberg, Arzberg/Oberfranken

Asahi Optical Co.Ltd, Tokyo (Japan)

Yoshiteru Asai, Nagoya (Japan)

Ascom Gfeller AG, Bern (Switzerland)

Assmann Informatik 2000 GmbH, Bad Homburg

authentics artipresent GmbH, Leinfelden-Echterdingen

Autographe S.A., Paris (France)

Bär und Knell Design, Bad Wimpfen

Baleri Italia, Bergamo (Italy)

BaByliss (UK) Ltd., Alton, Hampshire (England)

Bantam Doubleday Dell Publishing Group, New York (USA)

Herr und Frau Bareiss, Ottobrunn

Saul Bass, Los Angeles (USA)

B.A.T. Cigarettenfabriken GmbH, Hamburg

création baumann, Baumann Weberei und Färberei AG, Langenthal (Switzerland)

Baumann & Baumann, Schwäbisch Gmünd

Porzellanfabrik Weiden Gebr. Bauscher, Weiden/Opf.

Angelo Bazzi und Maria Gaffuri, Vertemate/Como (Italy)

Beiersdorf AG, Hamburg

Bo Bendixen, Aarhus (Denmark)

Ruth Berner, Munich

Bestform Brökelmann GmbH & Co. KG, Arnsberg

Beurer GmbH & Co., Ulm

Bieffeplast, Caselle di Selvazzano/Padova (Italy)

Bilumen, Milan (Italy)

Bisterfeld + Weiss GmbH, Kirchheim/Teck

Dr. Bernd Bittmann, Tutzing

Black & Decker GmbH, Idstein

BMW AG, Munich

Brand GmbH, Wertheim

Braun AG, Kronberg/Taunus

Brionvega S.p.A., Milan (Italy)

Prof. Dr. Michael Brix, Munich

Büchergilde Gutenberg, Frankfort

Helmut Feliks Büttner, Rostock

Bund Deutscher Radfahrer e.V., Munich

Burda GmbH, Munich

Busse Design, Ulm

Bute Fabrics Ltd., Rothesay, Isle of Bute (Scotland)

Edition Cantz, Stuttgart

Capedevila, Fuenterrabia (Spain)

Carrera International GmbH & Co. KG, Traun (Austria)

Casa-Möbel, Munich

Cassina S.p.A., Meda/MI (Italy)

Dorothea Chabert, Wolfsburg

Eric Chan (Ecco Design), New York (USA)

Cinova, Lissone (Italy)

Cive s.c.r.l., Empoli (Italy)

ClassiCon GmbH, Munich

Cloer Elektrogeräte GmbH, Arnsberg

Coca Cola, Brazil

Crival Products Denmark ApS (Christophe Walch), Horsens (Denmark)

Priscilla Cunningham, Hampton Bays, N.Y. (USA)

Cyan, Berlin

Daimler-Benz Aerospace MTU, Munich

Prof. Dr. Hans von Denffer, Munich

Designer's Agency, Rosenheim

Deutsche Grammophon/Polydor International GmbH, Hamburg

Horst Diener (Designpraxis diener), Ulm-Gögglingen

Digital Equipment GmbH, Munich

Driade S.p.A., Fossadello di Caorso (Italy)

Silvia Durst, Krailling

Durst Phototechnik GmbH, Brixen (Italy)

D.O.R.C., Dutch Ophtalmic Research Center, Geervliet (Netherlands)

Atsushi Ebina, Tokyo (Japan)

ECM Records, Munich

Wolfgang Ehrlich, Hofheim

Stasys Eidrigevicius, Warsaw (Poland)

Electro-domésticos Solac S.A., Vitoria (Spain)

électronique d 2, Paris (France)

Heinrich Ellermann Verlag, Munich

ERCO Leuchten GmbH, Lüdenscheid

Ernst & Sohn Verlag, Berlin

Eschenbach Optik GmbH & Co., Nuremberg

Dr. Hans-Jürgen Escherle, Munich

Thomas Esmyol, Munich

Raphie Etgar, Jerusalem (Israel)

Euro-Matsushita Electric Works AG, Holzkirchen

Prof. Stephan Eusemann, Nuremberg

Fauxpas, Munich

Festo KG, Esslingen

Fiskars Consumer Oy Ab, Billnäs (Finland)

Fissler GmbH, Idar-Oberstein

Flos S.p.A., Brescia (Italy)

Flughafen Munich GmbH, Munich

Fontana Arte S.p.A., Corsico/MI (Italy)

Fornara & Maulini, Gravellona Toce (Italy)

Hugo Freund GmbH & Co

Gartenwerkzeugfabrik, Wuppertal

Heinrich Fries Jun., Munich

Hubert Fritz, Munich

FSB Franz Schneider Brakel GmbH & Co., Brakel

FUBA Hans Kolbe & Co., Bad Salzdetfurth

Dr. Richard Fuchs, Gräfelfing

Fujitsu Deutschland GmbH, Munich

Shigeo Fukuda, Tokyo (Japan)

Henrik Gačnik, Burgdorf

Gardena Kress + Kastner GmbH, Ulm

Gar-Tek Transportmateriel A/S, Hvidovre (Denmark)

Prof. Christof Gassner, Frankfort

Studio Juan Gatti, Madrid (Spain)

Ivan Gazdov, Sofia (Bulgaria)

Geha-Werke GmbH, Hannover

Gelma Industrieelektronik, Bonn

Karl Oskar Ritter von Georg, Hamburg

Gilette North Atlantic Sharing Group, Boston, MA (USA)

Firma Klaus Gillessen, Langenfeld

Giro Ireland Ltd., Newcastle West Co., Limerick (Ireland)

Gottschalk & Partner Parfumerie-Kosmetik GmbH, Munich

Grässlin GmbH & Co.KG Feinwerktechnik, St. Georgen

Grassoler S.A., Cerdanyola del Vallès, Barcelona (Spain)

Ilse Greif, Fürstenfeldbruck

Urs Grünig, Bern (Switzerland)

Erhard Grüttner, Blankenfelde

Grupo T, Barcelona (Spain)

Stefan Grzimek, Berlin

Prof. Dr. Christoph Hackelsberger, Munich

Hackman Iittala Oy Ab, Iittala (Finland)

Hagri, Hans Grimberg Edelstahl GmbH, Essen

Hallen Company, Houston (USA)

Hamax AS, Fredrikstad (Norway)

Hubertus Hamm, Munich

Hanseatisches Wein- und Sektkontor Hawesko GmbH, Hamburg

Hans Hansen, Hamburg

hansgrohe GmbH & Co. KG, Schiltach

Harmann Deutschland, Heilbronn

Josef Haunstetter Sägefabrik, Augsburg

Klaus Peter Heim, Gräfelfing

Helit Preßwerk Westfalen, Kierspe

High Tech, Munich

Masaaki Hiromura, Tokyo (Japan)

Hitachi Europe GmbH Electric Components Div., Haar

Hoechst Ceram Tec, Selb

Prof. Erhard Hößle, Ebenhausen

Hans-Jürgen Hummel, Konstanz

Hyvälysti, Tokyo (Japan)

Idealspaten-Bredt GmbH & Co. KG, Herdecke

Takenobu Igarashi, Tokyo (Japan)

Igus GmbH, Bergisch Gladbach

Ine Ilg, Aalen

In situ Producciones, Barcelona (Spain)

Intent de Disseny S.A., Barcelona (Spain)

Interflex S.p.A., Meda (Italy)

Italiana Luce, Settimo Milanese (Italy)

Jutaro Ito, Tokyo (Japan)

Radovan Jenko, Celje (Slovenia)

Georg Jensen Solvsmedie AS, Copenhagen (Denmark)

Junghans Uhren GmbH, Schramberg

Kai Europe GmbH, Solingen

Kartell S.p.A., Noviglio, Milano (Italy)

Keiper Recaro GmbH & Co, Kirchheim

Der Kinderbuchverlag, Berlin

Klaus Kinold, Munich

André Kirchner, Berlin

Katarina Kissoczy, Prag (the Czech Republic)

Irmgard Klinger, Munich

Knoll International, Murr

Konica Europe GmbH, Hohenbrunn

Reyer Kras, Amsterdam (Netherlands)

Dres. C.F. und H.-J. Kreiner, Munich

Claude Kuhn-Klein, Bern (Switzerland)

Erik Theodor Lässig, Riemerling

Lammhults Mekaniska, Lammhult (Sweden)

Dr. Arnica-Verena Langenmaier, Munich

Gert Leufert, Caracas (Venezuela)

E. Levi & C. S.p.A., Milan (Italy)

Leybold AG, Cologne

Ligo Electric SA, Ligornetto (Switzerland)

Lindberg Optic Design A/S, Aabyhøj (Denmark)

Sen-hao Lo, Taipeh (Taiwan)

Uwe Loesch, Düsseldorf

Loewe Binatone GmbH, Langen

Irene von Lossow, Munich

Luceplan S.p.A., Milan (Italy)

Gustav Lübbe Verlag, Bergisch Gladbach

Deutsche Lufthansa, Köln

Prof. Franz Xaver Lutz, Munich

João Machado, Porto (Portugal)

Werner Maerz, Munich

Prof. Helmut Magg, Munich

Marsberger Glaswerke Ritzenhoff GmbH, Marsberg

Shin Matsunaga, Tokyo (Japan)

Deutsche Aerospace AG, MBB, Munich

MBB-AT, Angewandte Technologie GmbH, Medical Devision, Ottobrunn

Mendell & Oberer Graphic Design, Munich

Mercedes-Benz AG, Sindelfingen

Georg Messer, Weisenheim am Berg

Ilse Michel, Weimar

Prof. Ralph Michel, Schwäbisch Gmünd

Klaus Micklitz (Team Micklitz), Schwäbisch Gmünd

Midori Co. Ltd., Tokyo (Japan)

Millelire Stampa Alternativa, Rom (Italy)

Anne von Miller, Munich

Mobles 114 S.A., Barcelona (Spain)

Jonas Mohr, Munich

Karin Mollier, Kienraching

Mono Metallwarenfabrik Seibel GmbH, Mettmann

Nils Holger Moormann, Aschau i. Ch.

Movado Watch Co., Grenchen (Switzerland)

Rolf Müller, Munich

Municher Rückversicherungs-Ges., Munich

Naef AG, Zeiningen (Switzerland)

Kazumasa Nagai, Tokyo (Japan)

Nec Deutschland GmbH, Munich

Pierre Neumann, Montreux (Switzerland)

Gebr. Niessing GmbH & Co., Vreden

Ninaber/Peters/Krouwel industrial design, Leiden (Netherlands)

Nordica S.p.A., Trevignano, TV (Italy)

Noto-collezione Zeus, Milan (Italy)

Novo Nordisk A/S, Glostrup (Denmark)

Nuno, Tokyo (Japan)

nya nordiska, Dannenberg

Oakley Inc., Irvine, CA (USA)

Dr. Oettinger, Ebersberg

OK-Tech Paul Ossege Kunststofftechnik, Drosten

Oldenbourg Verlag, Munich

Olivari B. S.p.A., Borgomanero (Italy)

Olivetti S.p.A., Milan/Ivrea (Italy)

OMK Design Ltd., London (England)

Nicolaus Ott + Bernard Stein, Berlin

F.W. Oventrop KG, Olsberg

Panasonic Deutschland GmbH, Hamburg

Fab. Paustian A/S, Copenhagen (Denmark)

Payer Elektroprodukte GmbH, Graz (Austria)

Pentagram, London and New York

Volker Pfüller, Berlin

Philips, Eindhoven (Netherlands)

Piazza Battista 1865 SRL (Twergi), Crusinallo (Italy)

Kari Piippo, Helsinki (Finland)

Plan Créatif (Crabtree Hall), Paris/London/Geneva

Weverij de Ploeg NV, Bergeyk (Netherlands)

Santiago Pol, Caracas (Venezuela)

Pott GmbH, Solingen

Progetti s.r.l., Carate Brianza (Italy)

Punt Mobles, Paterna-Valencia (Spain)

Quadro, Hamburg

Rabo A/S, Fakse (Denmark)

Rado Watch Co. Ltd., Lengnau (Switzerland)

Hartmut Räder Wohnzubehör GmbH, Bochum

Raiffeisenbank Bidingen

Jan Rajlich, Brno (the Czech Republic)

Paul Rand, Weston, Conn. (USA)

Rasch Tapetenfabrik, Bramsche

Ludwig Rase, Munich

Ravensburger Bücherverlag Otto Maier, Ravensburg

Reemtsma, Hamburg

Reisenthel Programm, Munich

Weingut Balthasar Ress, Hattenheim

Rexite S.p.A., Cusago, Milan (Italy)

Ritter-Werk GmbH, Munich

Rösle Metallwarenfabrik GmbH & Co. KG, Marktoberdorf

Rohi-Stoffe GmbH, Geretsried

Rohleder GmbH, Konradsreuth

Firma Christian Romanowski, Berlin

Rosenthal AG, Selb

Wieslaw Rosocha, Warsaw (Poland)

Rossignol Ski S.A., Voiron (France)

Prof. Richard Roth, Munich

Rotring-Werke Riepe KG, Hamburg

Rowohlt Taschenbuch Verlag GmbH, Reinbek

Royal PTT Nederland NV, The Hagne (Netherlands)

Ruchay Zeichentechnik, Cologne

A/S Ruko, Herlev (Denmark)

Sabattini Argenteria S.p.A., Bregnano/Como (Italy)

Rolf Sachs, London (England)

Makoto Saito, Tokyo (Japan)

Salomon GmbH, Puchheim

Samsung Deutschland GmbH, Eschborn

Jil Sander AG, Hamburg

AB Sandvik Bahco, Enköping (Sweden)

Sanyo Büro-Electronic Europa-Vertrieb GmbH, Munich

Sanyo Energy (Europe) Corp. GmbH, Haar

Sanyo Fischer Vertriebs GmbH, Munich

Koichi Sato, Tokyo (Japan)

Taku Satoh, Tokyo (Japan)

Scheurich Keramik GmbH, Kleinheubach/Main

Hermann Schmidt Verlag, Mainz

Renate Schmidt, Berlin

Elisabeth von Schöfer-Salzmann, Munich

Schopenhauer S.p.A. (Gruppo Fontana Arte), Corsico (Italy)

Schott-Zwiesel-Glaswerke AG, Zwiesel

Ralph Schraivogel, Zürich (Switzerland)

Eckehart SchumacherGebler, Munich/Leipzig

Büro Schwaiger Winschermann, Munich

Seca Meß- und Wiegetechnik Vogel & Halke GmbH & Co., Hamburg

Firma Seitz & Zöbeley GmbH, Munich

Porzellanfabriken Christian Seltmann, Weiden/Opf.

Jun Shibata, Tokyo (Japan)

Shiseido Deutschland GmbH, Düsseldorf

S. Siedle & Söhne Stiftung & Co., Furtwangen

Ernst von Siemens-Stiftung, Munich

Siemens AG, Munich

Siemens Italia, Milan (Italy)

Sigg AG, Frauenfeld (Switzerland)

Silit-Werke GmbH & Co. KG, Riedlingen

Robert Skogstad, Starnberg

Prof. Peter Skubic, Gamischdorf (Austria)

Gisela Smith, Ebenhausen

Solari Udine S.p.A., Udine (Italy)

Spear & Jackson GmbH, Schorndorf

Georg Staehelin, Ottenbach (Switzerland)

Stage & Service OHG, Munich

Stankowski + Duschek, Stuttgart

Prof. Eberhard Stauß, Munich

Steininger Wohndesign, Munich

Dr. Adelheid Straten, Munich

Friederike Straub, Munich

Prof. Ute Stumpp, Nuremberg

Stuttgarter Gardinenfabrik GmbH, Herrenberg/Württ.

Suevia Uhrenfabrik GmbH, Sindelfingen

Swedese Möbler AB, Vaggeryd (Sweden)

Minoru Tabuchi, Kobe (Japan)

Kan Tai-Keung, Hongkong

Takara Shuzo Co. Ltd., Kyoto (Japan)

Ikko Tanaka, Tokyo (Japan)

Dr. Paul Tauchner, Munich

Tecno S.p.A., Milan (Italy)

Tecta, Lauenförde

Telefunken Fernseh und Rundfunk GmbH, Hannover

Telekom, Bonn/Darmstadt

Telenorma GmbH, Frankfort

LT Terraneo S.p.A., Erba Como (Italy)

Teunen & Teunen, Geisenheim

Thomas (Rosenthal AG, Selb), Werk Waldershof

Klaus-Werner Thümmler, Munich

Tiptel AG, Ratingen

Tirol Werbung, Innsbruck (Austria)

Rosmarie Tissi (Odermatt & Tissi), Zürich (Switzerland)

Dr. Ursula Tjaden, Dortmund

Toppan Printing Co. Ltd., Tokyo (Japan)

Toshiba Europa (I.E.) GmbH, Regensburg

Tranekaer Furniture A/S, Tranekaer (Denmark)

Troika Ltd., Stratford-upon-Avon (England)

Tsubame Shinko Industrial Co. Ltd., Tsubame-shi (Japan)

Hideko und Tokiyoshi Tsubouchi, Tokyo (Japan)

Tupperware Int. Services Premark Resources NV, Aalst (Belgium)

Oscar Tusquets Blanca, Barcelona (Spain)

Alexander Tutsek, Munich

Yasuyuki Uno, Tokyo (Japan)

Dr. Heinz Usener, Munich

Uvex Winter Optik GmbH, Fürth

Michael Vanderbyl, San Francisco (USA)

Ventura Design on Time SA, Wangen (Switzerland)

Vereinigte Stahlwarenfabriken, Gebr. Richartz + Söhne GmbH, Solingen

Gerd und Bernd Vieler KG, Iserlohn

Massimo und Lella Vignelli, New York (USA)

Villeroy & Boch, Mettlach/Saar

Vimar s.r.l., Marostica, VI (Italy)

Vitra International AG, Basel (Switzerland)

de Vivanco & Co. GmbH & Co., Ahrensburg

VKI Technologies Inc., Saint-Hubert, Quebec (Canada)

Dr. Gerd Völlinger, Freising

Gerhard Voigt, Halle

Vorwerk, Hameln

Vullierme S.A., Rumilly (France)

Linda Walz, Munich

Watch Company, Bremen

Gert M. Weber, Munich

Martin Weinbrecht, Neckarsteinach

Wella AG, Darmstadt

Werkhaus GmbH, Suhlendorf

Günter Wermekes Design, Kierspe

Georg Wiedemann, Venningen

Peter Wiese, Munich

Wilkens Bremer Silberwaren AG, Bremen

Wilkhahn, Wilkening + Hahne GmbH + Co., Bad Münder

Thomas Gabriel Will, Munich

WK-Erwin Hoffmann-Stiftung, Neu-Isenfeld

WMF Württembergische Metallwarenfabrik AG, Geislingen

Wolf-Geräte GmbH, Betzdorf/Sieg

Prof. Leo und Gretl Wollner, Vienna (Austria)

Xylo Buchstaben, Rudolf Prien GmbH, Munich

Kijuro Yahagi, Tokyo (Japan)

Zaket Accessoires, Lübeck

Zanotta S.p.A., Nova Milanese (Italy)

Carl Zeiss, Oberkochen

Eva und Peter Ziegler, Hemhof/Chiemgau

Zojirushi Corporation, Osaka (Japan)

Zumtobel GmbH & Co., Usingen

Exhibitions by Die Neue Sammlung
1990 to 1995

Künstlerplakate. Frankreich/USA. Zweite Hälfte 20. Jahrhundert.
Artist Posters. France and USA. Second Half of the 20th Century.
(14 December 1990 – 31 March 1991)

Already the first exhibition under the museum's new direction was
dedicated to a subject going beyond the narrow categories of traditional art viewing: From the comprehensive poster holdings of the
museum almost 200 characteristic works by French and American artists
were selected: including G. Braque, M. Chagall, H. Matisse, P. Picasso,
V. Vasarely, as well as J. Dine, K. Haring, J. Johns, R. Lichtenstein, or
A. Warhol.
Artist posters document particularly well that a strict drawing of boundaries between fine and applied arts is untenable. Almost all important
artists of classical modernism since 1945 have dealt with the medium
poster.
"Artist posters stand apart from the works of professional graphic designers as an independent group, having their own rules. Designers
are painters, sculptors, or architects: in other words, 'fine' artists – in so
far as that one can categorize artist posters, like print graphics, to the
area of the so-called fine arts. On the other hand, these works have like
any other poster a certain function; they were designed for a particular
occasion – usually for exhibitions – and thus belong at the same time
to the so-called applied arts."
The subject was selected very deliberately in view of the planned new
museum buildings in Munich and Nürnberg: the aspect of crossing
the boundaries between the arts is particularly relevant, since fine and
applied art are to be united there under one roof for the first time.
As has been the case since 1980 already, Pierre Mendell and Klaus Oberer
were responsible for the graphic design (exhibition poster, invitation,
catalog cover).

Press review: Münchner Merkur, 14.12.1990 (Simone Dattenberger); Der Neue Tag (Weiden),
15./16.12.1990; Süddeutsche Ztg., 17.12.1990; Abendztg. (Munich), 20.12.1990 (Peter M.
Bode); TZ (Munich), 20.12.1990 (Karl H. Prestele); 089 Magazin 1991, no.1, 30 ill.; Nürnberger Ztg., 03.01.1991 (Monika Reuter); Dolomiten, 05.01.1991; Die Zeit, 18.01.1991, no.4;
Frankfurter Allgemeine Ztg., 21.01.1991; Pan 1991, no.2, 14 ill.; Detail. Zs. f. Architektur +
Baukunst 1991, no.2, 124; Feine Adressen (Munich) 1991, no.2, 60 ill.; Journal München
1991, no.2, 77 ill.; Prinz (Munich) 1991, no.2, 84 ill.; Mittelbayer. Ztg., 15.02.1991 (Birgit

Abstraction and Color.
The Art of the Amish.
Quilts from the Ziegler
Collection.
April 1991 – June 1991

Sonna); Die Welt, 22.02.1991 (Peter Dittmar); Welt am Sonntag, 24.02.1991, no.8; Bayer. Staatsztg., 08.03.1991 (Bärbel Reitter); Weltkunst, 15.03.1991, no.6 (Florian Hufnagl)

Abstraktion und Farbe.
Die Kunst der Amischen. Quilts der Sammlung Ziegler.
Abstraction and Color.
The Art of the Amish. Quilts from the Ziegler Collection.
(17 April 1991 – 2 June 1991)

The key words of the title of the exhibition on Amish quilts – abstraction and color – describe the characteristics of these textiles. Standing in front of these quilts, one is always reminded of modern painting, particularly of the USA: perhaps of Josef Albers or Ad Reinhardt, Kenneth Noland, Barnett Newman, Frank Stella, or Victor Vasarely. These associations exist rightfully so and are at the same time false. Because in their clear geometry and radical abstraction, their strict principles of construction and their large planes of color, the quilts of the Amish do in fact come amazingly close to the above mentioned styles of the sixties and seventies of the 20th century.

The expression of the late 19th century Amish quilts, which appears so modern, stems, however, from the design intentions of a deliberately antiquated and isolated fundamentalist American Christian sect! Quilts, such as those shown in the exhibition, were already made at the time that Queen Victoria reigned: parallel to the lavishness of historicism, also parallel to the playfulness of Jugendstil and art deco. They thus stand in diametric opposition to the contemporary European and European-influenced American art. The view of the Amish, withdrawn from the world, their attempt at a life style striving for simplicity and order in harmony with nature, created in the second half of the 19th century a so-called folk art that anticipated the design principles of modern art of the 20th century.

The exhibition took up a theme that Die Neue Sammlung had explored for the first time in 1974 in the exhibition of the thing world of the Shakers, a Christian sect in the pioneering times of the United States.

Pierre Mendell and Klaus Oberer were responsible for the graphic design
for this exhibition as well.

Press review: Abendztg. (Munich), 19.04.1991; Abendztg. (Munich), 20./21.04.1991;
Mittelbayer. Ztg., 22.04.1991 (Bärbel Reitter); TZ (Munich), 23.04.1991; Münchner Merkur,
26.04.1991 (Simone Dattenberger); Abendztg. (Munich), 03.05.1991; Dolomiten, 07.05.1991;
Süddeutsche Ztg., 15.05.1991 (Claudia Jaeckel); Weltkunst, 15.05.1991 (Florian Hufnagl);
Bayer. Staatsztg., 17.05.1991 (Barbara Reitter); md. Möbel. Interior. Design 1991, no.8, 66
ill.; Mitgliederzs. der Patchwork Gilde e.V. 1991, no.23 (Marija B. Schmidt); Kunstmarkt
1991, no.6

Design und Kunst.
Burg Giebichenstein 1945–1990. Ein Beispiel aus dem anderen Deutschland.
Design and Art.
Castle Giebichenstein 1945–1990: An Example from the Other Germany
(3 July 1991 – 22 September 1991)

Design and Art.
Castle Giebichenstein
1945–1990: An Example from
the Other Germany
July 1991 – September 1991

The arts and crafts school Burg Giebichenstein, today Hochschule für
Kunst und Design, founded in 1915 in Halle/Saale, taught and teaches
fine and applied arts as well as design on an equal basis, like once
the Bauhaus or the Hochschule für Gestaltung Ulm. With selected
examples from 1945 to 1990 the integral concept of this school, which
even in the times of the German Democratic Republic did largely not
conform, was made clear.
In the opening speech it was said: "The goal of the present exhibition
was to show the completely different experiences and developments
in the two parts of Germany after 1945 on the basis of a typical example,
in order to thus make an open discussion possible, which is always a
pre-requisite for working together. While the development in design is
relatively well-known for the western part of Germany after 1945, the
thinking in the East was until recently completely unknown."
Thus the exhibition, which was worked out in close collaboration with
the Hochschule Burg Giebichenstein, entered new territory. It was opened
by the Bavarian minister for economy and traffic Dr. h.c. August R. Lang.
Sponsored by the Bavarian ministry for economy and traffic and in
cooperation with the Design Zentrum München as well as the Designforum Nürnberg, the exhibition was also shown on the fair grounds in
Nürnberg on the occasion of the "Consumenta '91" from 26 October
to 3 November. On the one hand, this offered the opportunity to address
new sections of the public, on the other hand, it meant that Die Neue
Sammlung was present in Nürnberg for the first time, and this a few
weeks before the jury of the competition for the planned new museum
building began to meet.

Press review: Mitteldeutsche Ztg., 26.02.1991 (Margit Boeckh); BPAR 1991, June, n.p.;
Mitteldeutsche Ztg., 18.05.1991; Textilforum 1991, no.3, 10 ill. (Friedbert Ficker); Art Aurea
1991, no.3, 100 ill.; Mitteldeutsche Ztg., 27.06.91; Halle Anders, 1991, no.7; Mitteldeutsche
Ztg., 03.07.1991 (Margit Boeckh); Mitteldeutsche Ztg., 04.07.1991; TZ (Munich), 04.07.1991
(Karl H. Prestele); Süddeutsche Ztg., 05.07.1991 (Claudia Jaeckel); TZ (Munich), 05.07.1991;
Abendztg. (Munich), 06./07.07.1991 (Peter M. Bode); Frankfurter Allgemeine Ztg.,
10.07.1991 (Wolfgang Pehnt); Nürnberger Nachrichten, 11.07.1991; Freie Presse (Chemnitz),
11.07.1991 (Friedbert Ficker); Dolomiten, 11.07.1991; Oberpfälzer Nachrichten, 11.07.1991;

Augsburger Allgemeine, 13./14.07.1991; Süddeutsche Ztg., 17.07.1991 (Christoph Wiedemann); Schwäbische Ztg., 18.07.91 (Klaus Colberg); Neue Ruhr Ztg. (Essen), 18.07.1991
(Marlis Haase); Neue Züricher Ztg., 23.07.1991; Highlights. Magazin f. München 1991, no.8,
23 ill. (Manuel Zalles); Interni 1991, no.422, 102 ill.; Detail. Zs. f. Architektur + Baukunst
1991, no.4, 358 ill.; Pan 1991, no.8, 12 ill.; München Mosaik 1991, no.4, 31 ill.; Kunstmarkt
1991, no.8 (Susanna Partsch); Applaus (Munich) 1991, no.8 (Bärbel Reitter); Kunst +
Handwerk 1991, no.4, 46; Mittelbayer. Ztg., 07.08.1991 (Barbara Reitter); Hannoversche
Allgemeine Ztg., 08.08.1991 (Christoph Gunßer); Bayer. Staatsztg., 23.08.1991 (Barbara
Rollmann); Der Standard (Vienna), 23.08.1991 (Robert Haidinger); Mannheimer Morgen,
24./25.08.1991 (Susanna Partsch); Süddeutsche Ztg., 28.08.1991 (Birgit Sonna); Prinz
(Munich) 1991, no.9, 104 ill.; ZuhauseWohnen 1991, no.9, 65 ill. (Monika Buttler);
Süddeutsche Ztg., 04.09.1991; Die Ost-West-Ztg., 06.09.1991 (Susanna Partsch); Süddeutsche
Ztg., 14./15.09.1991; md. Möbel. Interior. Design 1991, no.12, 75; Nürnberger Nachrichten,
26./27.10.1991 (Bernd Zadow); Hochparterre 1992, no.4, 54; ÖIT 1992, no.75, 17
Radio: Bayer. Rundfunk, Bayern 2, Kultur Aktuell, 02.07.1991 (Johanna Schmidt-Grohe);
Deutschlandfunk, Kultur heute, 04.07.1991 (Wolfgang Pehnt)
Television: Bayer. Fernsehen, Capriccio, July 1993

Design: Vignelli, New York.
(31 January 1992 – 5 April 1992)

The first exhibition in the German language region about Vignelli Associ-
ates showed key aspects of the work of the internationally significant
design office. At first working in Milan, amongst other places, Massimo
and Lella Vignelli moved to New York in 1965. Integral thinking, social
responsibility, clarity, noblesse, and undogmatic multiplicity characterize
their view of design. The intentionally broad range of work includes
posters, packaging, book design, and signage for buildings, as well as
furniture or things of everyday use made of metal, glass, ceramics, and
plastics; the works range from graphic systems – for example, corporate
identity programs – to fashion design down to the complex three-
dimensional area of interior design, for example, museum and exhibition
design. "Design: Vignelli" linked up with, for one, the exhibition "Italian:
Design 1945 bis heute", held in 1988, and for the other, it continued
a series of monographic exhibitions, which in previous years had ranged
from Hans Gugelot to Sep Ruf, Fritz Haller, and Mendell & Oberer down
to Armin Hofmann.
In the days after the opening the designer Massimo Vignelli lectured
at the Akademie der Bildenden Künste, amongst other places: an inten-
sification of the external activities of the museum targeted toward
an interested public as well as the academically trained specialists. Again
Pierre Mendell and Klaus Oberer were responsible for the impressive
visual presentation.
The exhibition had further venues in Prague and Paris.

Design: Vignelli, New York.
January 1992 – April 1992

Press review: Münchner Merkur, 31.12.1991/01.01.1992; Art Aurea 1992, no.1, 112;
Münchner Merkur, 31.01.1992 (Carin Steinlechner); Süddeutsche Ztg., 31.01.1992; Art Aurea
1992, no.2, 102 ill.; TZ (Munich), 01./02.02.1992 (Monika Reuter); Abendztg. (Munich),
01./02.02.1992 (Peter M. Bode); Süddeutsche Ztg., 03.02.1992 (Dorothee Müller); Abendztg.
(Munich), 04.02.1992; Süddeutsche Ztg., 05.02.1992 (Dorothee Müller); Neue Züricher Ztg.,
11.02.1992 (Susanna Partsch); Die Tageszeitung (Berlin), 26.02.1992 (Martina Kirfel);
Bayernkurier, 29.02.1992; Feine Adressen (Munich) 1992, no.3, 80 ill.; Highlights. Magazin f.

München 1992, no.3; Prinz (Munich) 1993, no.3, 86/87 (Patricia Engelhorn); Frankfurter Allgemeine Ztg., 05.03.1992 (Renate Schostack); Bayer. Staatsztg., 06.03.1992 (Barbara Rollmann); Handelsblatt, 13./14.03.1992, no.52; München Journal 1992, no.3, 77 (Angelika Irgens-Defregger); Kunsthandwerk & Design 1992 (March/April), 48 ill.; Münchner Stadtmagazin 1992, no.7, 99/100 ill. (Uta Klinger); Eyes (Nuremberg) 1992, no.7 (Jürgen Burck); md. Möbel. Interior. Design 1992, no.4, 92 ill.; Madame 1992, no.4; Form. Zs. f. Gestaltung 1992, no. 137, 129

Bayerischer Staatspreis für Nachwuchsdesigner 1992.
Bavarian State Prize for Young Designers 1992.
(30 April 1992 – 24 May 1992)

The Bavarian state government awarded the Bavarian State Prize for Young Designers in 1992 for the fifth time. The results of this German-wide competition, on whose jury Die Neue Sammlung sat as well, was presented in three of the five rooms of Die Neue Sammlung. The Bavarian minister for economy and traffic emphasized in his opening speech: "At a time of quickly changing fashion and design trends, the Bavarian State Prize wants to honor achievements of outstanding quality by young professionals. At the same time it wants to contribute to the development of a critical awareness of design, which is clearly differentiated from a throw-away mentality. It was under consideration of these points of view, that Die Neue Sammlung was selected as the site for awarding the prize and for the exhibition. The exhibition of the exponants in this renowned museum, which harbors the probably world-wide largest collection of design objects, is at the same time an honor for all applicants for this Bavarian State Prize."
The exhibition was carried out with the support of the Bavarian ministry of economy and the Design Zentrum München, at its second venue in cooperation with the Designforum Nürnberg, which showed the selection in the foyer of the Kreissparkasse Nürnberg (district savings bank) from 3 June 1992 until 26 June 1992.

Press review: Eyes (Nuremberg) 1992, no.8 (Jürgen J. Burck); Werk und Zeit 1992, no.2; Design Report 1992, no.20/21; Frankfurter Allgemeine Ztg., 30.04.1992; TZ (Munich), 30.04./01.05.1992 (Sabine Adler); Süddeutsche Ztg., 30.04./01.05.1992 (Antje Weber); Mittelfränkische Wirtschaft 1992, no.5, 34; Süddeutsche Ztg., 02./03.05.1992; Münchner Stadtanzeiger, 04.05.1992; Süddeutsche Ztg., 04.05.1992 (Karl Ude); Münchner Merkur, 05.05.1992; Deutsche Handwerks Ztg., 08.05.1992; Bayer. Staatsztg., 08.05.1992 (Barbara Reitter); Trostberger Tagblatt, 12.05.1992 (Joachim Goetz); Design Report 1992, no.20/21; Nürnberger Nachrichten, 04.06.1992, 26; Nürnberger Ztg., 04.06.1992, 33
Television: Bayerisches Fernsehen, Rundschaumagazin, 29.04.1992
Radio: Bayern 2, Kultur Aktuell, 30.04.1992

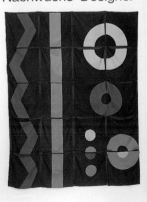

Bavarian State Prize for Young Designers 1992
April 1992 – May 1992
Volker Corell. People of Hollywood. May 1992

People of Hollywood:
Photographien von Volker Corell.
Photographs by Volker Corell.
(6 May 1992 – 24 May 1992)

The photographs of Volker Corell accompanied, as an independent presentation in two rooms of Die Neue Sammlung, the exhibition of the Bavarian State Prize for Young Designers. "People of Hollywood" showed works by the German photographer working in California, who tracked down eccentric people in the streets of Hollywood and made portraits of them for this series. The exhibition was conceived of by Dr. Reinhold Mißelbeck, head of the department of photography at the Museum Ludwig in Cologne, and was shown, after its first venue at Die Neue Sammlung, in Hamburg, Cologne, Vienna, and Berlin.
"Volker Corell's photographs of the people of Hollywood are not advertising photographs, and yet they can be linked in a very unique way with an extremely successful advertising campaign. It is particularly this aspect that I found so appealing that I wanted to have this exhibition for Die Neue Sammlung: that is, in the way that fine and applied photography metamorphose here, so to speak, as Siamese twins or as two faces of one and the same Janus head. I think I do not need to specially point out the provocation that the Benetton advertising has displayed, in order to indicate in how high a degree the world of advertising, the world of the media reality, and the world of our lived reality are bound up in one another and what an important role especially photography plays in this." (From the opening speech by F. Hufnagl.)
Beyond that the exhibition illustrated a central tendency of contemporary advertising and product photography that has meanwhile left its mark on numerous significant campaigns: the linking of "personalities" and public relations. Outstanding examples of this photographic movement – for instance, by Christian Coigny (see p. 182) – can also be found in the poster and photography collections of the Staatliche Museum für angewandte Kunst (i.e. Die Neue Sammlung).

Press review: Photo Technik International 1992, no.4, 3 (Hans-Eberhard Hess); München Journal 1992, no.5; Forbes 1992, no.5, 138 ill.; Highlights. Magazin f. München 1992, no.5 (Katharina Friedrichs); Münchner Merkur, 07.05.1992 (Susanne Hable); Ostthüringer Ztg., 13.05.1992; Süddeutsche Ztg., 13.05.1992 (Barbara Rollmann); Süddeutsche Ztg., 23./24.05.1992 (Birgit Sonna); European, 31.05.1992 (Anna Patricia Kahn); High Society 1992, no.6, 85 ill.; Münchner Stadtmagazin 1992, no.11, 58 ill. (Sabine Thienel)

M – Der Flughafen. Elemente des Erscheinungsbildes.
M – The Airport. Elements of its Visual Appearance.
(1 July 1992 – 13 September 1992)

The exhibition, prepared in cooperation with the architectural office of Professor Eberhard Stauß, presented the comprehensive design system of the new Munich airport, which was opened in the summer of 1992. Elements of its visual appearance – such as graphics, color, landscape, structures – were illustrated with sketches, drawings, plans, and posters, as well as with objects in the areas of furnishing, lighting, signage, clothing, etc. Aside from displaying the results, the design process was

M – The Airport. Elements of
its Visual Appearance.
July 1992 – September 1992

also shown on the basis of various phases of development over 20 years
of planning. The concepts openness, lightness, clarity, functionality describe the attitude striven for in this new type of complex corporate
design, which was supposed to apply throughout – from bridge railing to
signage down to the benches, from the color scheme to the writing.
Starting point and basis for these considerations was the surrounding
landscape; the structures of the whole complex, in general as well as in
detail, were derived from its characteristics. Within the framework of
many years of discussions about the Munich airport, the exhibition was
seen as a contribution to the discours, concentrating on the subject
matter. In addition, it linked up with a series of exhibitions of Die Neue
Sammlung on the theme "system design."

Press review: Süddeutsche Ztg., 24.05.1992 (Barbara Rollmann); Abendztg. (Munich),
02.07.1992 (Peter M. Bode); Süddeutsche Ztg., 08.07.1992 (Cornelia Gockel); Süddeutsche
Ztg., 21.07.1992 (Wolfgang Jean Stock); Raum & Wohnen 1992, no.4/5, 14; Süddeutsche
Ztg. (Landk. Erding), 22./23.08.1992; Prinz (Munich) 1992, no.8; Bayer. Staatsztg., 28.08.1992
(Florian Hildebrand); München Journal 1992, no.9, 74 (Angelika Irgens-Defregger);
Charivari Sept. 1992, 59; ID News, 01.09.1992; Neue Züricher Ztg., 08.09.1992 (Susanna
Partsch)

Japan: Hülle und Gefäß.
Tradition – Moderne. Yohji Yamamoto, Makio Araki, Mingeikan.
Japan. Shell and Vessel.
Tradition – Modernism. Yohji Yamamoto, Makio Araki, Mingeikan.
(25 November 1992 – 2 February 1993)

The exhibition "Hülle und Gefäß" was an event of international significance; the historical section was carried out in cooperation with the
Mingei museum in Tokyo. Guest curator Dr. Gabriele Fahr-Becker contributed decisively to the conception and organization of the exhibition,
assisted by Natsue von Stegmann-Hanada. Tradition and modernism of an
old cultural group was to be reflected in this exhibition. Thus objects of
daily life, outstanding examples of Japan's highly refined culture of forms
that have had a strong attraction for Europe for a long time already,

Japan. Shell and Vessel.
1992 – February 1993

were shown in three complexes: on the one hand, historical objects; on the other, objects finished today that are indebted to the traditional customs; thirdly, modern works, which do not, however, negate tradition throughout.

The historical works were selected examples from the holdings of the Mingei museum in Tokyo – objects, which have never before been shown outside of Japan: ceramic and metal vessels, lacquer ware and basket-work, but also textiles. Makio Araki, one of the most important packaging artists of Japan, created specially for this exhibition exponants that have gone into Die Neue Sammlung as a very special enrichment. They were exclusively packagings of paper and natural materials designed in a traditional manner. In these extraordinarily carefully worked things, whose appeal lies not least of all in the fact that they are at once artifacts and "pieces of nature," the singular importance, which is given packaging in Japan, becomes visible. The direct relationship to modernism was contributed by the internationally active fashion designer Yohji Yamamoto who, in collaboration with the film set designer Kan Taka-hama and the light designer Nihei, made a room installation on the theme "body and shell" for the exhibition. The 90-minute film essay on Yamamoto by Wim Wenders "Aufzeichnungen zu Kleidern und Städten" (1990) had given rise to the desire to let this artist, who rejects the fleetingness of the tastes of the times in his branch, design a room in Die Neue Sammlung.

The exhibition was realized with the support of Japan Foundation Tokyo and Ushio Inc. It was opened by the under-secretary of the Bavarian ministry for economy and traffic Alfons Zeller as well as the director of the Japanisches Kulturinstitut Köln. The Bavarian state ministry for economy and traffic invited to a series of lectures on Japanese product design that accompanied the exhibition.

Pierre Mendell and Klaus Oberer were once again responsible for the graphic presentation. The exhibition was hosted subsequently – with the exception of the loans from the Mingei Museum Tokyo, which were passed on to Rome – by the Hällisch-Fränkisches Museum in Schwäbisch

Hall and by the Atelier am Wasser in Zurich within the framework of the Japan weeks held there.

Press review: Art Aurea 1992, no.4, 92; Abendztg. (Munich), 13.08.1992 (Ulrike Reisch); AIT 1992, no.7/8; Form. Zs. f. Gestaltung 1992, no. 140, 92; Abendztg. (Munich), 18.09.1992; Münchner Merkur, 25.11.1992 (Carin Steinlechner); Abendztg. (Munich), 25.11.1992 (Peter M. Bode); TZ (Munich), 25.11.1992 (Monika Reuter); TZ (Munich), 25.11.1992 (Christiane Soyke); Abendztg. (Munich), 26.11.1992 (Rudolf Schröck); TZ (Munich), 26.11.1992; Süddeutsche Ztg., 26.11.1992; Thüringer Landesztg., 26.11.1992; Straubinger Tagblatt, 26.11.1992; Alt-Neuöttinger Nachrichten, 27.11.1992; Freie Presse (Chemnitz), 27.11.1992; Abendztg. (Munich), 28./29.11.1992; Nürnberger Nachrichten, 30.11.1992 (Monika Reuter); Südwest Presse (Ulm), 30.11.1992 (Alexander Hosch); Göppinger Kreisnachrichten, 30.11.1992 (Alexander Hosch); Giesinger Zeitung, 30.11.1992; Kunst u. Antiquitäten 1992, no.12, 50 u.84 ill.; Bauwelt 1992, no.47, 2642; Vogue 1992, no.12, 34 ill.; Schwäbische Ztg., 12.01.1993 (Joachim Goetz); Fränkische Landesztg., 03.12.1992; Donau-Kurier (Ingolstadt), 03.12.1992 (Barbara Reitter); Nordkurier (Neubrandenburg), 03.12.1992; Nürnberger Nachrichten, 03.12.1992; Ludwigsburger Kreisztg., 04.12.1992 (Alexander Hosch); Süddeutsche Ztg., 04.12.1992 (Dorothee Müller); TZ (Munich), 09.12.1992; Süddeutsche Ztg., 23.12.1992 (Barbara Rollmann); Mittelbayer. Ztg., 29.12.1992 (Barbara Reitter); Journal der Bayer. Staatsoper 1992/93, no.1, 18–29 ill.; Weltkunst 1993, no.1; Prinz (Munich) 1993, no.1, 92 ill.; Raum & Wohnen 1993, no.1; Feine Adressen (Munich) 1993, no.1, 84 ill.; München Mosaik 1993, no.1, 43 ill.; Frankfurter Allgemeine Ztg., 02.01.1993; Trostberger Tagblatt, 02./03.01.1993 (Joachim Goetz); Bayernkurier, 09.01.1993; Bayer. Staatsztg., 15.01.1993 (Hans Krieger); Darmstädter Echo, 21.01.1993 (Barbara Reitter); Gondroms Festspielmagazin Aug. 1993 (Monika Beer)
Radio: Bayer. Rundfunk, Bayern 2, Notizbuch (J. Schmidt-Grohe); Bayer. Rundfunk, Bayern 1, Morgenjournal (interview with Dr. Fahr-Becker)

Goldsmiths, Silversmiths.
Three Generations.
March 1993 – May 1993

Goldschmiede, Silberschmiede. Drei Generationen:
Franz Rickert, Hermann Jünger, Erhard Hößle, Ulla Mayer, Otto Künzli.
Goldsmiths, Silversmiths. Three Generations.
(3 March 1993 to 31 May 1993)

Franz Rickert (1904–1991), whose life spanned almost the whole 20th century, belongs, together with Karl Müller, Elisabeth Treskow, Andreas Moritz, Wolfgang Tümpel, and a few others, to the most important goldsmiths and silversmiths of modernism in Germany. His comprehensive œuvre, which the exhibition presented on the basis of a few selected examples, included, aside from such works of silver and non-ferrous metal as cutlery, everyday utensils, or liturgical instruments, also objects of the goldsmith art. As professor at the Munich Akademie der Bildenden Künste Rickert left his mark on more than one hundred and fifty goldsmiths and silversmiths, who have in part achieved international status. His immense significance as teacher is almost equal to that of his works. From the large circle of his students, Die Neue Sammlung exhibited those artists who succeeded Franz Rickert as professors at the Munich and Nürnberg academies: Erhard Hößle and Hermann Jünger, as well as their students and their successors as teachers Ulla Mayer in Nürnberg and Otto Künzli in Munich. Not only did the expansion from being nationally limited to self-understood internationalism thus become clear, the stylistic transformation as well as the changes in attitude as to what a goldsmith and silversmith is "allowed" to do became obvious. Hermann

Jünger uses unorthodox materials in classical silversmith tasks, Erhard Hößle possesses the gift of invention, Ulla Mayer experiments with new techniques in her art works, and Otto Künzli arrives at a new definition of jewelry by questioning the apparently matter-of-fact, he makes the step to concept art and lowers the barriers between fine and applied art. Die Neue Sammlung dedicated a whole room to each of the five goldsmiths and silversmiths. In addition to that, student works from the Staatliche Fachschule für Glas und Schmuck Neugablonz, which was directed by Günther Glüder, a former student of Franz Rickert as well, were shown in the foyer. Franz Rickert was himself committed to planning, establishing, and building up this educational institution in the fifties. The exhibition, opened by the Bavarian state minister for education, culture, science, and art Hans Zehetmair, marked the beginning of a whole series of events on the subject gold, to which numerous Munich cultural institutes dedicated themselves. The visual presentation was designed by the graphics office Mendell & Oberer.

Press review: Süddeutsche Ztg., 30.12.1992 (Eva Karcher); Art Aurea 1993, no.1, 105 ill.; Süddeutsche Ztg., 11.01.1993 (Birgit Sonna); Goldschmiede u. Uhrmacher Ztg. 1993 (February), 125; Art Aurea 1993, no.2, 68-74 ill.; TZ (Munich), 27./28.02.1993; Applaus (Munich) 1993, no.3, 75 ill.(Barbara Rollmann); Form. Zs. f. Gestaltung 1993, no. 141, 98; Focus 1993, no.9, 76 ill.; Kunsthandwerk & Design 1993, no.2; Prinz (Munich) 1993, no.3, 128 ill.; Charivari 1993, no.3, 57 ill.; Gold + Silber. Uhren + Schmuck 1993, no.1, 21; Münchner Merkur, 03.03.1993 (Simone Dattenberger); Münchner dpa-Meldung, 03.03.1993; Süddeutsche Ztg., 03.03.1993 (Claudia Jaeckel); Münchner Stadtanzeiger, 04.03.1993 (Barbara Bichler); Abendztg. (Munich), 04.03.1993; Süddeutsche Ztg., 05.03.1993; TZ (Munich), 05.03.1993 (Monika Reuter); Trostberger Tagblatt, 05.03.1993; Südwest Presse (Ulm), 05.03.1993 (Petra Kollros); Süddeutsche Ztg., 06./07.03.1993 (Christoph Wiedemann); Bayernkurier, 20.03.1993 (Reinhard Müller-Mehlis); Abendztg. (Munich), 20./21.03.1993 (Elisabeth Müller); Süddeutsche Ztg., 24.03.1993 (Christoph Wiedemann); Bayer. Staatsztg., 26.03.1993 (Barbara Reitter); Abendztg. (Munich), 27./28.03.1993; Kunstmarkt 1993, no.4, 10; Kunsthandwerk & Design 1993, no.4, 9–17 ill.; Detail. Zs. f. Architektur + Baukunst 1993 (April/May), 127; Frankfurter Allgemeine Ztg., 12.05.1993 (Brita Sachs); Süddeutsche Ztg., 26.05.1993 (Barbara Rollmann); Kritik (Munich) 1993, no.3, 69–73 ill.; Crafts Art Magazine July/Aug. 1993, 48/49 ill.; Antiquitäten-Ztg. 1993, no.9, 284/285 ill.

Marcello Morandini.
Bildhauer – Designer.
Sculptor – Designer.
(30 June 1993 – 26 September 1993)

Marcello Morandini.
Sculptor – Designer.
June 1993 – September 1993

The exhibition showed exemplary works by the internationally renowned Italian sculptor Marcello Morandini from the areas of design, sculpture, architecture, or urban planning. Working first as designer and graphic artist, Morandini turned soon to his "ricerche", research in the area of stereometry, perspective, movement, and transformation, which he translated in graphics, relief-like mural structures, or sculptures that can be freely walked around. In this Morandini proves to be a frontier crosser between fine and applied art, working since 1980 more intensely with architectural projects, the conception of public spaces, and design. "In ranging from visual art works, design bound to everyday things, and architectural or urban design, the œuvre of Morandini proves particularly well how obsolete the 'splitting of the arts' has become. Especially this oscillation between the poles of fine and applied art was one of the reasons for organizing the exhibition on Marcello Morandini in Die Neue Sammlung ... and exactly as the artist had himself conceived it. World-wide there has never before been an exhibition of his design works. Thus our exhibition is a premiere. And in that Morandini's work is now being presented in a museum for applied art, the perceptual perspective is turned around and other relationships become clear. For Die Neue Sammlung, design is of course the primary interest. But to understand it, the simultaneous exhibition of his sculptural works is absolutely essential." (From the opening speech.)
The exhibition was a continuation of a series of monographic events in Die Neue Sammlung, within which the work of Lella and Massimo Vignelli was the last shown. Thus a bridge could be thrown between the architects and designers Vignelli and the sculptor and designer Morandini. The design for the poster and the invitation were once again from the hands of Pierre Mendell and Klaus Oberer.
Further venues were Val Saint Lambert, Belgium (1993), Wilhelm-Hack-Museum, Ludwigshafen (1994), and Palácio Galveias, Lisbon (1994).

Press review: Architektur & Wohnen 1993, no.3; Elle Decoration 1993; Lufthansa. Express-magazin 1993, no.6; Münchner Merkur, 30.06.1993 (Claudia Teibler); md. Möbel. Interior. Design 1993, no.7, 61; Design Report 1993, no.1, 110 ill.; Abendztg. (Munich), 01.07.1993; Süddeutsche Ztg., 22.07.1993 (Birgit Sonna); Hochparterre. Illustrierte f. Gestaltung u. Architektur 1993, no.8; Architektur & Wohnen 1993, no.4, 154; Intercity. Das Magazin der Bahn 1993, no.8; Mensch & Büro 1993, no.4, 102 ill.; Ambiente 1993, no.4, 17 ill.; Kritik (Munich) 1993, no.3, 129; Journal München 1993 (August), 75 ill.; Mittelbayer. Ztg., 04.08.1993 (Barbara Reitter); Süddeutsche Ztg., 11.08.1993 (Birgit Sonna); Handelsblatt, 13./14.08.1993 (Beate Valentin); Trostberger Tagblatt, 19.08.1993 (Joachim Goetz); Lands-huter Ztg., 27.08.1993 (Joachim Goetz); Kultur. Kritische Blätter für Kenner u. Neugierige (Stuttgart) 1993, no.31, 19 ill. (Helmut Schneider); ZuhauseWohnen 1993, no.9, 156 ill.; Art Aurea 1993, no.3, 80 ill.; Bayer. Staatsztg., 03.09.1993 (Barbara Reitter); Neue Züricher Ztg., 15.10.1993 (Susanna Partsch)

Hans Finsler. Photography and
New Objectivity.
October 1993 – January 1994

Hans Finsler.
Photographie und Neue Sachlichkeit.
Photography and New Objectivity.
(29 October 1993 – 30 January 1994)

Hans Finsler (1891–1972) – pioneer of object photography – is one of the outstanding protagonists of the "new way of seeing" of the twenties. Photographs of products, architecture, and industry, as well as the illustration of mass production belong to his foremost subjects. Working at first in Halle, as of 1932 in Zurich, he founded in both places the first specialized classes in his profession at the arts and crafts academies. Since the fifties he decisively influenced, not least of all due to his immediate students, modern object photography, which is also one of the acquisition areas of Die Neue Sammlung. Hans Finsler's way of seeing as well as his selection of subject matter correspond to a great extent to the intentions of Die Neue Sammlung. With this exhibition the museum picks up on a tradition again, which had been interrupted for a longer period of time: after all, in the sixties and particularly in the seventies a series of photographic exhibitions had already taken place ranging from Robert Häusser to André Kertesz, Herbert List and Raoul Hausmann, to Bernd and Hilla Becher. The works shown by Hans Finsler stem from the holdings of the Staatliche Galerie Moritzburg Halle. Theo Immisch, head of the department of photography there, conceived the exhibition and opened it at Die Neue Sammlung. Before it came to Munich it had already been shown in Halle and Zurich, amongst other places. The graphic presentation including the invitation card and poster was designed by Pierre Mendell and Klaus Oberer.

Press review: Süddeutsche Ztg., 27.10.1993 (Claudia Jaeckel); Abendztg. (Munich), 29.10.1993 (Peter M. Bode); TZ (Munich), 29.10.1993; Münchner Merkur, 29.10.1993 (Carin Steinlechner); Journal München Nov. 1993; Handelsblatt, 26./27.11.1993 (Beate Valentin); AIT 1993, no.12, 7 ill.; Süddeutsche Ztg., 01.12.1993; Freie Presse (Chemnitz), 11.12.1993 (Markus Rinderspacher); Bayer. Staatsztg., 23.12.1993 (Barbara Reitter); Süddeutsche Ztg., 24.12.1993 (Claudia Jaeckel); Der Tagesspiegel, 31.12.1993/01.01.1994 (Bernhard Schultz); Intercity. Das Magazin der Bahn 1994, no.1; Design News 1994, no.1, 16 ill.; Antiquitäten-Ztg. 1994, no.1, 30 ill. (Florian Ganslmeier); md. Möbel. Interior. Design 1994, no.1, 82 ill.; Wohn-Design 1994, no.1, 8 ill.; Puccini (Munich) 1994, no.1, 45 ill. (A. Irgens-Defregger); Kultur. Kritische Blätter f. Kenner u. Neugierige 1994, no.36, 30 ill. (Helmut Schneider); Landshuter Ztg., 10.01.1994 (Joachim Goetz); Trostberger Tagblatt, 14.01.1994 (Joachim Goetz); Photopresse, 20.01.1994, 19/20 ill. (Alexander Hosch); Süddeutsche Ztg., 21.01.1994

Busse Longlife Design Award.
(8 November 1993)

On 8 November the "Busse Longlife Design Award 1993" presentation and exhibition of the prize winning objects took place in the rooms of Die Neue Sammlung. Already in 1990 this event was carried out in Die Neue Sammlung, opened on 22 October 1990 by the then Bavarian state minister for economy and traffic Dr. h.c. August Lang. The prize, awarded every three years since 1977, honors products that not only have excellent design, but have beyond that been on the market for at least nine years and of which at least 100,000 pieces have been sold. To view design as an enduring cultural expression, not as a short-lived phenomena, corresponds to the basic ideas and goals of Die Neue Sammlung, which was also represented on the jury. The Bavarian state minister of economy and traffic Dr. Otto Wiesheu presented the award and opened the exhibition in 1993.

Arne Jacobsen.
Designer. Architect.
(25 February 1994 – 29 May 1994)

The exhibition on Arne Jacobsen (1902–1971) showed the many-sided work of this internationally highly renowned Danish designer for the first time in Germany. Corresponding to Jacobsen's two major areas of work, the exhibition was structured in two parts and thus showed the close ties between architecture and design. The first complex included product design. Famous furniture pieces such as the armchair "Egg" and "Swan", which Jacobsen had designed for the SAS Royal Hotel in Copenhagen (see p. 148) were presented, furthermore metal works, glasses, lamps, textiles, instruments, etc. On the basis of sketches, models, prototypes, and so forth, the design process from the idea to the execution was illustrated. Particular attention was paid to Jacobsen's creative and critical exploration of the technological possibilities.

Arne Jacobsen.
Designer. Architect.
February 1994 – May 1994

In the second complex Jacobsen's architectonic œuvre was presented with the help of design sketches, plans, and photographs: the various types of buildings from Copenhagen, Berlin, London to Islamabad for which Jacobsen as passionate protagonist of the integral principle on several occasions designed the complete furnishing as well, indeed even the parks or gardens.

In addition, a video with an enlightening interview with Jacobsen, which includes statements on his buildings, his influences, and his working method, the use of color, etc., and which lets the personality of Jacobsen intensely show through, was shown in the foyer.

The exhibition, opened by the Danish consul general Carsten Schmidt, was organized by the Danish Design Centre, Copenhagen, and in the area of product design was designed in collaboration with the Danish architectural office Dissing + Weitling by Birgit Flügge and Mikael Fuhr, DDC. The architecture complex was curated by the Danish Centre of Architecture and Building Export. This cooperation gave us the first impression of how a collaboration between Die Neue Sammlung and the Architekturmuseum of the Technische Universität München in the planned new museum building – the Museum der Moderne – Kunst. Architektur. Design. – might work out (see p. 16).

The graphics office Mendell & Oberer was again responsible for designing the poster and invitation card. The exhibition continued on to the Design Museum London.

Press review: Mensch & Büro 1994, no.1, 107; md. Möbel. Interior. Design 1994, no.2, 82-85 ill. (Charlotte Blauensteiner); Art Aurea 1992, no.2, 97 ill. (Gudrun Meyer); Design Report 1994, no.2, 116 ill.; Design News 1994, no.2, 18; Architektur-Information (TU München), 15.02.1994; Münchner Merkur, 25.02.1994 (Simone Dattenberger); TZ (Munich), 25.02.1994 (M.R.); Süddeutsche Ztg., 25.02.1994; Abendztg. (Munich), 28.02.1994 (Peter M. Bode); Antiquitäten-Ztg. 1994, no.6; ZuhauseWohnen 1994, no.3, 130 ill. (Monika

Bavarian State Prize for Young
Designers 1994.
June 1994 – July 1994

Buttler); Kulturchronik 1994, no.3, 26 (kws); Baumeister 1994, no.3, 6 ill. (LTT); AIT 1994, no.3, 4 ill.; Focus 1994, no.13, 230 ill.; md. Möbel. Interior. Design 1994, no.3, 64; Kennzeichen ›D‹1994, no.30 (RH); IKZ Haustechnik 1994, no.3, 146 ill.; Elle Decoration 1994, no.3, 33; Süddeutsche Ztg., 02.03.1994 (Barbara Rollmann); Süddeutsche Ztg., 02.03.1994 (Dorothee Müller); Mainzer Allgemeine Ztg., 10.03.1994 (Susanne Armbruster); Bayer. Staatsztg., 11.03.1994 (Barbara Reitter); Landshuter Ztg., 16.03.1994 (Joachim Goetz); Frankfurter Rundschau, 19.03.1994 (Thomas Fechner-Smarsly); Hannoversche Allgemeine, 24.03.1994 (Gudrun Meyer); Trostberger Tagblatt, 28.03.1994 (Joachim Goetz); Der Standard (Vienna), 31.03.1994 (Gert Walden); Hausbau Magazin 1994, no.3/4, 10 ill.; Feine Adressen (Munich) 1994, no.4, 15 ill.; VfA Profil 1994, no.4, 28 ill. (Joachim Goetz); Detail. Zs. f. Architektur + Baukunst 1994, no.2 (CS); Form. Zs. f. Gestaltung 1994, no.145, 90 ill.; Ambiente 1994, no.4, 17; Design News 1994, no.4, 16; Wohn!Design 1994, no.2, 8 ill.; Kunstmarkt 1994, no.4; IKZ. Haustechnik 1994, no.4, 146; Der Architekt 1994, no.4; Journal München Apr. 1994, 80 (aid); Office 1994, no.4; Manager 1994, no.4; Morgenavisen Jyllands-Posten, 07.04.1994 (Jeannette Andersen); Pro (Prague), 07.04.1994 (ho); De Standaard (Brussels), 07.04.1994 (Valentijn Vandeweyers); Die Welt, 11.04.1994, 8 (mar); Neue Züricher Ztg., 23./24.04.1994 (Susanna Partsch); Bauwelt 1994, no.16/17, 866 ill. (Dorothea Baumer); Munich Found 1994, no.5, 20 u. 45 ill.; Bauwelt 1994, no.20, 1081 (Florian Hufnagl); Design + Design 1994, no.27, 26-35 ill. (Hans Irrek); Trödler & Sammler Magazin 1994, no.173, 153/154 ill.; Bündner Ztg. (Chur), 07./08.05.1994 (Lore Kelly); Passauer Neue Presse, 16.05.1994 (Alexander Hosch); Münchner Merkur, 29.12.1994

Bayerischer Staatspreis für Nachwuchsdesigner 1994.
Bavarian State Prize for Young Designers 1994.
(15 June 1994 – 5 July 1994)

Behind the awarding of the state prize, which was awarded in 1994 for the 6th time by the Bavarian state minister for economy and traffic, stands the recognition, that the factor design plays a decisive role to a large, indeed growing, extent in the economic future of the industrial state Bavaria. In view of this background the realization of the new museum buildings for Die Neue Sammlung, whose holdings illustrate and make the development of design on the basis of top achievements comprehensible, is not just a question of offering cultural programs, but is also an instrument for furthering the economy and securing the location. In the opening speech the director of Die Neue Sammlung emphasized: "One of the decisive characteristics of this state prize has particularly proven its worth with time: it is the only one in a number of similar competitions, which includes both areas of design, that of the craft as well as that of the industrial design. These two areas have always been part of the museum's concept of acquisition; because culture, and particularly our designed environment, is not divisible in separate parts! For both areas the saying is true: 'Design is art that makes itself useful.'" The exhibition was carried out with the support of the Bavarian ministry of economy and opened by Hans Spitzner, under-secretary in the Bavarian ministry for economy and traffic. Due to the repeated cooperation with the Nürnberg Design Forum, the basis for a later collaboration in the planned new museum's building in Nürnberg has been broadened. The visual presentation was conceived of by Pierre Mendell and Klaus Oberer.

Press review: md. Möbel. Interior. Design 1993, no.11.; Art Aurea 1994, no.2, 94 (aw); md. Möbel. Interior. Design 1994, no.5, 89; Nürnberger Nachrichten, 06.05.1994 (Walter Fenn); Bayer. Staatsztg., 13.05.1994 (W.F.); Kunsthandwerk & Design 1993, no.3, 28-31 ill. (Renate Luckner-Bien); Münchner Merkur, 18./19.06.1994 (Claudia Teibler); Süddeutsche Ztg., 29.06.1994 (Barbara Rollmann); Süddeutsche Ztg., 29.06.1994; Munich Found 1994, no.7; Artis Jul./Aug. 1994, 28; AIT 1994, no.7/8, 5 ill.; db. Deutsche Bauzeitung 1994, no.8, 10 ill. (gu)

Buchgestaltung in der Schweiz.
Book Design in Switzerland.
(20 July 1994 – 18 September 1994)

Internationally pathbreaking, of highest quality and often award-winning, Swiss books belong to the most beautiful books in the world. On the basis of characteristic examples, the exhibition illustrated the numerous styles. Every book was shown in various copies, so that different aspects of book design from typography and layout to cover design or paper selection could be displayed. Since visual enjoyment and tactile appeal are often indivisibly linked with a book, there was an extra copy of each book for leafing through.
A Tschichold citation makes the aims of the exhibition clear: "'I could be proud of the million Penguin books, for whose typography I was responsible. Next to them, the few luxurious books I have made mean nothing. We do not need any resplendent books for the rich, we need really well-made normal books.' That is exactly what it is about here as well: the well-made normal books, and in the end it has always been about that in the building-up of the department 'book art' in Die Neue Sammlung." (Extract from the opening speech by F. Hufnagl.)
The exhibited works were, as was the accompanying publication, selected and commentated by the internationally renowned Swiss graphic artist Jost Hochuli on commission of the Swiss cultural foundation Pro Helvetia. They supplement the graphic design holdings of Die Neue Sammlung superbly.
The exhibition, most positively acclaimed in specialist circles, was opened by the Swiss consul general Paul Studer. It travelled on to the Hochschule für Grafik und Buchkunst in Leipzig. The impressive motif of the poster and invitation card was designed by Pierre Mendell and Klaus Oberer.

Press review: Süddeutsche Ztg., 19.07.1994; Münchner Merkur, 20.07.1994 (Simone Datten-berger); Abendztg. (Munich), 21.07.1994 (Peter M. Bode); Süddeutsche Ztg. 23./24.07.1994 (Gerhard Matzig); Architektur-Information (TU München), 31.07.1994; Detail. Zs. f. Architektur + Baukunst 1994, no.4; Kunsthandwerk & Design 1994, no.4, 53; Focus 1994, no.33, 174 ill.; Landshuter Ztg., 09.08.1994 (Joachim Goetz); Alt-Neuöttinger Anzeiger, 31.08.1994 (Barbara Reitter); Börsenblatt f. d. Dt. Buchhandel 1994, no.69, 306–310 ill. (Georg Ramsegger); Novum Gebrauchsgraphik 1994, no.10, 70 (Michael Reiter); Münchner Merkur, 29.12.1994

Initiativ. Kunst. Kirche.
Initiative. Art. Church.
(18 October 1994 – 8 January 1995)

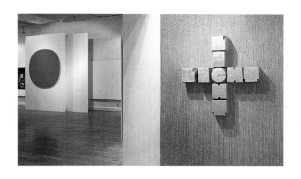

Initiative. Art. Church.
October 1994 – January 1995

The theme of the exhibition – future-oriented initiative in the artistic design of church spaces 1969–1994 in all of Germany – was illustrated primarily with large photographs of ensembles of works in the areas of painting, sculpture, arts and crafts, and design, as well as outstanding original works by Rupprecht Geiger, Rita Grasse-Ruyken, Arnulf Rainer, Norbert Radermacher, Brigitte Trennhaus, and Ben Willikens.
F. Hufnagl explained the intentions of this exhibition in his opening speech: "An institution like the church, which even today dares to ask, ... the question of (and demand) the absolute, cannot be satisfied with the mediocre, with arbitrariness, with that which is just well-meant, when it concerns presentation of its contents and values in the church space, it must seek the highest artistic quality. This conviction was the starting point for a Germany-wide competition announced by the Deutsche Gesellschaft für christliche Kunst (German Society for Christian Art), and was the basis for the prolonged work of the jury, upon which our exhi-bition is built.
Since some time fine and applied art have been placed by some of their interpreters in an unnatural polarity, indeed even a hierarchy. This view corresponds in no way to the historic facts. And in particular it should not arise in relation to sacred art – even today. Because in the area of sacred art ... a separation of fine and applied art has never existed. That is why the Staatliche Museum für angewandte Kunst, jointly with the Deutsche Gesellschaft für christliche Kunst, is carrying out this exhibition. It is our goal, to reopen with it the discussion on the status of applied art in general, as well as to further – in specific – applied art, especially sacred art, to set standards, and in illustrating the highest quality, to trigger the initiative for projects in the future."
The exhibition was opened by the Bavarian deputy prime minister and state minister for education, culture, science, and art Hans Zehetmair and by Friedrich Cardinal Wetter, archbishop of Munich and Freising.
The poster design for this exhibition by Pierre Mendell and Klaus Oberer was awarded the Grand Prix and was thus designated the "Best German Cultural Poster of 1994."

Press review: Münchner Merkur, 21.10.1994 (Claudia Teibler); Kath. Nachrichten-Agentur (Bonn), 22.10.1994 (Alice Potz); Sonntagsblatt, 30.10.1994 (Annette Krauß); Traunreuter Anzeiger, 04.11.1994 (Joachim Goetz); Bayernkurier, 05.11.1994 (Reinhard Müller-Mehlis); Sonntagsblatt, 06.11.1994; Landshuter Ztg., 25.11.1994 (Joachim Goetz); Süddeutsche Ztg., 07.12.1994 (Christoph Wiedemann); Bayer. Staatsztg., 09.12.1994 (Barbara Reitter);

The Urge to Travel. International Travel Posters from the Turn of the Century till Today. March 1995 – May 1995

Süddeutsche Ztg., 14.12.1994; Süddeutsche Ztg., 28.12.1994 (Barbara Rollmann); Kritik (Munich) 1994/95, no.4/1, 81–84 ill. (Joachim Goetz); München Mosaik 1996, no.2, 21/22 ill. Radio: Bayer. Rundfunk, Bayern 2, Kultur Aktuell, 17.10.1994 (Geseko, Lüpke)

Reiselust.
Internationale Reiseplakate von der Jahrhundertwende bis heute.
The Urge to Travel.
International Travel Posters from the Turn of the Century till Today.
(8 March 1995 – 25 May 1995)

The exhibition was recruited exclusively from the comprehensive holdings of Die Neue Sammlung. Far beyond the cultural-historical interest, the works illustrated – with the highest design standards – the art historical, or stylistic, development of the graphic medium poster on the basis of the travel poster. The exhibited international travel posters from the last 100 years reflected particularly obviously the yearning for distant shores, the history of travel, and of vacations – from the world of mundane resorts of around 1900 to the long-distance trains and luxury cruise ships of the thirties, from the development of the alps to tourism in exotic regions and foreign metropolises.
"To hold fast the history of the travel poster seems particularly urgent at a time when this medium has almost completely disappeared in travel advertising – replaced by brochures, magazines or television advertising. Those who, for example, go through one of the relevant trade fairs – such as the Caravan-Boot-Reisemarkt here in Munich – will see this con-firmed. Predominant are idyllic photographs blown-up to poster scale, which appear arbitrarily exchangable. Actually these works have nothing to do with 'poster' any more, they are only large photographs. Unfortunately the few other travel posters from recent times do not in general satisfy as poster graphics; there are few exceptions. Placing a thorn in the side, with a retrospective of examplarily designed works, is in my opinion one of the most appealing responsibilities of a museum for modern applied art like Die Neue Sammlung, which has always seen itself in a dialog with the immediate present." (Extract from the opening speech.) New, unexplored themes in the area of applied arts have already

been discovered by Die Neue Sammlung and worked up on numerous occasions, as for example film posters in 1965, product posters in the early eighties, or artist posters in 1990/91; this one was able to meaningfully continue with travel posters – again, art historically speaking, new territory.
The visual presentation was once again designed by Pierre Mendell and Klaus Oberer. The Mittelrhein-Museum Koblenz hosted the exhibition from 29 May 1995 to 3 October 1995.

Press review: Die Zeit 1995, no.13; In (Munich) 1995, no.12/13, 14 ill.; Süddeutsche Ztg., 01.03.1995; Süddeutsche Ztg., 08.03.1995 (Hanne Weskott); Mittelbayer. Ztg., 09.03.1995 (Barbara Reitter); Abendztg.v. 09.03.1995; TZ (Munich), 08.03.1995 (Barbara Welter); Donau Kurier (Ingolstadt), 10.03.1995 (A. Krauß); Münchner Merkur, 11./12.03.1995 (Claudia Teibler); Illertisser Ztg. (Augsburg), 11./12.03.1995 (Gernot Kirzl); Eberbacher Ztg.,14.03.1995 (Petra Kollros); Südwest Presse (Ulm), 14.03.1995 (Petra Kollros); Der Neue Tag (Weiden), 17.03.1995; Neue Züricher Ztg., 21.03.1995 (Susanna Partsch); Süddeutsche Ztg., 27.03.1995 (Gerhard Matzig); Munich Found Apr. 1995; Touristik Management Apr. 1995, 6; Trödler & Sammler Magazin 1995, no.186, 167 ill.; Detail. Zs. f. Architektur + Baukunst 1995, no.2, 181 ill. (CS); Madame 1995, no.4, 15 ill.; iwz. Illustrierte Wochenztg. 1995 (29.04.-05.05.1995), 37 ill.; Süddeutsche Ztg., 01./02.04.1995 (Heidi Rauch-Lange); Der Tagesspiegel (Berlin), 02.04.1995 (Rolf Brockschmidt); Frankfurter Allgemeine Ztg., 06.04.1995 (Renate Schostack); Bayer. Staatsztg., 07.04.1995 (Hans Krieger); Fränkischer Tag (Bamberg), 15.04.1995 (Monika Beer); Bayernkurier, 15.04.1995 (Reinhard Müller-Mehlis); Südkurier, 22./23.04.1995 (Henny Willenbrock); Kultur und Medizin 1995, no.298; Sammler-Journal 1995, no.7, 1010; Vital 1995, no.108; Charivari 1995, no.5, 55/56 ill.; Vereinsztg. d. AGV München 1995, no.3 (Ernst Siebler); Design Report 1995, no.5, 114 ill. (Is); Börsenblatt f. d. Dt. Buchhandel 1995, no.34, 151–153 ill. (Michael Reiter); Diners Club Magazin (Vienna)1996, no.1, 104–106 ill.
12 information screens at 6 Munich subway stations, exhibition information inserted every 6–8 minutes, e.g. on 10./11./12.03., 21.03.1995
Radio: Bayer. Rundfunk, Bayern 2, Das Notizbuch, 29.03.1995 (Johanna Schmidt-Grohe); Bayer. Rundfunk, Bayern 2, Mittagsmagazin, 07.03.1995
Television: Bayer. Fernsehen, Lesezeichen, 03.04.1995 (Otmar Engel); Deutsche Welle TV (Berlin), Boulevard Deutschland, 27.04.1995; Bayer. Fernsehen, Kultur Aktuell, 28.03.1995

Klaus Kinold.
Architektur. Photographie.
Architecture. Photography.
(13 June 1995 – 10 September 1995)

The historical retrospective – as can be read in the exhibition catalog – confirms the close link Die Neue Sammlung has with the areas of photography and architecture. From the very beginning the museum had taken on a forerunner role in the presentation and integration of photography. Since that exhibition on "Neue Amerikanische Baukunst" (New American Architecture) in the year 1926, which in the nature of things could be achieved only through the photographic medium, the outstanding tendencies of quality object and architectural photography has been followed and documented in Die Neue Sammlung. Thus the works of the architectural photographer Klaus Kinold – today one of the world-wide most sought-after protagonists of his profession – have found their place here. Kinold's subjects include works of classical modernism as well as of contemporary architecture: buildings by, for example, Le

Corbusier, Carlo Scarpa, James Stirling, Frank O. Gehry, or Tadao Ando. The architect and professor Karljosef Schattner, recipient of many awards, opened the exhibition. Standing on the point of intersection of the areas architecture and photography, this was the first joint project of Die Neue Sammlung and the Architekturmuseum of the Technische Universität München. At the same time the first perspectives for Munich's new museum building, and the future collaboration of the museums housed there, were demonstrated in an exemplary manner even before the corner stone has been laid. The exhibition had further venues at the Galerie der Stadt Kornwestheim (20 September 1995 – 19 November 1995) and at the Museum für Konkrete Kunst, Ingolstadt (17 March 1996 – 28 April 1996).

Press review: TZ (Munich), 26.05.1995 (Sabine Adler); Architektur-Information (TU Munich), 16.06.1995; Baumeister 1994, no.7, 9 ill.; Süddeutsche Ztg. 03.07.1995 (Dorothea Parker); Mittelbayer. Ztg., 08./09.07.1995 (Barbara Reitter); Donau-Kurier, 10.07.1995 (Joachim Goetz); Neue Züricher Ztg., 13.07.1995 (Susanna Partsch); Münchner Merkur, 23.07.1995 (Reinhard Müller-Mehlis); Landshuter Zeitung, 26.07.1995 (Joachim Goetz); In (Munich) 1995, no.32/33/34, 9 ill.; Stuttgarter Zeitung, 07.08.1995 (Joachim Goetz); Südwest Presse (Ulm), 09.08.1995 (Hanskarl, Neubeck); Fränkischer Tag (Bamberg), 17.08.1995 (Monika Beer); Detail. Zs. f. Architektur + Baukunst 1995 (Aug./Sept.), 632 ill. (CS); Design Report 1995, no.9, 117 ill. (Joachim Goetz); db. Deutsche Bauzeitung 1995, no.9, 28/29 ill.; Baumeister 1995, no.9, 64/69 (Wolfgang Jean Stock); Frankfurter Allgemeine Ztg., 01.09.1995 (Christian Marquart); Kulturchronik 1995, no.5, 32–34 ill. (Wolfgang Pehnt); Photo Technik International 1995, no.5, 12 (Hans-Eberhard Hess)

David Carson – Zeichen der Zeit.
Graphikdesign aus Kalifornien.
David Carson – Signs of the Times.
Graphic Design from California.
(12 October 1995 – 14 January 1996, extended to the end of February 1996)

With the – world-wide first – exhibition of works by the avant-gardistic graphic designer and art director, Die Neue Sammlung presented an exhibition that dealt for the first time with the changes that are taking place in graphics and visual communication in the era of digital technology, as exemplified by one of the outstanding protagonists of this radical change (see p. 204). Carson's expressive free style – heatedly discussed and much honored – his playful use of typography and the visual solutions, freed from all rules of the profession, would not be possible without the computer. The exhibition showed a cross-section of all working areas of the designer, from magazine design to television advertising spots, and included examples of his early works, with such papers from the scene as "Beach Culture", as well as recent commissions by large corporations. One key work was the magazine "Ray Gun" (The Bible of Music + Style), which in a short period of time rose to be the internationally most influential publication on contemporary graphic design and cult object of a young public. Carson's video essay "The End of Print", which had its world premiere at Die Neue Sammlung, illustrated the close relationships between the new means of presentation with cinematic perception and digital film technology.
The exhibition, curated together with Albrecht Bangert, was itself result

David Carson – Signs of
the Times.
October 1995 – March 1996

of this radical change: Carson designed the display walls as as large-scale graphics on the computer; these were blown-up in Germany by means of a digital and photographic process. Three-dimensional layerings, video projections, and monitor steles supplemented the presentation.

The accompanying publication, poster, and invitation were also designed by Carson; poster and catalog were reprinted three times during the period of the exhibition! Die Neue Sammlung passed the exhibition on to the Kunstmuseum Düsseldorf, where, in collaboration with Rempen & Partner, it can be seen from 19 April to 2 June. Subsequently it will be shown in Switzerland, further venues are being planned in France and the Netherlands.

Press review: Focus 1995, no.43, 342 ill.; Form. Zs. f. Gestaltung 1995, no.3, 3,12/13,90 ill. (Fabian Wurm); In (Munich) 1995, no.43/44; Page 1995, no.11, 15 ill. (jn); Abendztg. (Munich), 20.10.1995, 19 ill. (Peter M. Bode); TZ (Munich), 20.10.1995, 16 ill. (Sabine Adler); Münchner Merkur, 26.10.1995, ill. (Simone Dattenberger); Facts (Switzerland), no.43, 26.10.1995, 120–126 ill. (Hanspeter Eggenberger); Süddeutsche Ztg., 27.10.1995, 16 (Christoph Wiedemann); Neue Züricher Ztg, 27.10.1995 (Susanna Partsch); Design Report 1995, no.11, 112 ill. (ls); Focus 1995, no.44, 157–160 ill. (Gabi Czöppan); In (Munich) 1995, no.47/48, ill.; Bunte 1995, no.44, 10 ill.; I.D. (New York) 1995, no.11, 48–53 ill. (Rick Poynor); Werben & Verkaufen 1995, no.47 ill.; Fränkischer Tag (Bamberg), 07.11.1995 (Monika Beer); Bayer. Staatsztg., 17.11.1995, 12 (Barbara Reitter); Handelsblatt, 24./25.11.1995, 7 ill. (Elke Trappschuh); Münchner Merkur, 25.11.1995, 6 (SiDa); Art Aurea 1995/96, no.4, 6 ill.; Applaus 1995, no.12; Prinz (Munich) 1995, no.12, 106 ill. (Verena Richter); Münchner Stadtmagazin 1995, no.12, 99 ill. (Andreas Bildt); Applaus 1995, no.12, 83; Art Aurea 1995/96, no.4, 6 ill.; Artur (Augsburg) 1995, no.12, 3; Monthly Design (Korea) 1995, no.12, ill.; Hifivision 1995, no.12, 176 ill.; md. Moebel. Interior. Design. 1995, no.12, 76 ill.; ÖIF (Austria) 1995, no.6, 11 ill.; AGD Quartal 1995, no.4, 2/3 and 18 ill.; Kultur. Kritische Blätter f. Kultur u. Neugierde 1995, no.12 (Helmut Schneider); Wörkshop [sic!] 1995, no.6, 12/13 ill.; Süddeutsche Ztg., 01.12.1995; Frankfurter Allgemeine Ztg., 04.12.1995, 35 ill. (zek); Nürnberger Nachrichten, 06.12.1995 (Walter Fenn); Süddeutsche Ztg., 13.12.1995 (Cornelia Gockel); Südkurier, 20.12.1995; Nordbayer. Kurier, 21.12.1995 (Monika Beer); Süddeutsche Ztg., 27.12.1995 (Christoph Wiedemann); Photo Technik International 1996, no.1, 12/13 ill.; Männer Vogue

1996, no.1; Süddeutsche Ztg., 17.01.1996 (Barbara Rollmann); Süddeutsche Ztg., 23.02.1996 (ehh); Linie 4 1996, no.33, 8 ill.; Interni 1996, no.1, 162–167 ill. (Albrecht Bangert)

Online: Stadtnet München, Chat-Infoline, City Guide Munich, Kunst & Kultur, announcement from Oct.1995 to Feb.1996

Television: ARD, Kulturreport, 15.10.1995; ZDF, Länderjournal, 19.10.1995; 3SAT, Kulturzeit, 20.10.1995; Bayer. Fernsehen, Capriccio, 25.10.1995; Bayerisches Fernsehen, Lesezeichen, 04.12.1995; RTL 2, HotzPotz, 07.01.1996

Radio: Bayer. Rundfunk, Kultur Aktuell, 20.10.1995; Bayer. Rundfunk, Bayern 2, Zündfunk, 24.10.1995; Bayer. Rundfunk, Kultur Aktuell, 17.01.1996

External Exhibitions by Die Neue Sammlung 1991 to 1995

E.M. Lang – Auf der Straße nach Europa.
E.M. Lang – On the Road to Europe.
Brussels, former Embassy of the GDR
4 June 1991

In 1988 Die Neue Sammlung took over the whole body of political caricatures drawn by Ernst Maria Lang for the Süddeutsche Zeitung since 1947. Approximately 300 works, a fraction of the total holdings, were shown in the rooms of the museum already in the spring of 1990. In Brussels, a commentated selection served as inspiring supporting program for an event given by the Bavarian state minister for federal and European affairs Dr. Thomas Goppel in the rooms of the former embassy of the GDR and could count approximately 900 visitors on just one day. (see p. 234).

E.M. Lang – Der Weg zur deutschen Einheit.
E.M. Lang – The Way to German Unity.
Hamburg, the Inland Alster
3 October 1991

From their very first presentation at Die Neue Sammlung on, the caricatures of E.M. Lang were very popular with the public. They were thus sent on tours in varying quantities and with divergent themes on numerous occasions. The exhibition, initiated by the Bavarian state chancellery, included a selection of political caricatures from the years 1948 to 1991 on the theme of the German division and re-unification. It took place in a tent along the shores of the Hamburg inland Alster on the Day of German Unity, being celebrated for the first time, and was seen by approximately 10,000 visitors.

Objects Designed for Everyday
Use from the Late 18th Century
till Today.
Department Store. Munich 1992

Gestaltete Gebrauchsdinge des Alltags vom
ausgehenden 18. Jahrhundert bis heute.
**Objects Designed for Everyday Use from the
Late 18th Century till Today.
Munich, Department Store Beck am Rathauseck
4 May 1992 to 31 May 1992**

Die Neue Sammlung, severely restricted in its external impact due to the
limited exhibition possibilities, sought with this presentation unusual
means to reach a public that would otherwise not find its way to a
museum. In a well-known, culturally committed department store at the
Marienplatz, in the heart of the city, all display windows and exterior
display cases were cleared out and filled with objects from the hidden
vaults of Die Neue Sammlung.
Key objects in the development of design in unaccustomed surroundings
made tens of thousands of people aware of the museum with lightening
speed.

Moderne Keramik der Republik China auf Taiwan.
**Modern Ceramics from the Republic of China on Taiwan.
Weiden/Oberpfalz, Internationales Keramik-Museum
(Branch of Die Neue Sammlung)
11 December 1992 – 12 April 1993**

The Internationales Keramik-Museum, opened in May 1990, came into
existence within the framework of the museum development programs
adopted by the cabinet in 1979 and was conceived of by Die Neue
Sammlung. Ceramic objects of various periods from several continents
and in different techniques are displayed – but not in a static presentation, rather in combination with permanent and temporary exhibitions.
Other Bavarian state museums and collections that have their own
ceramic holdings also collaborate on these exhibitions on a rotating
principle. It is exactly in view of this background, that the influence East
Asian porcelain has had on the development of European ceramics can
be comprehended.

The temporary exhibition "Moderne Keramik aus der Republik China auf Taiwan," on the other hand, showed selected works of about 50 contemporary ceramic artists, which are particularly characterized by their unique and complicated glazes. In many objects a synthesis of century-old tradition and the present was created, others had completely new types of concepts. The exhibition was worked out in collaboration with the National Museum of History, Taipeh. In supplement to the exhibition, the young Chinese ceramist Sen Hao Lo was invited to demonstrate his skills at the wheel. The sudden increase in the number of visitors affirmed the new and lively concept of the branch museum.

Press review: Oberpfälzer Nachrichten, 12.12.1992; Der Neue Tag (Weiden), 12./13.12.1992; Der Neue Tag, 28.01.1993 (Christiane Schmidt)

Japan: Hülle und Gefäß. Tradition und Moderne.
Japan: Shell and Vessel. Tradition and Modernism.
Schwäbisch Hall, Hällisch-Fränkisches Museum
27 February – 25 April 1993
Zurich, Atelier am Wasser
4 September 1993 – 16 September 1993

The successful presentation of Die Neue Sammlung was taken over by two other sites in reduced versions. Schwäbisch Hall had to do without the selected holdings from the Mingei-Museum in Tokyo, which were being hosted in Rome at this time (Japanese Cultural Institute, 17 February – 9 April 1993). The exhibition at the Hällisch-Fränkisches Museum had more than 4,600 visitors and again received a good response from the press.
For the Zurich Japan weeks, which illustrated, amongst other things, cultural traditions and relationships, parts of the exhibition – packaging made by Makio Araki of natural materials and paper – were selected out and presented at the Atelier am Wasser. In this way a broad public could again be reached and addressed.

Press review: Heilbronner Stimme, 26.02.1993 (Peter Hohl); Haller Tagblatt, 26.02.1993; Sammler-Journal 1993, no.3; Hohenlohe Trends 1993, no.3; Haller Tagblatt, 01.03.1993 (Rainer Hocher); Haller Tagblatt, 02.03.1993; Stuttgarter Ztg., 03.03.1993; Haller Tagblatt, 23.03.1993; Hohenloher Tagblatt, 15.04.1993

Science and Technology
Reflected in Caricatures.
Bayerischer Rundfunk.
June – July 1993
(see p. 234)

Wissenschaft und Technik im Spiegel der Karikatur.
Science and Technology reflected in Caricatures.
Munich, Foyer of the Bayerischer Rundfunk (radio sender)
22 June 1993 – 11 July 1993

On the occasion of the 125th anniversary of the Technische Universität München, 18 leading European caricaturists – all internationally renowned critics of the times – were invited to comment on the theme in a selection of works. A scholarly framework of comprehensive bibliographic references and vitae of the illustrators, which included, amongst others, Ernst Maria Lang, Luis Murschetz, Pepsch Gottscheber, Ironimus (= Gustav Peichl), Paul Flora and Marie Marcks, rounded off the catalog of caricatures. Thus a comprehensive overview of the various trends and styles of contemporary caricature was created at the same time.

Press review: Münchner Merkur, 22.06.1993 (ib); Süddeutsche Ztg., 22.06.1993; Süddeutsche Ztg., 08.07.1993 (Franz Kotteder)

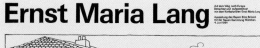

E.M. Lang – On the Road
to Europe. Brussels 1991
(see p. 231)

Ernst Maria Lang – Bayern und Ereignisse der Welt.
Ernst Maria Lang – Bavaria and World Events.
Oberammergau, so-called Pilatushaus
9 October 1993 – 1 November 1993
Schwabmünchen, Museum und Galerie der Stadt Schwabmünchen
27 March 1994 – 24 April 1994
Neuburg/Donau, Department of Culture of the City of Neuburg
26 June 1994 – 22 July 1994
Waldkraiburg, Studiogalerie im Haus der Kultur
22 September 1994 – 20 November 1994
Weiden/Oberpfalz, New City Hall
11 May 1995 – 11 June 1995

The great visual appeal and ingenious humor of the political caricatures E.M. Lang has been creating for the Süddeutsche Zeitung since 1947 are surely the reason that this travelling exhibition was so well received. In 1988 the original drawings of Lang became the property of the Free State of Bavaria and were given over to Die Neue Sammlung: an impressive body of work enlarged every year with the "running production." From the monographic exhibition, which took place in 1990, a concentrated distillation was created that – always supplemented by recent works – could be shown at various places. Lang made the selection himself together with Die Neue Sammlung. In this way his central concern could be made authentically clear: "Mockery is at the same time a binding solution, a cleaning solution, as well as a bit of stimulation."

Press review: Schwabmünchen: Schwabmünchner Allgemeine Ztg., 29.03.1994 (Siegfried Hasler); Stadtztg. (Schwabmünchen), 30.03.1994 (saw); Schwabmünchner Allgemeine Ztg., 23.04.1994 (zgw); Donau-Kurier, 01.07.1994 (Heinz Zettel); Neuburger Rundschau, 06.07.1994 (Stefan Schuch); Waldkraiburger Nachrichten, 16.09.1994; Alt-Neuöttinger Anzeiger, 17./18.09.1994; Die Woche, 21.09.1994; Blickpunkt, 21.09.1994, no.38; Waldkraiburger Nachrichten, 24./25.09.1994; Mühldorfer Anzeiger, 24./25.09.1994 (Hans Grundner); Alt-Neuöttinger Anzeiger, 24./25.09.1994 (us); Traunreuter Anzeiger, 07.10.1994; Der Neue Tag, 22./23.04.1995 (vok); Expuls – Regionalmagazin 1995, no.5, 4/5; Kulturkalender

Stadt Weiden 1995, no.5; Der Neue Tag, 11.05.1995; Oberpfälzer Nachrichten, 11.05.1995 (hzg); Oberpfälzer Nachrichten, 16.05.1995 (cw); Oberpfälzer Nachrichten, 16.05.1995 (hzg); Oberpfälzer Nachrichten, 22.05.1995 (on)

Ernst Maria Lang – 75 Jahre Freistaat Bayern.
Ernst Maria Lang – 75 Years Free State Bavaria.
Munich, Kuppelsaal in the State Chancellery
7 November 1993 and 27/28 November 1993

The exhibition was based on a selection of caricatures Ernst Maria Lang made in the time from 1947 to 1993, supplemented by historical drawings taken primarily from the satirical paper "Simplicissimus" as of 1918.
It was organized for two events of the Bavarian State Chancellery on the occasion of the anniversary of the founding of the Free State, which took place shortly after their new building had been completed at the Hofgarten. How useful and successful it can be to go new ways in bringing hidden treasures to light again and again, was demonstrated by the high number of visitors (about 4,800) in just three days.

Press review: Süddeutsche Ztg., 29.11.1993 (Burt)

Porzellan aus China. Die Sammlung Seltmann.
Porcelain from China. The Seltmann Collection.
Weiden /Oberpfalz, Internationales Keramik-Museum
Since 5 December 1994

The private collection acquired by the entrepreneur Wilhelm Seltmann – in view of his own important porcelain factories – was donated to the Internationales Keramik-Museum Weiden in 1993, and has been exhibited there since 1994. Through this the branch museum of Die Neue Sammlung owns, as the first of Bavaria's branch museums, its own collection of the highest quality. The collection consists primarily of vessels of the Qing period, that is works from the 17th century to the beginning of the 20th century. The earliest pieces thus stem from the time in which Chinese porcelain was "exoticism" par excellence and ruled the collecting passion of the European princes, while the latest objects stem from exactly that period in which the Seltmann porcelain factories were established in Weiden. Thus the holdings of the Seltmann collection build, so to speak, a bridge, an ideal link to our immediate present. The exhibition in the Internationales Keramik-Museum was opened on 5 December 1994 by the Lord Mayor of Weiden Hans Schröpf.
A comprehensive publication with numerous color plates as well as contributions by renowned experts on the historical background, technical conditions, and stylistic development introduces the approximately 140 objects for the first time. Particular attention was paid to the little researched porcelain of the 19th and early 20th century.

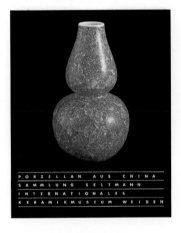

Porcelain from China.
The Seltmann Collection.
Internationales Keramik-
Museum Weiden.
Since December 1994

Press review: Der Neue Tag (Weiden), 30.11.1994 (ps); Der Neue Tag, 06.12.1994 (ps); Oberpfälzer Nachrichten, 06.12.1994 (fu); Aktuelle Oberpfälzer Rundschau, 08.12.1994, 2 (ka); Expuls-Regionalmagazin Dez. 1994, ill.; Der Neue Tag, 10./11.12.1994 (ps); Oberpfälzer Nachrichten, 31.12.1994, 19 (Reinhold Willfurth); Isar Aktuell, 08.02.1995; Oberpfälzer

Nachrichten, 09.02.1995 (on); Rhein-Neckar-Ztg., 01.03.1995 (Heide Seele); Der Neue Tag, 04./05.03.1995 (Marieloise Scharf); Die Schaulade March 1995, ill. (en); Neue Keramik - New Ceramic März/Apr. 1995, no. 8, 590 (G.W.); Expuls Mai 1995, 5; Sächsische Ztg., 21.07.1995; Buchhändler heute 1995, no. 11, ill.; Expuls Febr. 1996, 4 ill.; Der Neue Tag, 05.03. and 08.03.1996

Reiselust.
Internationale Reiseplakate von der Jahrhundertwende bis heute.
The Urge to Travel.
International Travel Posters from the Turn of the Century till Today.
Koblenz, Mittelrhein-Museum
29 June 1995 – 3 October 1995

In Koblenz, where in 1827 the Baedeker as "Führer durch das Rheinland" (Guide through the Rheinland) was first published, and thus in a region, which already before the development of the Riviera and the alps enjoyed a reputation of being one of the most important travel destinations, an exhibition on the subject tourism was certain of success. It was taken over in a slightly modified version from the Munich presentation.

Press review: Wormser Ztg., 17.05.1995; Tours & Tips 1995, no.11, 5 (dzt); Rhein-Ztg., 14./15.06.1995 (RED); Rhein-Ztg., 28.06.1995; Rhein-Ztg., 29.06.1995 (MS); Rhein-Ztg, 30.06.1995 (MS); Sammler-Journal 1995, no.7, 1010; Die Rheinpfalz, 01.07.1995 (Dagmar Gilcher); Rhein-Ztg., 11.07.1995 (Michael Stoll); Rhein-Ztg., 14.07.1995 (Michael Stoll); Stader Tageblatt, 17.06.1995; Rheinischer Merkur, 21.07.1995 (Ermano Hoepner); Kölner Stadtanzeiger, 26.07.1995 (Frank Rumpf); Kultur und Medizin 1995, no.298; Diner Club Magazin 1995, no.10; Lokalanzeiger, 02.08.1995 (roe)
Radio: SWF 4, Lieder. Leute. Landschaften, 29.06.1995; Deutsche Welle (Cologne), Mittagsmagazin Umschau, 12.07.1995; SDR, 29.06.1995
Television: SWF, Landesschau Aktuell, 28.06.1995

Exhibition Catalogs by Die Neue Sammlung 1990 to 1995

Wichmann Hans and Florian Hufnagl, Künstlerplakate. Frankreich/USA. Zweite Hälfte 20. Jahrhundert. In collaboration with Corinna Rösner. Die Neue Sammlung, München. Basel 1990. 320 pages with 229 color plates and 19 black-and-white illustrations.

Hufnagl Florian, Abstraktion und Farbe. Die Kunst der Amischen. Quilts der Sammlung Ziegler. With a contribution by Corinna Rösner. Die Neue Sammlung. München 1991. 60 pages with 19 color plates.

Hufnagl Florian (ed.), Design und Kunst: Burg Giebichenstein 1945–1990. Ein Beispiel aus dem anderen Deutschland. With contributions by Paul Jung, Renate Luckner-Bien, Eva Mahn, Horst Oehlke etc. Die Neue Sammlung. München 1991. 122 pages with 29 color plates and 64 black-and-white illustrations.

Hufnagl Florian (ed.), Design: Vignelli, New York. Die Neue Sammlung. München 1992. 80 pages with 40 color plates, often two-page spreads illustrating several objects, and 3 black-and-white illustrations. In German and English.

Bayerischer Staatspreis für Nachwuchsdesigner '92. Pub. by Bayerisches Staatsministerium für Wirtschaft und Verkehr. Die Neue Sammlung. München 1992. 71 pages with 14 color plates and 70 black-and-white illustrations.

Mißelbeck Reinhold and Rainer Wick (ed.), People of Hollywood. Photographien von Volker Corell. Die Neue Sammlung, München; Museum für Kunst und Gewerbe, Hamburg, etc. Frankfurt a.M. 1992. 136 pages with 67 black-and-white, mostly full-page illustrations. In German and English.

Hufnagl Florian (ed.), M – Der Flughafen. Elemente des Erscheinungsbildes. With a contribution by Christoph Hackelsberger. Die Neue Sammlung. München 1992. 104 pages with 63 color plates and 21 black-and-white illustrations.

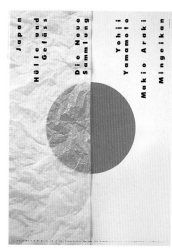

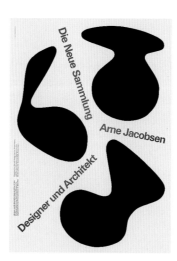

Examples of the graphic presentation
of Die Neue Sammlung 1990 to 1995.
Design by Mendell & Oberer,
Graphic Design, Munich

Franz
Rickert

Drei
Generationen
Gold- und
Silberschmiede

Erhard
Hößle
Hermann
Jünger

Die Neue
Sammlung

Ulla
Mayer
Otto
Künzli

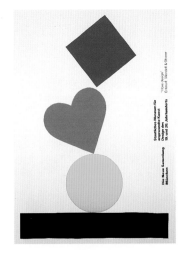

Reise
plakate
8.3.-
25.5.95

Die Neue Sammlung
Staatliches Museum
für angewandte Kunst

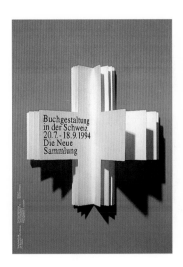

Buchgestaltung
in der Schweiz
20.7. - 18.9.1994
Die Neue
Sammlung

Hufnagl Florian (ed.), Japan: Hülle und Gefäß. Tradition – Moderne. Arbeiten von Yohji Yamamoto und Makio Araki. With a text by Wim Wenders. Die Neue Sammlung. München 1992. 69 pages with 17 color plates and one black-and-white illustration.

Mingei. Arbeiten anonymer Kunsthandwerker in japanischer Tradition. With a foreword by Florian Hufnagl. Pub. by Mingei Museum und The Japan Foundation, Tokio. Die Neue Sammlung, München. Tokio 1992. 129 pages with numerous color plates and black-and-white illustrations. In German and English.

Wissenschaft und Technik im Spiegel der Karikatur. 125 Jahre Technische Universität München. With an introduction by Christian Schütze. Technische Universität München; Bayerischer Rundfunk; Die Neue Sammlung. München 1993. 87 pages with 54 black-and-white illustrations.

Hufnagl Florian (ed.), Goldschmiede Silberschmiede. Drei Generationen von der Weimarer Zeit bis heute. Arbeiten von Franz Rickert, Hermann Jünger, Erhard Hößle, Ulla Mayer, Otto Künzli. In collaboration with Corinna Rösner and Katharina Kerscher. With a contribution by Ursula Keltz. Die Neue Sammlung. München 1993. 167 pages with 152 color plates and black-and-white illustrations.

Marcello Morandini. With contributions by Peter M. Bode, H. Heinz Holz, Florian Hufnagl and Wieland Schmied. Die Neue Sammlung, München. Mailand 1993. Vol. 1, Art: 141 pages; Vol. 2, Design: 165 pages. With numerous color plates and black-and-white illustrations. In German, English and Italian.

Hans Finsler. Neue Wege der Photographie. Ed. by Klaus E. Göltz, Theo Immisch etc. Staatliche Galerie Moritzburg, Halle. Leipzig 1991. 302 pages with 98 duplex plates and 540 black-and-white illustrations.

Tøjner Poul Erik and Kjeld Vindum, Arne Jacobsen. Architect & Designer. Pub. by Dansk Design Center, Kopenhagen. Die Neue Sammlung, München; Design Museum, London. Kopenhagen 1994. 132 pages with numerous illustrations, some in color. In English and Danish.

Bayerischer Staatspreis für Nachwuchsdesigner '94. Pub. by Bayerisches Staatsministerium für Wirtschaft und Verkehr. Germanisches Nationalmuseum Nürnberg; Die Neue Sammlung. München 1994. 65 pages with numerous illustrations, some in color.

Hochuli Jost, Buchgestaltung in der Schweiz. Pub. by Pro Helvetia Schweizer Kulturstiftung. Zürich 1993. 159 pages with numerous illustrations.

Initiativ. Kunst – Kirche. Forewords: Florian Hufnagl, Gebhard Streicher. With contributions by Paul Hoffmann, Aloys Goergen, Rainer Volp, Friedhelm Mennekes, Peter P. Steiner etc. Deutsche Gesellschaft für christliche Kunst and Die Neue Sammlung. München 1994. 160 pages with 107 illustrations, some in color.

Hufnagl Florian (ed.), Porzellan aus China. Die Sammlung Seltmann. With texts by Arnulf Stößel and Nora von Achenbach. Die Neue Sammlung, München; Internationales Keramik-Museum, Weiden. Heidelberg 1994. 162 pages with numerous, mostly full-page, color plates and 4 black-and-white illustrations.

Hufnagl Florian (ed.), Reiselust. Internationale Reiseplakate von der Jahrhundertwende bis heute. With a contribution by Corinna Rösner. Die Neue Sammlung. München 1995. 76 pages with 37, mostly full-page, color plates and 5 black-and-white illustrations.

Hufnagl Florian and Winfried Nerdinger (ed.), Klaus Kinold. Architektur-Photographie. With contributions by Wolfgang Pehnt and Ellen Maurer. Die Neue Sammlung and Architekturmuseum der Technischen Universität. München 1995. 64 pages with 51 duplex plates.

David Carson – Zeichen der Zeit. Graphikdesign aus Kalifornien. With a foreword by Florian Hufnagl. Text: Lewis Blackwell. Die Neue Sammlung, München. München/Schopfheim 1995. [n.p.] 160 pages with numerous, mostly full-page, color plates and black-and-white illustrations.

Index

Photo Credits

Artifort, Maastricht
p. 166

Bang & Olufsen, Struer
p. 197

Bayerischer Rundfunk, Munich
p. 233

Fa. Beck, Munich
p. 232

Belux, Wohlen
p. 178, 179

BMW Archives, Munich
p. 99

Braun, Kronberg
p. 138

Office Stephan Braunfels, Munich
p. 24, 26, 27, 35

Angela Bröhan, Munich
p. 16 bottom, 39, 41, 47, 48, 49, 53,
54, 55, 57, 59, 60, 61, 63, 66, 68, 69,
71, 73, 75, 76/77, 79, 81, 85, 86, 91,
93, 101, 103, 104, 105, 106, 107, 111,
113, 116, 117, 119, 120, 121, 125, 127,
132, 133, 135, 137, 141, 144, 145, 147,
149, 150, 151, 155, 157, 159, 160, 161,
163, 164, 165, 169, 172, 173, 175, 176,
177, 181, 189, 191, 201, 219, 221, 222,
223, 224, 226, 227

Cassina, Meda/Milano
p. 187

Christian Coigny, Lutry
p. 182

Electronique d2, Paris
p. 195

Max Factor, Tokyo
p. 185

Hans Finsler
p. 89

Flos, Brescia
p. 139

Galerie Artificial, Nuremberg
p. 170, 171

Galerie Objekte, Munich
p. 167

Bjarne Geiges, Munich
p. 230

Giro Sport Design Inc., Santa Cruz, USA
p. 202

Sophie-Renate Gnamm, Munich
p. 16 top, 94/95, 212, 213, 214, 215,
217

Hans Hansen, Hamburg
p. 152/153

Klaus Kinold, Munich
p. 18/19

Professor Friedrich Kurrent, Munich
p. 10, 11 right

Eberhard Lantz, Munich
p. 8, 15, 17, 32, 33, 42, 45, 67, 74,
82/83, 87, 96/97, 131, 205, 234, 235,
238, 239

Bernhard Limberger, Munich
p. 7, 36/37, 208/209

George Meister, Munich
p. 128, 129

Willi Moegle
p. 143

Office Paolo Nestler, Munich
p. 9

Archives of Die Neue Sammlung, Munich
p. 11 top, 123

Oakley, Irvine/Calif.
p. 203

Olivetti, Ivrea
p. 194

OMK Design, London
p. 199

Pratt & Whitney Archives, USA
p. 108/109

Bernd Schaier, Munich
p. 218

Office Volker Staab, Berlin
p. 28, 29, 30, 31

Anton Stankowski, Stuttgart
p. 88

Vitra, Weil am Rhein
p. 183 (Photo Andreas Sütterlin), 193

© VG Bild-Kunst, Bonn 1996
p. 67, 94/95, 131, 137, 165, 166, 175,
189